GLUED TO THE TUBE

The Threat of Television Addiction to Today's Family

Cheryl Pawlowski, Ph.D.

SOURCEBOOKS, INC.
NAPERVILLE, ILLINOIS

This publication is designed to provide accurate and authoritative information in regard to the subject matter covered. It is sold with the understanding that the publisher is not engaged in rendering legal, accounting, or other professional service. If legal advice or other expert assistance is required, the services of a competent professional person should be sought. —*From a Declaration of Principles Jointly Adopted by a Committee of the American Bar Association and a Committee of Publishers and Associations*

All brand names and product names used in this book are trademarks, registered trademarks, or trade names of their respective holders. Sourcebooks, Inc., is not associated with any product or vendor in this book.

Published by Sourcebooks, Inc.
P.O. Box 4410, Naperville, Illinois 60567-4410
(630) 961-3900
FAX: (630) 961-2168

Library of Congress Cataloging-in-Publication Data
Pawlowski, Cheryl.
    Glued to the tube: the threat of television addiction to today's family/
Cheryl Pawlowski.
      p. cm.
    Includes bibliographical references and index.
    ISBN 1-57071-459-2 (alk. paper)
      1. Television and family—United States. 2. Television and children—United States.
        3. Television addiction—United States. I. Title

    HQ520 .P38 2000
    302.23'45'0973—dc21

                                                              00-041978

                Printed and bound in the United States of America
                  BA   10 9 8 7 6 5 4 3 2 1

This is dedicated to the one I love: John

Acknowledgments

This book is the direct result of some wonderful people in my life who have supported, encouraged, and sometimes even cajoled me into making it happen. Among those I would like to thank are Dominique Raccah, president of Sourcebooks, for her vision and confidence in my abilities; Todd Stocke, editorial director, for his wise guidance; Jennifer Fusco, associate editor, for taking my initial manuscript to new levels of professionalism; and the entire staff at Sourcebooks for their hard work and creativity. I'd also like to thank my editor and friend, Michael Laughlin. Without his brilliant editing and friendship, this book would never have been possible.

There are so many others who have been instrumental in the writing process: my dear friend Mary Ann Keatley, who provided priceless emotional support; my research assistant Joanna Liebelt for her loyalty and dedication; New York University professor Neil Postman, who served as both advisor and mentor during my studies, and as a role model for my continuing work in media ecology; my professors Christine Nystrom and Joseph Giacquinta, whose advice, guidance, and groundbreaking efforts helped lay a foundation for this book; my daughters Crystal and Debbie, for their interest, encouragement, and sacrifice of valuable shopping time to provide indispensable input; my dad, whose excitement and enthusiasm have inspired all my work; and, most of all, my husband John. His love, his wisdom, his advice, and his humor were, and continue to be, the bedrock on which all my efforts are built.

Table of Contents

Preface

There are many books that deal with television. Most talk about TV violence or television's effect on child development. These subjects shouldn't be ignored, and you'll find discussions on them in this book as well. But the fact that TV violence can be damaging to children and may even play a role in many of the social problems we see today has almost become old news.

At some level, I think most viewers accept that watching too much TV is bad for you. But it seems like so many things can harm us that after a while we stop paying attention to all the warnings, studies, and "experts." And television has become such a pervasive influence in our lives, I think many people feel powerless to change the course of TV programming, their families' viewing patterns, or even their own television habits.

That's why I wrote this book. Because despite all the pressures to just let television take over our lives, we do have some choices. And it's a lot easier to make those choices when we realize what it is we're up against. The fact is, most families are competing for the attention, devotion, and well-being of their loved ones. And that competition is being waged in our living rooms, dining rooms, and bedrooms, and wherever else families used to congregate. It's being fought against a technology that has, for better or worse, become a member of our family, against a technology many of us have come to even…love.

I began to think about television in a more critical light almost twenty years ago when I studied anthropology, sociology, and communication at Western Connecticut University. Like many young people in the communication field, I had visions of a career in advertising or public relations—something that would pay well and be fun.

As I went on to pursue a master's degree at Fairfield University in Fairfield, Connecticut, I began to understand that television and other modes of mass communication create an environment of their own. Back then, most people hadn't heard about this almost-but-not-quite-real world. We now know it as "virtual reality," and although it's usually associated with computers, television is a big part of the artificial ecology in which many of us spend most of our existence. I also started to look at how the media is used to not only market products, but to change the way we think and feel and act. Frankly, it was a little disturbing.

At about that time, I began to teach interpersonal communication, and later, mass communication at various universities. I was able to witness firsthand how television and other media were shaping future generations. I realized, as well, how profoundly TV had impacted my own generation and how, in many ways, it had begun to replace the functions performed by previous generations such as those of my parents and grandparents. They were becoming obsolete! My students weren't turning to adults for advice and guidance—they were getting all the information they thought they needed from television!

As I went on to pursue my Ph.D. in media ecology and family communication theory at New York University, I began to better understand the relationship between television and family dynamics. On one level, that relationship is actually quite simple. When the TV is "on," family interaction is "off." People stop talking to one another, they stop doing other activities. Their minds are basically on autopilot.

But on another level something even more profound is occurring. People's needs don't cease simply because television is in their lives. If people are spending as much as six or eight hours a day alone in the virtual world of television, where are they getting the vital emotional and cultural nutrients previously provided by family members? The answer, of course, is television. The obvious next question is, how well is TV doing?

That's what this book is all about.

Although much of *Glued to the Tube* is based on my own observations, study, and research, there's a lot of good information in here for which I can't take credit. I've been fortunate enough to study and work with a number of experts in the field of media and family such as Neil Postman, Christine Nystrom, Murray Bowen, George Gerbner, and many others. Their thoughts and research helped shape my approach to investigating television's assumption of key family roles.

At the end of this book, you'll find a list of organizations that families can turn to for help in managing their TV viewing habits. You'll also find a pretty comprehensive bibliography, which represents the collective work of hundreds of people who have studied various facets of television's impact on individuals and society, as well as research into sociology, psychology, anthropology, family communication, and other topics that relate to TV's influence on the family. Each of these authors and organizations contributed to my knowledge of this vital field, and I am grateful to those who have gone before me and paved the way for *Glued to the Tube*.

Part One:

How Did We Get Here?

The Electronic Family

I t cuddles up next to us on the family room sofa. It's our know-it-all dinner companion, dominating table conversation and even suggesting the menu. It climbs into bed with us, interrupting our most intimate and loving moments. It's our children's favorite playmate. It provides solutions to our problems and even tells us what bathroom products to use, from deodorant and toothpaste to toilet tissue and hemorrhoid medication. Although "it" sounds very much like a family member—sometimes loved, sometimes annoying—it is, in fact, just a box full of circuits and wires. "It" is television.

In the past four decades, television has become a part of the American family in ways even the most beloved family pet has been unable to achieve over thousands of years. More American households have TVs than have indoor plumbing.[1] It demands more of our attention and, in many cases, influences our behavior more profoundly than any other member of the family unit. We have accepted it into our homes, learned to speak its jargon, and often mimicked its culture.

Unfortunately, we've also turned over many of our roles as fathers, mothers, sisters, and brothers to what has become the most powerful technology humankind has ever known.

Like a favorite aunt or uncle, we hang on its every word. We live by its moral code and delight in its ability to entertain us. But what price do we pay by giving this medium—a medium whose primary purpose is commerce—such an esteemed place in our families?

Many scholars have decried television's specific influences—the effects of its violence on children, its increasing sexuality, and its consumerist bent. As early as 1970, famed anthropologist Margaret Mead, for example, predicted that TV would become a second parent to many children.[2]

She was right. Television is, by far, America's favorite babysitter and companion. If both parents work, statistics show a child probably will spend more time in front of the television than with mom and dad combined. Studies suggest that children ages two to five spend an average of twenty-five to thirty-two hours per week in front of the tube.[3] And this daily pattern of television viewing—which can quickly develop into television addiction—often lasts a lifetime. That means today's average child will eventually spend about ten years of his or her life watching TV![4]

Godfrey Ellis, a respected researcher on television and the family, labeled television a "significant other" even before the phrase came into vogue.[5] Other researchers identify TV as a teacher or a house guest. Each of these experts anthropomorphizes television, giving it human characteristics…and for good reason. These researchers understand that TV is as influential in society as any human being.

Yet, most studies have failed to examine how television actually becomes a part of the family. Unfortunately, the majority of investigations treat television as an isolated phenomenon and ignore the impact of this medium on family processes and responsibilities.

For all of humankind's history, the family has been the primary tool to ensure the survival and success of the species. Families nurtured, taught, and protected their members. They served as standard-bearers for the greater society, and family members played specific roles designed to accomplish the natural goals of the family unit. Although imperfect, such a system allowed humankind to survive and thrive in a hostile environment. It provided the basic foundation and building blocks for the progress and prosperity we now enjoy.

Despite this tremendous responsibility, the role of the family has never been cast in stone. The ways in which family members interact and support one another constantly are evolving. Throughout history, the responsibilities of individual family members have changed and, in some cases, have been taken over by other societal elements and technologies. Communities, churches, synagogues, and other religious institutions, for example, have, at different stages in history, been dynamic forces in the lives of family members. They have assumed the roles of teacher, nurturer, moral guide, and more.

The advent of the printing press and a steadily climbing literacy rate allowed individuals to seek out the knowledge of others without filtering it through the family. Each new, more efficient mode of transportation reduced the family's long-term impact on individuals. The wagon, the train, the automobile, and the airplane have all allowed individuals to experience the influences of different societies. They also have separated many people from family and community traditions, values, and advice about life decisions.

But no other technology has succeeded in changing our family roles with the power and speed of television. Past technological break-throughs usually have focused on the utilitarian aspects of life. Although the motivation behind such discoveries may have ultimately been money or power, new technologies usually fulfilled a specific need. They reduced manual labor, increased productivity, or took over dull and repetitive chores. They were designed to reduce the work involved in day-to-day living.

Broadcast media took an entirely different approach. Radio and television tapped into a need most of us didn't know we had—the need for entertainment. But more importantly, at least from a business perspective, the purpose of broadcasting was to market products and services to a wider audience—ultimately an audience so large and so eager, even the most ardent capitalist could scarcely imagine it at the time. Marketing wasn't a new concept, but never before had a single marketing tool been so effective, so pervasive.

Broadcast media's truly unique role can be found in its ability to capture consumers' attention. Radio and TV were the first technologies truly attuned to the buyers' desires. More than any previous media, broadcast technologies can embed sales pitches into other messages—often to the point that consumers fail to recognize they're being targeted as a buyer.

Not designed to augment or reduce labor, TV simply occupies those times between work and sleep…and does so in a way no technology has ever achieved. Ironically, early critics of television cited its ability to simply consume time as a reason for predicting its quick demise. "The problem with television is that people must sit and keep their eyes glued on a screen; the average American family hasn't time for it," claimed an editorial in the March 21, 1939, edition of the *New York Times*.[6]

Rather than simply occupying some of the relatively few slack periods in most people's lives, however, TV quickly gobbled up enormous blocks of time previously spent on other activities. For most people, television viewing takes up more time than all other activities except sleep and work.

Television isn't inherently bad. In fact, television, at its best, can be a force for good. TV has the power to teach, to inform, and to inspire, and many programs have demonstrated the positive side of TV's potential.

Making a value judgment on an inanimate technology—whether it's good or bad—is a waste of time. Rather, as consumers, we must determine what role TV plays in our lives and whether that role is worthwhile. Ultimately, the responsibility for television's effects on society are as much in the hands of the consumers as the producers.

Although the dangers of television appear to have blossomed in the 1980s and 1990s, researchers began running up the warning flags more than forty years ago. By the 1960s and 1970s, it seemed clear that America as a nation and a culture had become addicted to the tube. While the average American household in 1950 viewed about four and one-half hours of television per day, only 9 percent of homes had TVs. By 1970, the amount of time spent on television had increased to almost six hours per day…but 95 percent of households had at least one TV.[7] A 1979 study by respected media scholar Edward Medrick noted that when families members are home, the TV is usually on. He described television as America's "number one obsession."[8]

Researchers study television for two basic reasons: to understand its effects on viewers, and to calculate its efficacy in attracting viewers and selling products. For those investigating television's societal effects, TV's power can be disturbing. And for those studying television's marketing potential, its allure is enticing beyond imagination.

The Electronic Family

Past research has focused primarily on television's effects on children or as a sociological phenomenon in which large segments of society are studied as a whole. These studies revealed the increasingly destructive nature of television, but failed to examine this technology in the most common context. Researchers have, too often, overlooked television's biggest competitor, the family. They have failed to investigate thoroughly how TV can affect, subvert, or usurp this most basic societal component.

Families are made up of individuals who, in the past, have performed specific roles that prepared children to contribute to society. The family unit also supported adult members as they coped with daily life.

In most families, formal and informal roles are assigned that meet the family's practical, social, and emotional needs. Some members act as family managers, guiding the household toward common goals and ensuring day-to-day responsibilities are met. Others are cultural narrators, relaying valuable information that maintains the continuity of the family and society at large. Parents, spouses, and older siblings may act as gender mentors and sexual advisors, helping all members understand and cope with their sexual urges and the possible roles they may occupy in the greater community. One or more members may serve as hero figures, defining integrity and upholding key values. Some family members are arbitrators, determined to keep the peace and assist in problem-solving. And finally, many members may be friends, providing comfort and companionship.

These roles are not always easily recognizable, but can be identified with careful research. They are key indicators of how well a family functions. I will attempt to more fully define these roles and illustrate how television has assumed many responsibilities historically held by individual family members.

In 1983, researcher Edward Palmer asked several children to draw pictures of their families. Perhaps the most accurate response came from a little girl whose rendering depicted a family grouped around a very prominent television set.[9] This simple drawing illustrates a basic trend: that television has become the centerpiece of the family unit; that today's family is organized around a single, incredibly powerful technology. Is television truly a member of the family? For better or for worse it can be argued that TV is not only a part of the family, but has become its dominant member.

It seems clear that television has assumed the responsibilities we once held as family members. Sometimes we may even feel that we're no longer needed. But as parents, as husbands and wives, as grandparents and children, we must ask ourselves, "Do we want to give up our family responsibilities to TV, and is television really doing a better job than we could?"

A Brief History of the Media

The late twentieth century has brought new meaning to the term "technology." The word now evokes visions of microchips, cellular phones, and laptop computers no larger than an Etch A Sketch. The term, however, actually covers a broader spectrum of inventions and ideas.

Technology, for instance, can encompass devices as simple as the sundial or as complex as the space shuttle. In the world of communication, the term "technology" can cover everything from satellite downlinks to the archaic pictographs of ancient Egypt.

Researcher Harold Innis explains that technologies act in three ways to produce new ideologies. First, technologies alter the structure of our interests—the things we think about. Second, they alter the symbols we use to formulate and communicate ideas—the tools we think with. And finally, technologies alter the nature of community—the arenas in which thoughts develop.[10] "We become what we behold," anthropologist Edmund Carpenter contends. He adds that each technology creates a totally new human environment, and all communication media create new perceptions and habits.[11]

The Technology of Communication

Language itself was the first significant form of communication technology. The sophistication of human language set us apart from the rest of the animal kingdom. It defined our world, our relationships, and our interpretation of life itself. Communication technologies not only provide us with material to think about, they also offer new tools with which to think.

"Language is not only a vehicle of thought," adds philosopher Ludwig Wittgenstein, "it is also the driver of the vehicle." He contends that individual languages create foundations for the cultures that use them. These languages define the cultures' perceptions of the world around them, specifying what constitutes an event, action, or thing. Language even designates the importance of each object or action.[12]

Most of us are typically unaware of how language controls our mental conceptions. Neil Postman emphasizes that "we live deep within the boundaries of our linguistic assumptions, and have little sense of how the world looks to those who speak a vastly different tongue." He explains what we think of as reasoning is determined by the character of our language.[13]

Reasoning in English is not the same as reasoning in Japanese, Italian, or German. Most of us assume others think in patterns similar to those we use. But reasoning is, in fact, a function of knowledge, and knowledge is gained and processed in the context of culture. It is in this context that culture is defined and communicated through language.

The technology of communication took a giant leap forward with the invention of the printing press, which changed the face of Western religion as a social framework. Protestant Reformist Martin Luther understood the power of the printed word. The printing press took the Bible out of the hands of the church elite and placed it in the hands of the masses. Luther described the printing press as "God's highest and extremist act of grace, whereby the business of the Gospel is driven forward."[14]

Despite Gutenberg's genius in creating the printing press, it's unlikely he would have embraced Luther's sentiments. As a devout Catholic, Gutenberg probably would have been horrified to learn how his invention was used by Luther to undermine the power of the Catholic Church.

In a sense, each technology we create has a blind spot. Inventors can dream of how their inventions will be used, but they can never know for certain the full implications of their discoveries. The mechanical clock is a powerful example of this "technological blindness." The clock was invented to bring precise regularity to the daily routines of medieval monks. The paradox, of course, is that a technology invented as a tool to worship God has become a veritable deity itself.

Still, it's not the responsibility of the inventor or the technology itself to understand and control the consequences of its existence. "No one expects a technology to understand or care about the ideological consequences of its own presence," says Postman. "Technology, in other words, changes without understanding. It is our task to understand so that what may be changed will serve ourselves and not technology....Without such understanding we are adrift in a technological sea without maps or compasses, and no sense of our destination."[15]

To comprehend the effects of communication technologies on society, we must first understand how the technologies evolved. We also must investigate the impact of new technologies on the societies that created them.

The history of communication technology can be divided into four major epochs. The first occurred when early humans began to string grunts and squeals together to form a rudimentary language. The power of complex language is humankind's most fundamental characteristic. It provides us with the tools to create ideas and to then communicate them to others. Imagine trying to form even the simplest thought without words!

The next major era in the communication technologies of the Western world occurred between 800 B.C. and 500 B.C. when the Greeks first began to use the phonetic alphabet—the written word—as a means of common communication. Writing was a major advancement in humankind's ability to communicate over significant distances. No longer were men and women bound by face-to-face communication and the amount of information they could memorize. The written word allowed a major leap in the precision of communication. Unlike oral traditions, facts could be recorded, then communicated days, weeks, or years later with reliable accuracy.

The advent of the printing press in the Middle Ages signaled another major milestone in the technology of communication. It opened to the masses a profusion of information previously restricted to the educated and wealthy. Knowledge was no longer confined to those with the money and power to access rare handwritten volumes.

Finally, the telegraph, invented in 1843, launched the current era in communication technology—electronic media. The immediacy of the telegraph and later the telephone expedited both commerce and social interactions, and played a major role in the Industrial Revolution.

Some scholars, perhaps rightly so, believe the advent of the television and computer signal another era, separate from earlier electronic media, the "Information Age."

The Written Word

The transition of humankind from an oral society to one that utilized the written word for common communication was a defining point in the civilization of the masses. Early oral cultures required a tribal mentality with histories defined by family or clan perspectives. Writing allowed a broader, even global perspective to emerge.

In approximately 800 B.C., Greek scholars began to use the phonetic alphabet primarily to record historical facts for religious purposes. It wasn't until about three hundred years later, however, that enough scholars could read and write to allow use of the alphabet for general communication by a wider, if still well-educated, population. Poetry, philosophy, and dramatic literature became more publicly disseminated, resulting in a body of common information, and ultimately, a solidification and clarification of the Greek culture.

The Greek philosopher Plato noted in the third century B.C. that the written word created a new environment, leading to logical thinking and reduced emotionalism. He predicted that writing would expand the human intellect. Plato realized that the thoughts, ideas, and information captured in these representative symbols could now stand on their own, independent of the writer.[16] Writing allowed scholars to build upon others' ideas rather than devoting their efforts to the memorization of a confined set of thoughts passed down through previous generations by oral tradition.

Much like an engineer may not fully comprehend the technology behind a microchip but can use that technology to create software that offers computer users new functions, writing also created a new paradigm. It recorded and communicated bodies of knowledge that provided foundations for other areas of investigation. These sets of knowledge could be utilized without complete mastery or memorization of all facts comprising the set. The bodies of knowledge also could be combined, manipulated, and expanded to create new ideas and technologies. The written word thrust humankind into a new age of learning, an age defined by a surge of technological advances.

Not all scholars welcomed the advent of the written word, however. Socrates argued against writing as destructive to Greek culture and society. He predicted writing would destroy humankind's capacity to memorize information. Socrates claimed writing would eradicate local dialects, presumably resulting in a global language, and would lead to a decline in oral participation.[17] Finally, he predicted that writing would end individual privacy.[18] While the same could be said of television, the written word introduced new vistas of knowledge to segments of Greek society that previously had little education. On the other hand, television, although it has the potential to educate, has rarely been used for that purpose. It would be interesting to hear Socrates' opinions about TV!

In early societies, writings frequently clarified and codified existing traditions and methods. The written word opened new paths for European nobility, although the general population remained largely illiterate. Even if commoners could read, few people but scholars had access to even the most rudimentary texts. Books, duplicated by scribes, were precious and rare treasures.

Among the nobility of the late sixteenth century, such texts profoundly affected social development and structure, bringing a new level of uniformity to the Elizabethan family. "Views of how family life should be conducted in a well-ordered household were relatively casual as long as reliance on unwritten recipes prevailed," explains media historian Elizabeth Eisenstein. "Elizabethans who purchased domestic guides and marriage manuals were not being given new advice—but they were receiving old advice in a new way and in a format that made it more difficult to evade."[19]

Eisenstein explains that written guides resulted in significantly more standardized roles. No longer relying on a hodgepodge of gossip and advice that conveyed random, sometimes conflicting expectations, books provided precise codes of behavior that were strictly observed. Such formalized standards produced a new, collective morality. These codified family roles eventually trickled down to the masses. Family roles were often diluted, however, since the harsh life of European peasants did not allow for the same level of sentimentality practiced by the nobles.[20]

Between the end of the Middle Ages and the seventeenth century, children of nobility won a place beside their parents. The home became a personal refuge, and its role as the primary socializing agent of children was significant. This bestowed upon the family its principal modern characteristics, distinguishing it from the medieval family, says Philippe Ariés in his book, *Centuries of Childhood: A Social History of Family Life*.[21]

Children became indispensable elements of everyday life. Parents worried about their education, careers, and futures. Although children had not yet attained the pivotal status bestowed upon youth during the mid-twentieth century, they were an important characteristic of the seventeenth century family. Families during this period were extremely social. Entertainment primarily consisted of parties and other gatherings. Seventeenth century life was lived in public.[22]

For all its reliance on communication technologies, from televisions and telephones to the computer, today's family is comparatively isolated, relatively alone in facing life's most daunting challenges. Most American families are now detached groups of working and/or single parents and children struggling to survive and thrive economically. Many of these family units have relatively little, if any, contact with neighbors or extended family members.

Although such a structure may appear practical, it fails to provide a foundation of values that honor the collective good. In its isolation, today's typical family promotes individual achievement but often gives little status to working toward the well-being of the family unit or society at large.

The Printing Press

The invention of the printing press signaled the next technology-based change in societal and family roles. Much like television, the printed word was primarily a one-way avenue of communication. This characteristic distinguished books as relatively indisputable sources of information, sources not easily contradicted by verbal feedback.

On a wide front, many scholars believe the printing press was a foundational element of the Protestant Reformation. It undermined the Catholic Church's monopoly on information by making the Bible available to the masses.

The printing press brought information to the common man, allowing a linear organization of information and ideas, and stimulating abstract thought. The ability to read required a significant increase in individual attention span, resulting in a higher degree of intellectualization practiced by the masses. It also served as a mighty tool for political discourse. It brought like-minded people together and allowed factions to emerge that contradicted the "truths" offered by ensconced leaders.

The printed word positioned the family as society's primary information manager. As books on every conceivable subject became available, parents stepped into the roles of guardian, protector, nurturer, and arbitrator of taste and rectitude. They defined what it meant to be a child primarily by excluding from the family domain information that undermined its purpose as an independent, productive unit and an incubator for society as a whole.[23]

The printing press also helped define and even extend childhood. Prior to the printing press, the key skill that defined adulthood was the ability to speak. The use of printed materials required a higher level of education. Children earned adulthood by achieving literacy. Earlier cultures usually featured tutor/student or apprentice/master learning environments. The printing press redefined the learning process. Education rapidly became a formalized institution. It would be difficult to imagine the concept of a public school system without printed materials.

The printing press also helped isolate the family unit. Fathers and mothers, rather than the community, became the family's primary moral agents. This was especially true for Protestant families. While Catholics were required by the church to rely on a priest for scriptural interpretations, the printed Bible allowed Protestant fathers—and later, mothers—to interpret scripture for their families. This trend was, in many ways, a foundation of the Protestant Reformation. While reformers put a high value on church participation, personal knowledge of the scriptures served as a check to the previous absolute power of the clergy under Catholicism.

Eisenstein in her book, *The Printing Press As an Agent of Change*, points out that the printing press elevated the father's role in the family from provider to spiritual and moral leader. It allowed widespread distribution of the Bible, turning the home into God's temple, with father providing guidance directly from the scriptures. Fathers were duty-bound to conduct household services for the family and its servants. "A 'spiritualization' of the household occurred....Ordinary husbands and fathers achieved a new position in Protestant households that Catholic men entirely lacked," says Eisenstein.[24] She explains that while Catholics were encouraged to depend upon priests for guidance, upper-class Protestants were bound—in some cases by law—to possess and study the Bible.[25]

The printing press also produced a variety of manuals on family-related subjects from home care and health to manners and education. As a result, folk remedies and "old wives' tales" were replaced by science, however primitive.

The printed word ultimately formalized the rules of home behavior. As the Western family structure evolved during the late eighteenth century, it became responsible for the emotional protection of its members from a cold and competitive social structure. This function produced separate religious traditions, individual languages and dialects, local lore, and other traditions.

Such changes were a direct result of the family's new role as the primary socialization agent. The family became a clear, if informal, structure for the management of information, allowing children access to facts only as appropriate in the context of the socialization and maturation process.

Electronic Media

Although many of us view radio and television as the primary modes of electronic media, the first true electronic communication technology was introduced in the mid–nineteenth century. Although the telegraph didn't share many of the characteristics common to more current forms of electronic media, it's introduction in 1843 whet consumers' appetites for immediate access to information. It also provided a foundation for the telephone in 1876, the phonograph in 1878, film and movies in the late 1800s and early 1900s, radio in 1919, and television in 1925.

The invention of electronic media changed the face of communication perhaps more than any other technological event since the advent of the written word. And unlike previous advances in communication technology, electronic media's widespread use occurred with unprecedented speed. It also allowed numerous other technological and societal changes.

The telegraph, for example, enabled America's massive westward expansion in the mid-1800s. It made areas previously perceived as remote and inhospitable more inviting to families. Earlier pioneers often had little hope of ever seeing or even hearing from family and friends left behind. The almost instantaneous nature of the telegraph provided contact, however brief, with important family ties "back home," allowing families to venture out into the great unknown with at least some vehicle to communicate with those left behind.

The telegraph also helped shape America's psyche. No longer content with local gossip, citizens began to view themselves as part of a national community. News, previously confined to local perspectives, assumed a nationwide viewpoint.

Although the telegraph set the stage for other electronic media, it wasn't until the advent of the telephone and the radio that society felt the real impact of a cultural transition.

Electronic media's power stems from several key characteristics that set it apart from oral, written, and print media. First, and perhaps most powerful, is the electronic media's sense of reality. Voices or pictures heighten the technologies' ability to create ideas that appear quite authentic. It therefore becomes much easier for the communicator and the consumer to blur the lines between reality and fantasy. The 1938 radio drama *War of the Worlds* was a prime example. Orson Welles' broadcast, based on the H.G. Wells story, sent much of the nation into a real-life panic. Listeners were convinced that Earth was being invaded by aliens based on the realism embedded in the radio play.

Although the printed word has always held sway as an authoritative source of information, the graphic, intensely human nature of electronic media enhances the belief that if it's on the air, it must be true.

Electronic media also disseminate information with unprecedented speed, evoking a sense of immediacy. While the written word inherently allows the reader to contemplate ideas, a broadcast call to action, by its nature, is a recommendation to "act now." This immediacy, combined with the emotional power conveyed through voice inflection and body language, creates a powerful propaganda tool.

Radio and television require users to do nothing more than press a button to receive a broadcast message. And, of course, that message is invariably condensed into a time slot that fits neatly between commercial breaks.

Postman contends that electronic media are more than just extensions of our senses. "They are ultimately metaphors for life itself; directing us to search for time-compressed experiences, short-term relationships, present-oriented accomplishments and simple, immediate solutions," he explains.[26]

Despite this fundamental flaw as a key communication media, television has become a particularly powerful tool for setting the agenda of our society. TV offers us a paradigm of how we should think and live, and what we should expect from our lives, mates, jobs, friends, and children.

TV works to create a new consciousness in which contemplative, orderly, and reasoned discourses lose their standing and are replaced by a form of fragmented imagery which stresses immediacy, subjectivity, and emotionalism. Several researchers have actually likened television to a drug. "It is, in fact, the parents for whom television is an irresistible narcotic, not through their own viewing (although frequently this, too, is the case) but at a remove, through their children, fanned out in front of the receiver, strangely quiet," says Marie Winn, author of *The Plug-In Drug*. "Surely there can be no more insidious a drug than one that you must administer to others in order to achieve an effect for yourself."[27]

Perhaps even more alarming, TV has the potential to destroy the very existence of childhood as a separate and distinct period in human development. Children learn significantly more about the adult world through electronic media than through printed documents, notes Joshua Meyrowitz in his book *No Sense of Place*. He explains that written materials feature a built-in censoring mechanism that radio and television do not possess.[28] Printed documents, by their nature, require specific levels of education and maturity to comprehend. A college textbook, for example, would be nearly incomprehensible to a child, and the words and sentence structure of an adult novel would probably confound or bore most young readers.

In the pre-broadcast media age, printed materials could be rationed more easily, providing a natural age-appropriate filter through which information was strained. Print media also allowed parents to limit children to an "onstage" view of the adult world. The "backstage"—doubts, anxieties, fears, sex, arguments, illnesses, etc.—could be revealed to children as they became emotionally ready to face life's more daunting challenges. The distilled environment possible before the advent of electronic media may not have been completely accurate, but it provided an emotionally reassuring setting in which to nurture offspring.

Broadcast media, on the other hand, cater to the lowest common denominator in an effort to capture the widest possible audience. They thrust everyone into a common communication system that not only offers children a keyhole into the adult world, but also the key with which to open that door.

Unlike the printing press, broadcast media reduce the amount of autonomy and control parents have over the family unit. They change the patterns of information flow into and within the household. More importantly, they lack the complex access paths that written documents provide to exclude young consumers. TV speaks in a language all age groups easily can translate.

Meyrowitz notes that unlike the traditional invited houseguest, parents have little control over television. While parents may control real-life child-guest relationships, television is an uninvited guest that broadens children's pool of information without parental consent.[29]

Computers

Although computers currently appear to be a separate and distinct technology from television, manufacturers and service providers within these two communities are rapidly forming some powerful alliances. The impending marriage of TV and computers has significantly more potential to further erode the roles of individual family members than either technology alone.

The dangers inherent in the combined technologies of computer and television are also their most attractive features. We have already discussed TV's allure. Computers possess many of the same characteristics. In addition, however, they allow immediate and relatively private consumer responses that require little effort or thought. Consumers are presented with an array of wares on the Internet. They can request those products without the moral filter of public purchase. The computer is the ultimate business tool, and is rapidly evolving into an incredibly powerful apparatus to control the consumer.

What makes computers so powerful is their inherently invasive nature. Unlike television, online sponsors can get immediate feedback on consumers' wants, needs, and desires without complex market research. The interactive nature of computers allows online companies to gather highly personalized information about specific consumers without the user's consent or knowledge—no questionnaires, no pesky telemarketers. It then becomes a relatively simple matter for online businesses to tally up which products and services sell the best, and provide more of the same.

Although the computer's potential to permeate American culture is, in some ways, even more powerful than television, the telephone, or radio, the government has been reluctant to impose significant controls on the Internet.

Before television, the word was humankind's most powerful communication tool. This supremacy has been challenged, however, by the introduction of images—powerful, realistic, moving images—into everyday communication. The combination of words and images offered by television, in tandem with the interactive power of the computer, will profoundly and forever affect the structure and character of society. It will also affect individual communication skills and our capacities to think and reason.

Ozzie and Harriet vs. The Simpsons

By tradition—a tradition that has served society well throughout history—each individual within a family holds specific roles. These roles support and enrich the family, and also help its members learn and practice the functions they must play within the greater society.

Family interaction usually defines how children are socialized into the dominant culture. As early as 1934, researcher George Herbert Mead noted that children learn their social roles during interpersonal interactions with family members.[30]

Family roles most certainly vary, and admittedly few parents, siblings, or other members completely fulfill their given responsibilities. However, the family, once considered to be the major institution for the socialization and control of the young, seems to be losing ground.

Human development scholar Uri Bronfenbrenner, in an essay on family life, argues that the contemporary family is characterized by a lack of involvement or sustained interaction between parents and children. He blames this destruction of family bonds on increased occupational and social demands and speculates that when children and parents are home together, they are absorbed with TV.[31]

Researcher Edward Shorter agrees. He explains that the instability of the couple, reflected in disturbingly high divorce rates, has contributed to parents' loss of control over their children. Shorter adds that other agencies now hold much of the responsibility for socializing and controlling the young.[32]

When interaction between family members is reduced or nonexistent, children and adults alike will turn to their most faithful companion for cues on societal roles and behavior. That companion is usually television.

The vicarious experiences offered by TV—accurate or not—teach social skills that are frequently generalized to fit other life situations. Christine Nystrom, professor of communication and culture at New York University, explains that as family members' experiences with each other decrease, television's lessons become increasingly more significant.[33] If television has replaced the family in this socialization process, what kinds of roles are family members adopting?

To truly grasp television's impact on family relationships, we must understand how the entertainment industry defines the family. In many ways, this definition shapes our own picture of the family unit and acts as a model for real-life family interaction.

It's also important to recognize that many of the initially "unique" social situations devised to create interesting television plots eventually become commonplace both on the screen and in real life. Some may argue that television's creative community is simply astute, identifying social trends early and using them to create dramatic or comic situations. It seems more likely, however, that at least in some cases television acts as a catalyst for social change, both positive and negative.

In many ways, this ability to create an ever-widening definition of family is indicative of television's integration into the American household. As family interaction continues to decrease,[34,35] television's assumption of family roles increasingly allows the medium to shape society's views on family life.

Idealized Roles

The expectation that mom is always "there" dressed in gingham and an apron, baking cookies, and keeping the house spic and span is unrealistic for most families. And dad, as the ever-stable breadwinner and patient teacher imparting sage advice is more often a character in a 1950s sitcom than the fathers most of us have known.

Nonetheless, these roles, idealized on television, in books, and by other forms of media, mirrored not only the desires of those in charge of the media, but often reflected much of post–World War II society's desire for stability and harmony. TV was particularly adept at amplifying and exaggerating these roles—often turning them into characterizations that bore little resemblance to reality.

While many characters and story lines on early television reflected prevailing stereotypes and the repression of women and minorities, families were typically depicted as supportive, harmonious, and, generally, intact. Home was a safe, lively place with plenty of interaction between family members. Equally important, early television programming generally adhered to a moral code that, while naïve by today's standards, did emphasize a sense of personal responsibility.

By the late 1950s and early 1960s, however, the Civil Rights movement, the women's movement, and later, the Vietnam War were prominent features on the evening news. The real-world unrest and violence of this era contradicted the bucolic world created by entertainment shows. Programmers soon discovered a market for more realistic depictions of family life. Unfortunately, they also discovered that conflict sells.

TV writers found fertile ground in the skirmishes produced by our failure to achieve a perfect family life. As the more risque *Peyton Place* (1964–1969) brand of programming competed with and eventually replaced the wholesome *Leave It to Beaver* (1957–1963), the roles espoused by centuries of tradition were presented as unattainable and undesirable. The undisputed message: don't even try to be Ward Cleaver. Television made it clear: fast cars and faster women were easier and more fun to attain than lasting relationships and an enduring sense of integrity.

Rather than providing a more balanced depiction of family life—or for that matter, life in general—television began to swing toward increasingly more angst-ridden, and even violent, portrayals of the world than actually existed. That trend continues today, as TV depicts a world filled with murder, rape, intrigue, betrayal, and sexual conquest that is no more reflective of reality than the perennially sunny, trouble-free world of *Ozzie and Harriet*. And just as early television normalized the roles and values it espoused, so too is modern TV normalizing its current messages.

The Age of Innocence

World War II was barely over when the first network television broadcasts began in 1946. The war had placed tremendous stresses on families. The men were gone, and the women were plunged into the workforce to support the war effort. When the war ended, much of society was anxious to reclaim a sense of normalcy, and television programming reflected this hope.

Whether Hollywood was inherently more friendly to the family is debatable, but television executives understood that the adult viewers of heartland America were their bread and butter. Traditional families made up the bulk of the market that bought the soaps, foodstuffs, appliances, automobiles, and other consumer goods that paid for programming. Sponsors were eager to support shows that reflected their ideal consumers: well-off, secure, and ready to buy.

Some critics rightly claim that early TV families pandered to the consumer market of the era. Shows depicting middle-class family life were especially adept at displaying the proper deference to consumerism and taught viewers how to have the perfect family by buying the right products. "The magically spotless kitchens of…June Cleaver, Harriet Nelson, and Margaret Anderson, amply stocked with all the latest durable goods, encouraged viewers to become model consumers and, by extension, model families," explains Ella Taylor of the University of Washington, Seattle, School of Communication.[36]

But equally important from a social perspective, the wholesome images conjured by this new medium also reflected the hopes of the American public. Programs that depicted happy, functional families were second in popularity only to the variety shows that had dominated radio. As television came into its own as a separate and distinct medium, family programs became a TV staple.

With the exception of the time-honored soap opera, which also made a successful transition from radio, most family programs during the 1950s and early 1960s were garden-variety situation comedies that focused on day-to-day family life. The 1952 comedy *The Adventures of Ozzie and Harriet* went so far as to feature an actual real-life family, portraying a television family, the Nelsons. Even their TV house was modeled after the family's actual home.

The program's fourteen-year run (not to mention an eight-year stint on radio preceding the television version) allowed America to watch Ozzie and Harriet Nelson's two children, David and Ricky, grow from small boys to adults with their own families and careers.

Hollywood in the 1950s focused on the most endearing qualities of traditional families. During this period, the entertainment community employed a "least objectionable" approach to programming, which was designed not to challenge viewers, but rather, to comfort and even flatter consumers. And although TV families were never accurate depictions of contemporary family life, they did present many positive role models for real-life viewers to emulate.

But postwar America was changing. Women who entered the work-force during World War II were often reluctant to return to more traditional arrangements. Although some traditionalists balked at the notion of a two-career family, many households grew comfortable with the unprecedented affluence that an extra paycheck provided.

In many ways, early television represented the most conservative forces within society—forces eager to preserve the status quo. *The George Burns and Gracie Allen Show* (1950–1958), for example, featured the wry observations of Burns as a contrast to Allen's zany antics. At some level, these shows attempted to reestablish the male-dominant social order. And the ever-present variety programs such as *The Ed Sullivan Show* (1948–1971), *The Milton Berle Show* (1948–1967), and *The Red Skelton Show* (1951–1971) all cast males in dominant roles.

Situation comedies such as the 1954–1962 series *Father Knows Best* generally depicted traditional nuclear families. Clad in a well-pressed suit or comfortable cardigan, dad, wise and strong, patiently dispensed sage advice to his wife and children.

Mom's role was also clearly defined. Despite its name, even *The Donna Reed Show*, which ran on ABC from 1958 to 1966, cast women in supporting roles. On television, at least, mom's job was to back up dad and provide a warm and loving home for the family. Rarely did a woman have a career beyond homemaking.

Children on early television were generally well-behaved and loyal. They rarely faced serious challenges involving issues such as sex, alcohol and drug abuse, or violence. On shows such as *Leave It to Beaver,* the innocence and naïveté of youth were central to most plot lines. Comedic or dramatic situations typically centered around relatively innocuous issues that supported the concept of a strong nuclear family and provided moral training. Such family shows reflected the optimism characterized by the baby boom of the 1950s.

The creative teams that produced early TV programs were able to generate entertainment from everyday situations. They didn't rely on unlikely or bazaar circumstances, depressing characters on the edge of a breakdown, random violence, or even bitingly cruel repartee. Instead, they used simple circumstances, predictable plots, and uncomplicated characters to create engaging, even beloved programs that continue to entertain subsequent generations of viewers in countless reruns.

Characters with an Edge

The 1950s saw most family-oriented TV shows set in upper–middle-class suburbs, a euphemism for homogeny and contentment. These shows tended to ignore the downside of suburban life—long commutes, the requirement for double incomes, and shrinking family time. Adults on these shows tended to spend most of their time engaged in leisure activities and solving innocuous domestic problems. Household chores were often performed by domestic help on shows such as *Beulah* (1950–1953), *Hazel* (1961–1966), and *Grindl* (1963–1964).

Those programs set in urban areas frequently carried a much stronger bent toward conflict. The 1951 hit *I Love Lucy,* for example, depicted a sharper quality to American family life. In the genre of slapstick comedy, *I Love Lucy* centered around the gaffs of its star, Lucille Ball. The more outrageous the situation the better. A key plot element during the show's prime-time run was husband Ricky's angry reactions to Lucy's antics. In the end, however, Ricky always lived up to the show's title.

A forerunner of the strong, competent women of later TV families, Lucille Ball managed to walk a social tightrope for the time. Many of the show's most hilarious situations focused on Lucy's desire to establish her own identity and test the limits of stereotypical womanhood. Although these situations usually resulted in disaster, they managed to both reassure more conservative viewers that a woman's place was in the home and articulate the desires of many women who wished to venture out into more male-dominated territories. Part of Lucille Ball's universal appeal was her ability to portray both vulnerability and strength in a single comedic character.

Like *The Adventures of Ozzie and Harriet*, elements of Ball's actual family life spilled over into the series, which further reinforced the nation's growing relationship with television. Husband Ricky was played by Ball's real-life spouse, Desi Arnaz. And when the TV Lucy gave birth to "Little Ricky" on the same night Ball and Arnaz's real-life son was born, the nation followed with the kind of breathless anticipation reserved for close family members.

The Jackie Gleason comedy *The Honeymooners* (1952–1957, 1958–1959) also tried to break new ground by depicting a grittier side of life. *The Honeymooners* was not much of a hit during its first run. The series depicted two middle-aged couples, Ralph and Alice Kramden (Gleason and Audrey Meadows) and Ed and Trixie Norton (Art Carney and Joyce Randolph).

Neighbors in a run-down Brooklyn apartment building, the Kramdens and the Nortons were far from the happy middle-class families portrayed in most 1950s series. Ralph Kramden was basically a cranky, loud-mouthed loser, and Ed Norton was his bumbling but lovable sidekick. Most of the comedy surrounded Ralph and Ed's failed attempts to make a quick buck or otherwise raise their social status.

What also made *The Honeymooners* different from other family comedies of the era was its portrayal of female characters. Wives Alice and Trixie were significantly wiser than their male spouses and demonstrated their superiority with acerbic criticisms of their husbands.

Although Gleason revived *The Honeymooners* with a revised cast in 1966, only thirty-nine of the original 1950s episodes were ever filmed. These episodes are now considered by many to be classic TV comedy, but their lack of popularity when first aired may attest to America's distaste during the 1950s for so-called "realism" in family entertainment.

Changing Tastes

In many ways, the 1950s acted as a kind of "breather" from the wartime stresses of the 1940s, and the burgeoning Cold War gave America an excuse to look outward and avoid too much self-examination. By the 1960s, however, it was rapidly becoming clear that the status quo excluded too many segments of society from the post-war prosperity that marked the preceding decade.

The social unrest of the 1960s forced much of Western society to reassess its values. And although most entertainment programming remained optimistic, these shows were in stark contrast to the news media's role of communicating, and even shaping, social conflicts and resulting public policies. This dichotomy between the messages of news programs versus entertainment shows could not exist indefinitely.

Eventually viewers' tastes began to change in ways that reflected both the media's power to influence popular discourse and the public's own admission that things weren't quite as rosy as they appeared on entertainment TV. Television programmers responded by shifting to a "demographic" approach, focusing on shows relevant to specific groups of viewers, such as suburbanites or young married couples—the viewers most likely to spend money on consumer goods.[37]

Interestingly, *The Flintstones* (1960–1966), a prime-time cartoon originally targeting adult audiences, was in many ways an animated, suburbanized version of *The Honeymooners*, which only four years earlier had bombed as a series. Its principals, Fred and Wilma Flintstone and Barney and Betty Rubble, were almost identical to *The Honeymooners'* characters. The 1961 program became the longest-running animated series in television history, in part by poking fun at the sanitized TV families of the previous decade.

By this time, television had become an ingrained part of American culture. The synergy between the media and society had become so entwined, it is difficult to determine how much society's tastes influenced programming decisions, and how much television influenced society's tastes. However, it was during this era that television began to "push the envelope," challenging many long-standing stereotypes and institutions.

Unlike most earlier depictions of women as dependent and submissive, *Bewitched* (1964–1972) and *The Dick Van Dyke Show* (1961–1966), for example, each offered strong female characters. Samantha (Elizabeth Montgomery) on *Bewitched* may have had to use magic to resolve problems, but she was usually competent and level-headed when compared to her beleaguered and sometimes bumbling husband, Darrin (Dick York from 1964 to 1969 and Dick Sargent from 1969 to 1972).

Like *Bewitched, The Dick Van Dyke Show* also portrayed a nuclear family, but wife Laura (played by Mary Tyler Moore) was both intelligent and sophisticated. In many ways, the characters on this show were suburbanized versions of John and Jackie Kennedy. Moore's character even looked suspiciously like the First Lady. As a couple, Van Dyke and Moore's characters demonstrated a level of teamwork and equality not found in many earlier shows.

Another key member of the cast, Rose Marie, played one of Van Dyke's coworkers. Like most employed women on television during this period, Marie was cast as single and man-hungry. In this instance, however, Marie created a character that was also savvy, independent, and street-wise. She broke the stereotype in other ways, as well, depicting a writer, rather than the typical secretary, teacher, or maid.

Most working women on TV during this period were portrayed as misguided, bemused, unfortunate, or immature. These characters frequently performed roles that simply supported male characters. Lucille Ball, for example, served as the zany and generally incompetent secretary to banker Theodore Mooney (Gale Gordon) on *The Lucy Show* (1962–1968). A host of other shows from *The Farmer's Daughter* (1963–1966) and *The Brady Bunch* (1969–1974) to *Good Times* (1974–1979), *The Courtship of Eddie's Father* (1969–1972), and *Hazel* (1961–1966) cast females as single, domestic employees. Such depictions contrasted reality, as well-educated, middle-class married women entered the workplace in droves, making up more than a third of the total workforce during this period.

The Family Structure

For a mix of reasons, television's family structure began to include a variety of forms. The extended family, and sometimes even a spouse, were left behind. Reflecting America's newfound mobility, the late 1950s and the 1960s found little room for extended families. The recently constructed U.S. interstate highway system opened new vistas for families, and a new family structure capable of going along for the ride was rapidly evolving.

The patriarch of this system was embodied by CBS newscaster Walter Cronkite, accessible to viewers no matter where they roamed. Cronkite's calm, almost folksy manner comforted the country through some of its defining moments, such as the loss of President John F. Kennedy. "When the President was assassinated, people did not go to church or to meetings. They came to their televisions, and everybody who was watching was, in a sense, holding hands. They were saying 'Father Walter, tell us everything will be OK,'" says Don Hewitt, executive producer of *60 Minutes* in 1968.

Kennedy's death was a profound media experience for many viewers. The first president to fully utilize the power of television, Kennedy personified the nation's optimism. To many, his death shattered the illusion of America's invincibility, and acted as a portent to the dark days of civil unrest and war that would characterize the latter half of the 1960s.

While Cronkite may have served as a surrogate grandfather to many viewers, only a handful of programs during the 1960s actually depicted extended family members. These shows usually cast grandparents, aunts, and uncles as quaint and unsophisticated. Families depicted on shows such as *The Real McCoys* (1957–1963), *The Andy Griffith Show* (1960–1968), *The Beverly Hillbillies* (1962–1971), and *Petticoat Junction* (1963–1970) all relied on extended family members for support—and all were set in rural America. Such shows often poked fun at the extended family, but usually cast elder relatives as possessing an earthy wisdom. Other shows such as *The Munsters* (1964–1966) and *The Addams Family* (1964–1966) also depicted extended family members, but only in the most bizarre circumstances.

The late 1950s and the 1960s also saw a strong emergence of a relatively infrequent family situation at that time: the single-parent household. The 1960 U.S. census reported that just 9 percent of all real-life households were headed by a single parent. But an analysis of four decades of television conducted by the University of Dayton Department of Communication reveals that between 1950 and 1959, 40 percent of television families lived in single-parent homes. "This study of family portrayals suggest that television has been and remains clearly out of sync with the structural characteristics of real working families," say Thomas Skill and James D. Robinson, who conducted the analysis.[38]

More a plot device than an acknowledgement of social reality, the single parents of early television were usually well-healed, middle- or upper-class males. In fact, while only 1 percent of all real-life families were headed by single fathers in 1960, 28 percent of all TV families in the 1960s were led by single dads.[39] Only *The Lucy Show*, a 1962 spin-off of *I Love Lucy*, dared take the then-audacious step of portraying a struggling female single parent.

In 1960, two new comedy series portraying single fathers emerged. *My Three Sons (1960-1972)* and *The Andy Griffith Show* joined *Bachelor Father* (1957–1962) in depicting dads going it alone. *My Three Sons* cast Fred MacMurray as the widowed father of three boys, assisted by a gruff but loving live-in relative (William Frawley from 1960 to 1965 and William Demarest from 1965 to 1972). Set in a midwestern suburb, *My Three Sons* was fairly contemporary and sophisticated for its time.

The Andy Griffith Show contrasted this sophistication with an idealized version of small-town life. Andy Griffith, a.k.a., Sheriff Andy Taylor, played dad to Ron Howard's young character, Opie. Like many programs depicting male single parents, Griffith was assisted by a surrogate mother figure, in this case, Aunt Bea, played by Frances Bavier. Such depictions, also seen on later shows such as *The Courtship of Eddie's Father* (1969–1972), acknowledged the prevailing notion that raising children was ultimately "women's work." The 1966 comedy *Family Affair* did little to improve the status of child rearing, relegating it to the butler, Giles French, played by Sebastian Cabot, and reinforcing the notion that parenting was a servile responsibility.

One true anomaly on many levels was the 1968 comedy-drama *Julia*. Actress and singer Diahann Carroll portrayed Julia, an African-American woman whose husband was killed in Vietnam. Unlike previous shows that frequently depicted people of color as domestics or other ancillary characters, Julia was an intelligent, highly competent nurse who lived in a modern apartment with her son.

Julia opened the door to the increasing reality of female single parents. The 1970 hit *The Partridge Family* cast Shirley Jones as single mom to five young rock musicians who traveled the country in a psychedelic bus. Although the premise was unlikely, the show, which lasted four seasons, was both upbeat and in tune with the pop culture of the early seventies. Only Jones and her real-life stepson, David Cassidy, were actually musicians, and the show launched Cassidy on a highly successful career in bubblegum rock recording.

To be sure, the plots of *The Brady Bunch* were also inane. They even spawned a series of movies and reunion episodes lampooning the show's almost satirical naïveté, but the 1969–1974 comedy did acknowledge one social reality few other programs dared tackle: the blended family. Unfortunately, the series did little to illuminate the real-life challenges of merging two families. It also failed to address other issues common in modern stepfamilies such as ex-spouses, former in-laws, and multiple sets of grandparents.

The Brady Bunch reflected the unspoken rule of television during the 1950s and 1960s: single adults were either never married or widowed. Although the early 1970s saw television begin to take a more liberal approach to its depiction of families, divorce still made many viewers uncomfortable.

It wasn't until the mid-1970s that a series portrayed a divorced single parent. Actress Bonnie Franklin played divorced mom Anne Romano on the CBS series *One Day at a Time* from 1975 to 1984. Not only did Romano have to resolve the day-to-day problems of her two headstrong teenage girls, she was also tasked with building a career and love life of her own.

While the series tackled a set of far more realistic issues than most family programs of its era, the behind-the-scenes aspects of *One Day at a Time* were even more indicative of the social problems facing contemporary families. Throughout the series, actress Mackenzie Phillips, who played daughter Julie, battled a real-life drug addiction and eating disorder, and was twice written out of the script to seek rehabilitation.

Once the door was opened by *One Day at a Time*, a flood of shows depicting single parents quickly ensued. In fact, throughout the 1980s, single-parent TV families actually became significantly more prevalent than in real life, accounting for more than 42 percent of all families with children depicted on television, versus 19.7 percent in real life.[40]

Hearkening back to an earlier era, the 1980s saw single dads become an especially popular theme—but with a twist. Shows such as *Full House* (1988–1995), *Who's the Boss?* (1984–1992), and *My Two Dads* (1987–1990), for example, all placed men squarely in the role of primary nurturers, with full domestic responsibilities.

Few TV single parents generated as much interest as the character Murphy Brown. The 1988–1998 comedy of the same name literally leaped into the political arena in May 1992 when Brown, played by Candice Bergen, gave birth to a baby boy, opting to reject marriage proposals by both the child's father and her current boyfriend. The day following the episode, Vice President Dan Quayle delivered a speech in San Francisco on the deterioration of family values in America, citing the show.

"It doesn't help matters when prime-time TV has Murphy Brown, a character who supposedly epitomizes today's intelligent, highly paid professional woman, mocking the importance of fathers by bearing a child alone and calling it just another lifestyle choice," said Quayle.[41] His tirade did little to advance the cause of the traditional family structure, however, and in fact it actually boosted the ratings of the CBS show.

Trouble Brewing

By the 1970s, it was clear that TV's traditional nuclear family was in big trouble. Norman Lear's *All in the Family*, which was produced from 1971 to 1983, took a decidedly contemporary approach to its depiction of the family unit. In Lear's version of family life, home may be where the heart is, but only because it's been eviscerated by sharp barbs and cutting exchanges.

Billed as a "reality-based" show, *All in the Family* sparked controversy from its first episode. Whether it was a reflection of typical household interaction or family life at its worse is debatable, but it certainly could not be accused of sugarcoating the traditional family.

The CBS series basically pitted actor Carroll O'Connor, as Archie Bunker, against the world. Bigoted, stubborn, and ultraconservative,

Bunker represented to many viewers all that was wrong with American society. Truly the antithesis of the 1950s genre of family comedies, *All in the Family* created a picture of home life riddled with marital, intergenerational, ethic, gender, and political conflicts.

Interestingly, however, *All in the Family* became one of the true all-time television hits. It was able to transcend its controversial reputation in part by satisfying two very diverse groups. Although the show was basically meant to skewer the status quo and point out the ignorance inherent in prejudice, many viewers actually saw Bunker as a hero.[42] Archie Bunker articulated these viewers' gut response to what was then seen as an attack on the white Anglo-Saxon male and the perceived ultraliberal agenda of popular culture.

CBS effectively tapped into the popularity of *All in the Family* with women and minority communities by creating several spin-offs, including a female liberal version of the show, *Maude* (1972–1978), and a black version of the show, *The Jeffersons* (1975–1985). Sherman Hemsley's irascible character, George Jefferson, had already appeared on *All in the Family* as the Bunker's African-American neighbor. George's bigotry, as virulent as Archie's but aimed at non-blacks, was tempered by his levelheaded wife, Louise, played by Isabel Sanford. Family conflict swirled around George's failure to accept an integrated world, even as his son dated and eventually married the daughter of an interracial couple.

The '70s also saw the emergence of a truly new genre of television shows based upon the move toward "reality programming." The 1970 network debut of *Phil Donahue*, with its focus on supposedly ordinary people and their extraordinary circumstances opened the door to a steady and increasingly bizarre stream of similar shows, launching the talk show careers of Oprah Winfrey, Sally Jessy Raphael, Jenny Jones, Maury Povich, and Jerry Springer. Although not specifically "family" programs, talk shows seem to make a point of highlighting family conflicts and the seamier sides of contemporary family life.

A Return to Tradition

"Reality" was a popular television theme during the 1970s. And although many in television's creative community seemed bent on exposing the gritty side of family life, the popularity of a handful of programs also reflected a growing nostalgia for positive depictions of family life.

The 1972–1981 dramatic series *The Waltons* struck a chord with family viewers as it depicted an imperfect but loving family struggling through the Great Depression. Like most other extended television families, the Waltons lived in a rural setting—the Blue Ridge Mountains of Virginia. Rather than satirizing the family, however, this drama was respectful of family life and the vital socializing roles played by siblings and grandparents. The Waltons faced serious problems, from poverty and illness to the children's budding sexuality, with both dignity and authenticity.

Little House on the Prairie (1974–1982), based on the *Little House* books of Laura Ingalls Wilder, tended to sanitize and romanticize family life a bit more than *The Waltons* but was equally popular for its positive depictions of the nuclear family.

By the mid-1970s, pop culture's free sex and drugs mantra had begun to take its toll on the American family. Many baby boomers began to long for the perceived simpler life of their childhood. The 1974–1984 series *Happy Days* fit the bill. At one level, *Happy Days* satirized the 1950s *Ozzie and Harriet* genre of TV fare, but at another level, it paid homage to the supportive nuclear family.

Ron Howard, who portrayed Richie Cunningham on the series, was already a veteran of television family life, having played son Opie on *The Andy Griffith Show*. The transition to TV teen was a natural for Howard, and many viewers took comfort in watching "Opie" grow up into a wholesome adolescent. Nonetheless, *Happy Days* became the top-rated TV program of the 1976–1977 season. The show eventually spawned successful spin-offs including *Laverne & Shirley* (1976–1983) and *Joanie Loves Chachi* (1982–1983). The show also fit well into the "family viewing hour" concept enacted by the National Association of Broadcasters in 1975.

The NAB voluntarily instituted the family viewing hour restrictions on prime-time violence and sex in response to a growing drive by Congress to institute mandatory guidelines. But the Writers Guild of America, led by top producers including Norman Lear, sued the U.S. Federal Communications Commission, charging that the agreement violated the First Amendment. The hour was struck down in 1977 by a federal judge who found "the existence of threats, and the attempted securing of commitments coupled with the promise to publicize noncompliance...constituted per se violations of the First Amendment."[43,44] In other words, it was unconstitutional to prevent certain shows from being aired at certain times.

Still, recognizing the success of *Happy Days, The Waltons*, and other family programs, television programmers pumped out a variety of "family" shows throughout the late 1970s and early 1980s. By far, the most successful was *The Cosby Show*, which aired from 1984 to 1992.

Partially owing to the popularity of its star, Bill Cosby, the show's phenomenal success was also a product of its format. *The Cosby Show* presented contemporary family life as both wholesome and hip. Although the cast was almost exclusively African-American, the program rarely tackled serious racial issues. In addition, while the characters occasionally displayed ethnic identities, the overall premise of *The Cosby Show* was sufficiently generic to attract a multicultural audience.

Cosby and his TV wife, Clair, played by Phylicia Rashad, became role models for many parents. Their savvy, no-nonsense but loving approach to parenting (mixed with an appropriate amount of wit) made sense to a generation of new parents unsatisfied with the laissez-faire approach to parenting espoused by the pop culture of the 1960s and 1970s.

Growing Pains (1985–1992) also attempted to create the idealized family of the 1980s. *A Father Knows Best* for the consumer decade, *Growing Pains* offered up Dr. Jason Seaver, played by Alan Thicke, as a wise and good-natured dad who moves his psychiatric practice to a home office to keep an eye on the kids while wife Maggie (Joanna Kerns) went off to work. Although the series occasionally tackled serious issues such as teen suicide, drug use, and drunk driving, most episodes focused on safer topics such as dating and sibling squabbles.

Like the 1970s, the 1980s had a brief flirtation with nostalgia. *The Wonder Years* (1988–1993) focused more on the music of the era than actual social issues. Twelve-year-old Kevin Arnold, played by Fred Savage and narrated by Daniel Stern, recounted the challenges of coping with school, young love, a hippy sister (Olivia d'Abo), and the constant wrath of his older brother (Jason Hervey). The one phenomenon the show depicted that reflected the realities of contemporary family life was Kevin's relationship with his parents. Unlike earlier nostalgic family shows, family relationships on *The Wonder Years* were both distant and stormy. This was especially true with Kevin and his father, Jack Arnold, played by Dan Lauria. The elder Arnold was almost always depicted as overworked, tired, and cranky.

The 1980s were also the age of the family dynasty. Tapping into the consumerism of the era, nighttime soaps such as *Dallas* (1978–1991), *Dynasty* (1981–1989), and *Falcon Crest* (1981–1990) gave newfound respect to the idea of an extended family living under one roof—albeit a very large roof. Infighting, betrayal, and intrigue were popular topics on these shows, but in the end, these TV families invariably united for a single purpose: to make money.

The financial theme even trickled down to situation comedies during this period. Baby boomers had begun to reach full maturity and "Reaganomics" became the decade's mantra. Perhaps no other program captured the dichotomy of 1980s greed versus 1970s and 1960s social consciousness better than the situation comedy *Family Ties* (1982–1989). Set smack in middle America—Columbus, Ohio—the sitcom pitted ultra-conservative teen Alex Keaton (Michael J. Fox) against his former flower children parents, Elyse and Steve Keaton, played by Meredith Baxter-Birney and Michael Gross. The show tackled a variety of themes—sometimes with dramatic overtones—but the central plot almost always focused on the conflict between fiscal conservatism and social idealism. Although both sides took plenty of ribbing, Fox's uptight, preppy character by far was most likely to be skewered.

Thirtysomething (1987–1991) took a more dramatic approach to consumerism, portraying a group of stereotypical yuppies. The show depicted the ideal viewer sponsors were hoping to reach: upwardly mobile young parents who were ready to buy. The show also demonstrated the angst of the era, as characters spent much of their time seeking a deeper meaning in their career-driven lives and patching up perpetually unstable relationships.

Reality with a Vengeance

During the late 1980s, so-called "reality-based" comedy came into vogue. In 1988, *Roseanne* debuted, turning the wholesome ideal of family life on its ear. Although the program's writers attempted to imply that the working-class Conner household was basically loving, the dialogue was nothing less than razor-sharp. Mom, played by Roseanne Barr, frequently joked that she hated kids and wasn't averse to suggesting to her offspring, "Go play in traffic."

If *Roseanne* was truly reality-based, it depicted a particularly harsh reality. In its defense, *Roseanne* wasn't afraid to tackle serious family issues such as adultery, drugs, and teen sex. But its stinging family interaction and cynicism also gave credence to the notion that a harmonious family life was out of reach for most American households.

Roseanne's success opened the door to even more cynical views of the family. The 1987 Fox sitcom *Married...With Children* (1987–1997) offered viewers the Bundy family—a depressing picture of total dysfunction. Al Bundy, played by Ed O'Neill, slogs through a dismal career as a shoe salesman. He's disdainful of his greedy, oversexed wife Peg (Katey Sagal), and both parents are indifferent to their ditzy, promiscuous daughter (Christina Applegate) and dull but conniving son (David Faustino). Although clearly a satire, *Married...With Children* has been one of the most telling social commentaries on how Hollywood sees the contemporary American family. In television's eyes, the institution of marriage and family life are a dismal failure.

This message isn't confined to adult-oriented comedies. The 1989 animated series *The Simpsons* offered a similar message to America's youth. Like many contemporary television shows such as *Home Improvement* (1991–1999) and *Buffy the Vampire Slayer*, (1997–) the children in this series are savvy and street-smart. Parents—especially fathers—are generally depicted as naïve buffoons. Few Americans fail to recognize Bart Simpson's trademark spiked hair and belligerent self-introduction: "I'm Bart Simpson! Who the hell are you?"

While some may argue that programs such as *The Simpsons*, *King of the Hill* (1997–), *Futurama* (1999–), *Family Guy* (1999–), and *The PJs* (1999–) are satirical in nature, and may even offer some moral statements, their animated formats make them particularly appealing to young viewers. This can be problematic, since often any moral messages are cloaked in sophisticated satire that young children may not understand. The ultimate message of, say, *The Simpsons* may be that inappropriate behavior is undesirable. But less analytical viewers such as young children simply may see that telling the school principal to "eat my shorts" or insulting religious neighbors and the elderly is fun.

Moreover, by depicting poor and even tasteless behavior and then successfully resolving it within a half-hour time slot, young viewers may be receiving the message that such behaviors have few consequences. It may be obvious to adults that a child who behaves like Bart Simpson will probably end up with a serious criminal record. But young audiences may not be capable of making the distinction between television and reality, and may be tempted to emulate such behavior.

In addition, the satire in many television family depictions is often based upon other TV portrayals of family life. In a sense, these series actually bite the hand that feeds them by poking fun at television as a medium. But such copious pop-culture references also require that viewers watch increasing amounts of television in order to form a basis for their humor.

Full Circle?

Television at the turn of the century has seen a small but telling backlash to the negative portrayal of families on television. Some in TV's creative community seem to have experienced a religious conversion that centers around traditional family values. Dramas such as *Promised Land* and *7th Heaven*, both premiering in 1996, for example, centered around relatively large families with strong religious faiths.

An offshoot of *Touched By an Angel* (1994–), *Promised Land* depicts a working-class Vietnam veteran (Gerald McRaney) who takes his family on the road after losing his job. Traveling the country in a beat-up Chevy Suburban and Airstream trailer, the Greenes help the people they meet tackle tough issues from drug and alcohol abuse to gang violence.

The WB network's *7th Heaven* is surprisingly wholesome, given the fact that it's an Aaron Spelling production (the same company that produced the Gen-X series *Melrose Place*). *7th Heaven* casts Stephen Collins as a minister and father of seven. Although the show espouses traditional family values, the plots frequently deal with serious social issues. The family is depicted as loving and supportive, however, fairly authentic squabbles break out frequently. What sets these depictions of "reality" apart from shows such as the less family-based series *NYPD Blue (1993–)* is their ability to resolve problems through positive interaction as opposed to violence. Also, these shows may touch upon sexual issues, but they resist dwelling on the sexual act in favor of examining the potential consequences.

Unlike *Promised Land* and *7th Heaven*, which target conservative adult and early and pre-teen audiences, relatively few programs aimed at Generation X during the 1990s actually depicted family life. Instead, a new genre of sitcom emerged: the surrogate family. These programs brought together groups of unrelated individuals who either lived together or spent significant amounts of time with one another in family-like situations. It seems apparent that such programs reflected the weakened family ties experienced by many Gen-Xers.

Seinfeld (1990–1998), *Friends* (1994), and *Melrose Place* (1992), for example, rarely depicted the characters' families. Instead, these characters relied on one another for the kind of support usually provided by the family. Other programs aimed at young viewers such as *Beverly Hills 90210* (1990–2000), *Dawson's Creek* (1997–), and *Buffy the Vampire Slayer* may have acknowledged the existence of a family, but parents and siblings rarely played significant roles in the main characters' lives. Ensemble profession-oriented shows such as *ER* (1994–), *The Practice* (1997–), *Law & Order* (1990–), *Ally McBeal* (1997–), and *NYPD Blue* also reflected the growing TV trend toward making relationships outside the home the primary means of support.

The New "Healthy" Family

Our idea of what constitutes a healthy family has been shaped by modern television. In the early days of this medium, television reflected those family characteristics we believed were most valuable. Realistic or not, TV depicted our ideal of the family, those traits that made families supportive structures for both adults and children.

Beginning in the 1960s, however, the family of mother, father, and children—and even grandparents—became fodder for comedy writers. Such families often are portrayed as outmoded and out of touch with reality.

Today's "real" family, as depicted by television, is usually portrayed as fraught with conflict.

Fathers are often depicted as distant, violent, or bumbling. And TV frequently communicates the belief that close relationships with mothers are typically dependent and manipulative. In dramas such as *Law & Order* and *ER*, children are commonly the victims of abusive parents. And in comedies, kids possess intellects that quickly outshine that of mom or dad. Children's repartee is no longer innocent or endearing—it's now witty and cutting, often bordering on cruel.

Television has gone head-to-head with the age-old notion that elders are fonts of wisdom. In its place, TV creates a portrait of grandparents and other senior citizens as outdated at best, and often simply doddering old fools. Television's message? The elderly have little to contribute to today's society. "Old people today are generally not appreciated as experienced 'elders' or possessors of special wisdom; they are simply seen as sometimes remaining competent enough to be included in the unitary role category of 'active citizen,'" notes media scholar Joshua Meyrowitz. "Old people are respected to the extent that they can behave like young people, that is, to the extent that they remain capable of working, enjoying sex, exercising, and taking care of themselves."[45]

It is no secret that technology has, in some ways, outpaced us all. Children do have more knowledge when it comes to technological matters. More important, however, are the societal implications of this trend. Now more than ever, society needs the wisdom of its elders in dealing with the complicated societal changes that technology has wrought.

Anthropologist Margaret Mead postulates that cultural continuity depends on the living presence of at least three generations. As grandparents are removed from the family setting, children's links to the past and preparations for the future are weakened by the absence of a full generation.[46]

Mead pointed out as early as the 1960s that technological changes appear to be making grandparents and elders obsolete. "Elders used to say, 'You know, I have been young, and you never have been old,' but today's young people reply, 'You never have been young in the world I am young in, and you never can be.'" Mead adds, however, that the emerging system is faulty because it provides no real-life guides to cultural awareness.[47]

Ultimately, then, the culture begins to be defined by the children rather than the elders. Such a model creates a highly unstable environment, since children may wield technological savvy but not the cultural and interpersonal skills of older, more experienced generations. "We must create new models for adults who can teach their children not what to learn, but how to learn," says Mead, "and not what they should be committed to, but the value of commitment."[48]

The world around us may be changing rapidly, but human social needs have remained fairly constant. The interpersonal and cultural experiences of older generations can still apply to many of today's situations, and their wisdom is still valuable in helping younger generations come to terms with their own relationships.

Without this wisdom, social structures begin to erode. We can already see the early effects of a society that no longer values social norms and constructs. As we enter the twenty-first century, we have broken down the social and cultural structures of our ancestors and erected a technological structure in their place.

Marriage is a popular target for TV. Rarely does television portray matrimony as something to be valued, as an institution that is supportive and loving. More often, it depicts marriage as fraught with bickering and unreasonable demands. Numerous evaluations of popular shows that depict families portray home as a distress-filled place peopled by characters who frequently verbally attack or belittle each other.[49] An analysis of twenty-three prime-time programs featuring families reveals, for example, that conflicts arise at a rate of nearly nine per hour. Surprisingly, sitcoms featured the most amount of conflict at 11.75 per hour, compared with family dramas at 5.44 per hour.[50] This is particularly alarming since some studies suggest that real-life couples actually use television as a model for their own relationships. "Not only do television portrayals of marriage affect the way in which people think about marriage and the family," say researchers William Douglas and Beth Olson, "but both married and divorced persons report using such portrayals to guide their own marriage behaviors."[51]

Television often opts in favor of cohabitation and sexual promiscuity outside the "confines" of marriage. While TV is adept at portraying sex, it only rarely depicts sexual activity with a long-term partner. Nearly half of all contemporary shows depict sex outside of marriage in a positive light, and another third pass no moral judgment.[52] In addition, a 1999 study published by Michael Morgan, Susan Leggett, and Shanahan James in the respected journal *Mass Communication & Society* suggests that television viewing changes viewers' perceptions about illegitimacy and single parenthood and is "contributing to the fraying of traditional family values."[53]

Noted media critic Michael Medved, in his book *Hollywood vs. America*, points out that antifamily images "have become so deeply ingrained in our national consciousness that few Americans can summon the courage or the strength to dismiss them as the destructive distortions that they are."[54]

The family structure provides children with vital tools—tools now on the brink of extinction. These skills help children become healthy adults capable of relating to others in work, play, and other social situations. They provide scripts for friendship, marriage, and child rearing. They help individuals define their roles in society. By offering up a mix of generations, ages, and sexes, the family structure provides a model for society. But many television depictions of families contradict this role, portraying the family as incapable or unprepared to socialize its youngest members.

"The experience of television children appears to have deteriorated across time," note researchers Douglas and Olson, who studied the perceptions of 267 subjects who viewed a variety of programs broadcast between 1954 and 1994. They noted that participants rated modern programs as portraying families as more conflict-ridden, less cohesive, less supportive, and less stable. "In addition, modern families were rated as less able to manage day-to-day life and less able to socialize children effectively."[55]

Recurrent Themes

One of the great ironies of television family life is that few TV family members watch much television. Those who do are invariably depicted as unsophisticated and dysfunctional. There is a simple explanation for this disparity between the average real-life family—which typically lives in what respected media scholar Edward Medrick describes as a "constant-television household"[56]—and the TV-averse television family. When families watch TV, little else happens. People stop talking; they stop moving; they stop interacting in almost every way. Simply put, watching people watch television is boring.

Television also does a poor job of integrating work and family. Most shows are set either in the workplace or at home and there is little crossover between the two. One study by the University of Washington, for example, found that only thirteen of 150 television shows depicted any sort of work/family interaction. In addition, the research found most shows fail to depict the reality of working mothers. For example, while two-thirds of real-life moms work for pay, just one-third of TV mothers do. And when television moms do work, they usually face few professional or career concerns. Katherine Heintz-Knowles, who conducted the study, notes that on programs such as *The Cosby Show*, for example, the mother's career was rarely discussed. She adds that women in middle-and lower-class jobs garner even less air time.[57]

It's also interesting to note the cyclic nature of television's depiction of the family. An analysis reveals a fairly steady movement toward increasingly negative depictions of family life. This trend is interrupted every few years by a backlash of programs that attempt to revive the notion that the nuclear family is still relevant and viable. The popularity of these programs and the huge success of cable channels such as Nickelodeon that air reruns of more wholesome fare indicate that many contemporary parents and younger viewers seem to have an innate hope that the family can and will survive an onslaught of programs that portend its demise. A 1996 study published in the respected journal *Communications Research* examined the perceptions and viewing preferences of 240 viewers ages nineteen to forty-eight. The participants were asked to assess the family relationships in eight popular television shows: *The Cosby Show*, *Family Ties*, *Who's the Boss?*, *Growing Pains*, *Roseanne*, *Family Matters* (1989–1998), *Full House,* and *Home Improvement*. Although most of these TV families were evaluated in comparatively positive ways, two families in particular, the Connors on *Roseanne*, and the Taylors on *Home Improvement*, were seen as having serious relational problems, including lack of supportive behaviors, high levels of conflict, and low ability to socialize children effectively.[58]

A 1992 Gallup Poll found that almost two-thirds of Americans are dissatisfied with contemporary family life.[59] It appears that the viewing public still cherishes a more idyllic picture of the family, and when Hollywood responds to this longing, the results are often quite remarkable—and profitable. Although *All in the Family*, *Roseanne*, *The Simpsons*, and other "reality-based" programs have attracted significant audiences, there is still a place in America's heart for *The Cosby Show*, *The Waltons*, and, yes, even *The Adventures of Ozzie and Harriet*.

Part Two:
Stolen Roles

Family Manager

Before television, parents were tasked with managing the household. They determined the physical layout of the home; made key decisions on how family members utilized their time; regulated and filtered many communications, often establishing appropriate conversation topics; managed conflicts among family members; rewarded and punished offspring, determined how family resources were to be used; and generally set the tone for other key family characteristics. Simply put, their job was to impose order over the household.

Among the most vital roles we play as parents and spouses is "family manager." No business, no group, and no country will last long without some form of leadership and guidance. Every effective organization requires a structure for making decisions, and families are no different. Members must decide how the family income is spent, what to have for dinner, where this chair or that table is placed in the living room, who feeds the family pet, when Junior should be home, and thousands of other issues that keep a household running. Sometimes these decisions are shared. In other households, one person makes most of the decisions and the rest follow. In contemporary America, however, television is often in charge.

This is not to say that the TV feeds the dog or buys the groceries. What it does mean is that, often, we rely on television to tell us what choices we should make, to provide us with key decision-making information that previously required a more personal investigation. The question this acquiescence raises is, "Whose wisdom, knowledge, and guidance are we relying upon?"

TV and Time Use

Literally thousands of studies have confirmed that when parents and children are at home, they spend most of their waking time with TV. The University of Maryland's "American's Use of Time Project,"[60] for example, polled a nationally representative sample of Americans on how they spent their time. The study found that when it came to leisure activities, the amount of time spent watching television was more than three times that of its nearest competitor, visiting with others. While most of us seem to face an increasing time crunch, this study indicated that our "spare" time has actually increased by more than five hours per week since the mid-1960s.

So why do we feel so pressured? The University of Maryland study found that for every hour of leisure time we gained, we watched at least one more hour of television.[61] Currently, most people spend about fifteen hours per week or about 38 percent of their free time watching TV. And if you include "secondary" and "tertiary" viewing—time spent doing other activities while watching TV or having the television on, TV viewing captures more than half of all free time. No wonder we feel overwhelmed by all the responsibilities of life. We're trying to jam them into a smaller window of opportunity, simply so we can watch more TV!

In many families, television plays the primary role in how members organize their time, arrange their environment, and talk to one another. A U.S. Department of Agriculture study titled "Use of Time in Rural and Urban Families"[62] found, for example, that while mom and dad spent an average of 136 minutes and 124 minutes per day respectively watching TV, teens were the biggest consumers, racking up an average of 147 minutes of TV every day.

Not surprisingly, research indicates the presence of television typically results in less play, reading, socializing, conversation, and even sleep. One study funded by the Children's Television Workshop and conducted by researchers at the University of Texas at Austin and the University of Kansas looked at the activity patterns of 236 young children (ages two to four) over a four-year period.[63] The researchers found that while children spent about twenty-two minutes per day reading, they spent nearly three hours per day with the TV. The children spent a similar amount of time playing, but often that play occurred in front of the television. While younger children may mix television viewing and play, other research, such as the Department of Agriculture study, suggests that as children age, their viewing patterns become exclusive of other activities.

Although the University of Texas and University of Kansas study was not designed to measure if television displaces other activities, it appeared to confirm other research in British Columbia, South Africa, the Netherlands, and Australia.[64] The researchers in these studies investigated the introduction of television into communities that previously did not have access to TV, and how television changed the amount of time spent on various activities. In South Africa and Australia, for example, children were less likely to play outdoors after the introduction of TV. A three-year study of 1,050 Dutch elementary school children published in the respected journal *Human Communication Research*[65] found that television significantly reduced the amount of time kids spent reading books. The research also suggested two alarming causes for the drop in reading: that TV appeared to erode positive attitudes toward reading and that it also reduced children's ability to concentrate on books and magazines.

Conversely, it's interesting to note that the 1997 winners of both the U.S. National Spelling Bee and the Westinghouse Science Talent Search were children who grew up without televisions in their home.[66]

Reading habits such as these tend to carry into adulthood. While the "American's Use of Time Project" notes that most adults now spend only about three hours per week reading, other research suggests that nearly 60 percent of Americans never read another book after leaving school.[67]

The University of Maryland study noted that the total time spent in religious activities has also dropped about half an hour per week[68] and that people who own a TV sleep an average of fifteen minutes per day (or one hour and forty-five minutes per week) less than those who shun the tube.[69]

Many studies suggest that television viewing reduces creativity, as well as participation in sports and extracurricular activities. A 1974 study of a Canadian town that was introduced to television profoundly demonstrated this pattern.[70] In addition to reading less, within two years of being regularly exposed to TV, community members' superior scores on creativity tests plummeted to the level of children in towns that had been watching television for much longer periods of time. Moreover, the children were less inclined to participate in sports, dances, and club activities.

The Electronic Classroom

Television's fast-paced images and short sound bites also alter our ability to assimilate large bodies of abstract ideas. Consequently, frequent TV viewers may find it difficult to process complex information.

Studies have shown that children who are heavy television viewers are less able to think in abstract terms.[71,72,73] These children also demonstrate lower levels of imagination than those who spend similar amounts of time reading. "While television hasn't killed the imagination, it has hurt it," says Kate Moody in her book, *Growing Up on Television: The TV Effect*.[74] Some research even suggests that television alters how we use our cognitive abilities and may even impact the physiology of the human brain. "The eye and brain functions employed in TV viewing likely put demands on different parts of the brain than those used in reading, causing incalculably different kinds of cognitive development at the expense of reading and writing aptitude," says Moody.[75]

The average child now starts school with a minimum of fifteen hundred hours of TV–watching experience under his or her belt. And by the time most children finish high school, they will have spent about eighteen thousand hours with the "TV curriculum" and only twelve thousand hours with the school curriculum.[76] One television program—billed educational by its network, PBS—specifically targets pre-verbal children, ages one and two. The creator of the British series, *Teletubbies* (1998), notes that its surreal characters may have as much in common with their medium as their audience. "The Teletubbies are not children but constructs," says Anne Wood. "They're technological babies."[77]

The characters' stomachs are actually TV screens depicting real children. At a very early age, fans are being encouraged to identify with characters who feature television as part of their anatomy—a telling message for parents who allow their children to become frequent TV viewers.

Once children reach school age, research shows they still spend twice as much time in front of the television as they do in the classroom. As a result, teachers now deal with a student population characterized by an epidemic of attention disorders and significantly shorter attention spans than that of previous generations. Nearly 20 percent of America's students now suffer from some form of learning disability, and more than a fifth of all educational resources are poured into remedial programs.[78]

Critics who rightly argue that educational television programs are so fast-paced that they may be of limited value to young viewers should also take a look at shows aimed at older audiences. The average scene from *Sesame Street* (1969) for instance, lasts about ten seconds, while MTV programming comes in at an alarming three seconds per shot.[79]

To maintain a sustainable social structure we must go beyond TV's sound-bite mentality. For both children and adults, popular media should be encouraged to provide programs involving complex thoughts that take more than a few seconds to fully comprehend.

Psychologist Sidney Segalowitz of Canada's Brock University points out that the growing visual and aural power of television threatens children's ability to control their own attention processes. He adds that TV viewing inhibits "self-monitoring," a psychological response that helps children learn how to behave in various social settings.[80]

Addicted to the Tube

If television viewing is so potentially destructive, why has TV use grown so rapidly over the past few decades? It seems to have little to do with technology. While the introduction of color TV in the 1960s seemed to boost viewership slightly, there were no dramatic increases in viewing among households with the introduction of more channels, more television sets, cable TV, or VCRs.[81,82] The fact is, television viewing has expanded to fill as much free time as we can possibly spare—and then some.

Apparently, television viewing really does act like an addiction. "Not unlike drugs or alcohol, the television experience allows the participants to blot out the real world and enter into a pleasurable and passive mental state," notes respected media researcher Marie Winn, author of *The Plug-in Drug*.[83] Linus Wright, former undersecretary of education, agrees.

"Television is addicting, like tobacco, and parents should never let their children get hooked."[84]

TV's lure is especially powerful among the lonely and emotionally vulnerable. A Rutgers University study, for example, examined the viewing habits of employees at five Chicago-area companies.[85,86] The researchers found the highest viewership among those who felt most alienated, particularly subjects who were divorced or separated. The researchers speculated that these distraught viewers turned to television to avoid examination of conflicts and internal turmoil. "Television programs and commercials, after all, provide parasocial experiences and are constructed to keep the viewer's attention focused on the TV and not on the self,"[87] notes Robert W. Kubey, who led the study.

TV is frequently used to punctuate time and as a framework for the family schedule. We wake up to TV news and morning programs. We rush home for lunch to catch a favorite soap opera. Our children cut playtime short to watch their afternoon cartoons or talk shows. Dinner is timed to coincide with the evening news or a favorite game show. Nightime activities are scheduled around dramas or comedies. And by bedtime, when you'd think we'd had enough TV, we're faced with the decision to watch the news and a late-night talk show, or sleep. Guess what often wins out.

Most contemporary households effectively build their living space around an average of three televisions. Often, family rooms or other gathering places are not organized in a circular arrangement that facilitates conversation and family interaction. Rather, furniture is placed in a U-shaped or linear arrangement to ensure a clear view of the TV. "For people in the room, television viewing is not just an option but a directed option," notes Arizona State University family and human development researchers Patricia Wilson and Scott Christopher. A similar phenomenon occurs in other living areas such as the dining room, kitchen, or bedrooms, where the TV becomes the primary factor in deciding room layouts.[88]

Communication Regulator

As a media ecologist, it's my job to investigate and understand how communication media affect and influence human relationships. The ways in which we communicate are what make us human. They are the vehicles through which interpersonal relationships are developed and maintained. Family scholars agree that communication is the foundation of family interaction and the Rosetta stone for understanding family dynamics.

In some ways, it appears we communicate more than ever—by phone, fax, pager, etc. Yet, the family as a social institution is losing ground. It appears that this breakdown is directly related to changes in the way humans communicate.

Conversations between family members that go beyond simple maintenance and regulatory functions have declined, and, in some families, ceased altogether. "Like the sorcerer of old, the television casts its magic spell, freezing speech and action and turning the living into silent statues so long as the enchantment lasts," says psychologist Uri Bronfenbrenner. "The primary danger of the television screen lies not so much in the behavior it produces as the behavior it prevents—the talks, the games, the family festivities and arguments through which much of the child's learning takes place and his character is formed."[89]

A study of seventy-six Madison, Wisconsin, families by researchers Judith Walters and Vernon Stone[90] found more than half of all respondents reported little or no conversation when the TV was on—similar to a 1951 study by media researcher Eleanor Maccoby and the 1982 conclusions of the National Institute of Mental Health.[91] The Wisconsin study, published in the respected *Journal of Broadcasting*, found that talking varied with the programming in another 32 percent of the families. Overall, only 12 percent of participating families reported talking frequently, and 4 percent talked "most of the time" the TV was on.

Research by Robert Kubey of 107 adults indicated that TV reduced conversation about 40 percent.[92] The subjects in this study also reported feeling less challenged, less skilled, more relaxed, less alert, less strong, and less active when the TV was on.

When the family is gathered at home, it may be together, in a physical sense, under one roof. But the dynamics of family interaction appear to be changing as a result of the increasing attention we pay to television. Researchers at the University of Georgia studied the interactions of twenty-seven families while viewing TV and during other activities.[93] They found that both children and fathers interacted with other family members in profoundly different ways when the TV was on. The kids and dads participating in the study talked less during viewing than during family play, and both dads and kids visually oriented toward each other less. Fathers also smiled less frequently during viewing. The changes in mothers' behaviors were less dramatic, but one finding was particularly interesting and appeared positive at first blush: both parents increased physical contact with their children during viewing.

While television advocates may point to this discovery as an encouraging sign, the Georgia researchers speculated that the increase in touching may reflect an unconscious sensitivity of parents to the fact that they are not interacting with their children in other ways. In a sense, such touching, then, may be considered compensation for, or even a guilt reaction to a decrease in verbal and visual communication.

Those who tout the increase in touching while viewing TV as positive also ignore another profound statistic—that a majority of children now have TVs in their rooms, making viewing an isolated, and non-tactile, activity. For example, a study of three thousand children for the highly respected Henry J. Kaiser Family Foundation, which funds healthcare and media research, found that more than 65 percent of eight- to eighteen-year-olds had a television in their room and spent as much as seven hours a day consuming TV and other electronic media.[94]

Equally disturbing, a two-year study of 271 five-year-olds by the University of Kansas found that when parents and children do watch TV together, they generally watch adult programming.[95] The study noted that although the young subjects viewed television with other people about 85 percent of the time, those co-viewers were usually siblings. The children watched TV with their mothers about 27 percent of the time and with dad about 18 percent of the time. Although the study was not designed to examine how the parents' programming preferences impacted those of the children, the researchers did note that children whose parents encouraged them to view specific programming did watch more educational shows and less "entertainment" programming, such as cartoons.

Studies such as the University of Maryland's "American's Use of Time Project" point out that television is America's favorite companion—beating out spending time with friends by a wide margin. In another poll of more than one thousand Americans conducted by Louis Harris & Associates,[96] only 13 percent of participants said they prefer spending time with family over other activities, including watching TV. Although these preferences may be attributed to the fact that almost everyone seems busy, they also reflect a choice—either conscious or unconscious—to watch the tube rather than interact with others. Simply put, TV is easier than socializing with real people, as Robert Kubey's research points out.

Even researchers who make a point of seeking out the positive effects of television must concede that TV is a powerful force in family dynamics. Media scholar James Lull, for example, classifies television as a social resource that enhances communication and social learning. Yet, he notes, it is rarely mentioned as a vital force in the construction or maintenance of interpersonal relationships.[97]

Researcher Francis Ianni claims that television encourages conversation and social interaction within families.[98] Studies suggest that television viewing is often the one activity in which all family members participate. Television provides topics of conversation among family members who may have few other mutual interests. Such research raises more questions than it answers, however. Why do many families have so little in common? Where is the interaction that builds commonalties? When did family members' experiences become so exclusive, so personal, so disconnected?

In eras that predate electronic media, home entertainment often consisted of reading as a family, playing games, engaging in conversation, or listening to live music performed by a family member. Such entertainment, as well as the common economic needs of the household, was the focus of family discussions.

In modern society, however, television reigns as the primary, often exclusive, mode of entertainment. Its role of enhancing family communication is clear. In some households, talk turns to televised sports, while other family members may discuss the latest soap opera developments or events covered by the evening news.

In households that maintain open lines of communication, the sexual material and adult language found in many TV programs may also spur conversations about these topics—particularly among children. Other families may spend time analyzing characters, motives, and topics found in the wide variety of dramas, comedies, and movies that make up the typical evening television schedule.

These observations support Ianni's contention that TV provides topics of conversation among family members, thus stimulating interaction. Other researchers such as E. Katz and D. Foulkes found viewing television as a family activity can stimulate a feeling of family solidarity by sharing emotional reactions such as laughter, sorrow, or anger.[99] Such solidarity and opportunities for communication may seem quite desirable, but there is a less positive side to this interaction. First, given the external nature of the television viewing experience, family solidarity is often fleeting. Time spent in the passive act of watching TV detracts from the family's abilities to share common, real-life experiences. While members may agree upon the quality of a made-for-television movie, they may be less inclined to discuss more mundane subjects that have a greater impact on the family such as school, work, relationships, or even who will take out the trash.

In addition, family discussions of sensitive subjects depicted on TV may open up topics that otherwise would not be tackled until a later, more age-appropriate time. Prior to TV, sexual curiosity often occurred on a natural timetable as a child faced puberty or the attention of the opposite sex. TV, however, creates a premature curiosity and interest in sex that neither parents nor children may be prepared to face. More than two-thirds of parents surveyed by the Kaiser Family Foundation say they are concerned "a great deal" that TV exposes their children to too much sexual content, and that number is on the rise.[100]

As effective as television may be at provoking—for better or worse—conversation, it is more frequently a tool to halt family interaction dead in its tracks. In today's multi-television households, many families have no idea about, or interest in, other member's viewing tastes. Even when household members view television as a family, some members may become so engrossed in the programming that all conversation ceases.

Conflict and TV

For many families, television is often the sole source of levity as well. While this role may seem unimportant, humor is a powerful stress reducer and also can be used as a form of mediation, reducing tense situations.

Several studies confirm that television has the power to increase or decrease family tensions. TV becomes an arbitrator in many families, acting as a significant factor in family adjustment.

University of Minnesota psychology researchers P. C. Rosenblatt and M. R. Cunningham found a strong relationship between the amount of time the television is on and self-reported conflicts and tensions within the family.[101] The family researchers examined sixty-four households and found that television can create tense situations in a number of ways. First, the sheer noise and visual stimulus of television can create distractions that make it difficult to carry on other family interactions near the TV set. Families also quarrel over programming decisions. Moreover, TV is used by many family members to withdraw from negative interpersonal relationships such as arguments, disagreements, or complaints.

While departure from negative relationships may sound like a positive function, such a situation can, in fact, impede family members' social development and increase family stress. Says respected family scholar Irene Goodman, "For example, father may be experiencing dissatisfaction with his job; when he gets home he does not want to interact with other family members. His coping mechanism is to turn on the set and 'tune out.' This may or may not be effective; his constant watching and ignoring other family members may exacerbate family tensions."[102]

Home has traditionally served as a training ground for resolving conflicts. Although withdrawing from an untenable situation may occasionally be the best course, eventually we must face problems and use our interpersonal skills to develop solutions. Constant withdrawal hinders our abilities to hone social skills in the relative safety of our homes—skills we'll eventually need in a sometimes cruel and unforgiving world. People who lack such abilities may find it difficult to hold a job or maintain healthy marital relationships. They may also pass their dysfunctional communication patterns down to their offspring.

Although television may act as an anesthetic in many families—numbing painful family interactions—it can also be a source of significant conflict and turmoil. Which TV to use, what shows are approved, which rental films are acceptable, and the amount of time devoted to TV viewing are common issues that often provoke combat.

Even attempts to reduce TV's prominence in the lives of family members or change program choices to more positive fare can actually result in a painful, conflict-ridden "withdrawal" period. "Conflict may occur when values expressed on television and embraced by one or more family members—perhaps due to peer pressure—are contrary to family values," notes Goodman.[103] TV plays such a pivotal role in so many American households, conflict regarding television has become a significant aspect of the typical family process.

The most common solution to conflicts over television is to buy more TVs so everyone can watch their favorite programs separately. Although this solution may resolve conflicts, it obviously also results in significantly less family interaction and an overall sense of alienation.

The destructive power of television on family communication and interaction unfortunately makes it an easy scapegoat for personal problems that may have little to do with the medium. Sometimes other issues within the family are not being confronted because it's easier and safer to blame TV. Fighting over television is simpler and less dangerous than facing more difficult problems. But it is merely a temporary solution. Ignoring such problems rarely results in a permanent cure, and these conflicts usually only continue to fester.

The presence of television often creates a circular effect in which it becomes increasingly difficult to identify the source of family problems. TV may alienate family members or provide negative role models, resulting in increased family conflicts. TV then provides an escape for family members by allowing them to tune out problems while they tune in to more television. This additional TV viewing further alienates family members and offers more negative role models.

Some family members may attempt to use television viewing as a temporary buffer to avoid conflict with another member of the household, or even to punish a spouse, parent, or child by withdrawing attention and giving it to TV. The other party in the conflict may then try to disrupt the first member's "relationship" with television. In this respect, TV fits well into the family systems theories of pioneer family therapist Murray Bowen. Under Bowen's "triangled other" theory, for example, a wife may view television as an enemy when her husband uses it to avoid an argument. He may view a football game as more pleasant than a marital dispute, while she perceives the television as "the other woman."[104]

Many men are, in essence, having an affair with television, devoting up to twenty hours each weekend to televised sports. And the proliferation of cable sports channels such as ESPN are now threatening to take over weekday evenings as well. Television effectively robs couples of the real-life attention, love, and affection characteristic of healthy marital relationships. "When he's watching eight hours of football on Sunday it's like 'there goes an entire day I could have had with him'," complains one sports widow interviewed on ABC's *20/20* about "sports junkies."[105]

Divorce lawyers point to the growing trend of women leaving home because they feel their spouses care more about TV sports than about their marital relationship. One survey of five hundred men and women conducted by author and former TV sports addict Kevin Quirk found that many women were so angry at television, they added extra pages to the survey just to "vent."[106] Quirk, whose own marriage ended in divorce, notes that during one Super Bowl, his wife became so angry she walked in, knocked over the TV, pulled out the plug, and walked out. He simply plugged the TV back in and watched the rest of the game.

Televised sports is often such an intensely emotional experience, many viewers are unable to interact with other family members beyond the occasional grunt or angry outburst. Many of the men who responded to Quirk's survey, while denying their addiction to TV sports, admitted that nothing else in their lives evoked an equal amount of passion. A wife complained, "I would try and talk to him and he would not even hear me. And everything was about the TV and the remote control."

"If you asked me a question I wouldn't even hear it," admitted one sports addict. Some men in the survey identified their wives as the problem because their spouses didn't know enough about sports to share their husbands' interests.

Psychologist William S. Pollack of McLean Hospital, Balmont, Mass., says many men turn to TV sports to "reconnect" with their own fathers.[107] It may be the only place they remember actually spending time with their dads, he explains. Pollack, who authored the book *Real Boys* and specializes in masculinity issues, adds that other men are trying to recapture the glory days of their youth when they played sports.[108]

Although the last decade supposedly produced the "'90s sensitive male," it appears unlikely that the patterns of television sports viewing will change significantly in the foreseeable future. According to a study conducted by the Amateur Athletic Foundation of Los Angeles, 90 percent of boys now watch televised sports.[109] And with its male-dominated "cast," TV sports provides some unique and powerful messages about masculinity—including the idea that aggression and violence among men is exciting and rewarding behavior. Televised sports has its own language, usually drawn from the field of battle, featuring words such as "kill," "detonate," "explode," and "shotgun." And, as noted, relatively few women appear in televised sports. When they do, it's usually as supporters, such as cheerleaders, prizes, or sex objects.

Interestingly, research has confirmed that men who are avid TV sports fans produce elevated levels of testosterone during viewing. One study by the University of Utah's Educational Psychology Department indicated that testosterone levels rise as much as 20 percent when an avid fan's team wins.[110] Some might conclude that this phenomenon should result in a more amorous husband—at least when his team is victorious. It's not the case, says Pollack. "To some extent he's having a falling-in-love or sexual-like experience with the TV," he explains. "There's another woman all right, but it's sports on TV."[111] Conversely, the Utah study showed that testosterone levels may drop nearly 20 percent when the fan's team loses, which may account for the depression some devoted fans experience following their team's defeat.[112]

Pollack goes on to suggest that men's passion for sports may be triggered by a lack of ability to be emotionally intimate. "For many boys, sports is the one place where they sense it's all right to show what they really feel and who they really are," says Pollack. "Because the source of their feelings is external and obvious—a missed goal, a great shot, a huge win, a narrow loss—the shame they usually experience if they show these feelings can sometimes fall away."[113]

The "triangled-other" relationship many family members form with television is artificial at best and does little to resolve underlying problems. In this complex situation, TV becomes both a scapegoat and stress-reducer, but its effects are only temporary. A triangled-other situation only allows participants to postpone the inevitable conflict while tensions continue to build. "If men wait five or ten years to talk, often there will be no one to talk to," says Pollack. "The reason men change isn't because the women make them, they change because after they start to talk about it, they discover that there is something empty or missing too."[114]

Reward and Punishment

Discipline is a natural part of parenting, and in an age when children are spending an increasing amount of time in front of the tube, it's only natural that many parents use America's favorite pastime as a tool of authority. TV may be granted or taken away as a technique to manipulate children's behavior.

The problem with using TV as a reward or punishment is that it significantly increases the importance of the medium. We all tend to crave that which we cannot have. Children are especially prone to this phenomenon, and parents may be sending them a subtle message by using TV as a power tool. They're telling children that television is something of value, something to be cherished and protected. In this atmosphere, television takes on a larger-than-life aura, and its role in the lives of families who use TV as reward and punishment becomes exaggerated.

Imposed Control

Beyond using television as a tool to reward or punish children, studies indicate relatively few parents actively control their children's TV viewing. In a study of 5,167 fourth- through ninth-graders, P. J. Mohr, associate professor of speech and coordinator of graduate studies in communications at Wichita State University, Kansas, found 84 percent of the children surveyed reported receiving "no advice" regarding their evening viewing selections. And lest you think the children may be underreporting their parents' involvement, 85 percent of moms and dads polled during the study admitted to not providing any advice.[115]

Simply put, a laissez-faire attitude toward television permeates most American homes. According to Edward Palmer, head of research for

Sesame Street, "parental concern and meaningful involvement in discriminating viewing have never been more warranted or more critically needed than they are today."[116]

Lost Childhood

A key element of parents' responsibilities is to filter information coming into the home—especially information directed toward children. It seems obvious that while an important function of childhood is to learn, some information remains best processed by more mature, discerning minds.

Many experts believe that television has weakened the family's structure and authority by eliminating vital information barriers.[117] Children today are bombarded with knowledge and experiences previously restricted to adults. And in case you think TV's influences are offset by school or other factors, consider that most kids spend more time in front of the tube than they do in a classroom.[118]

Television has created an "adult-child," says Neil Postman. "Through the miracle of symbols and electricity, our own children know everything anyone else knows—the good with the bad. Nothing is mysterious, nothing is awesome, nothing is held back from public view. It means...that in having access to the previously hidden fruit of adult information, they are expelled from the garden of childhood."[119]

Children are biologically constructed to learn rapidly. But because they have not fully developed the ability to discern between fact and fiction, right and wrong, children can be manipulated easily. Just as kids are susceptible to illnesses because their immune systems are still under construction, they also have an especially low immunity to the suggestive messages imparted by the entertainment industry. While they are absorbing the informaion TV sends, they cannot yet process it on a mature level.

In the fact- and opinion-filled world of television, children rapidly develop a premature sexuality. They also pick up the hyper-consumerism carefully crafted by an army of marketing experts, as well as the world-weary cynicism that seems to dominate the media.

Few children are prepared for the onslaught of information and ideas television conveys. Children lack the wisdom and anatomical maturity to cope with television's constant barrage of sexual messages.

Family Resource Manager

During 1996, the advertising industry spent more than $181 billion trying to convince us to buy specific products. That's about $12 per person, per week, and that doesn't include the millions of dollars spent on market research.[120]

Television often tells us to buy products we either don't need or that cost more than equally effective, cheaper substitutes. And the success of thousands of pricey name-brand products indicates that we often listen. TV tells us we need more credit cards, and we respond by picking up the phone and applying. It suggests our dinner menu, and we purchase it, even when we know that the choice is neither healthy nor economical. It convinces us that lottery tickets will lead to wealth, and we buy them, even when common sense and simple statistics point to the obvious folly of such purchases. It implies that most teens have no curfew and can stay out as late as they want, having sex or slaying vampires, and that's "normal." And little by little, we loosen our grip on the responsibilities we once held and hand them over to the tube.

Interestingly, TV ads rarely attempt to convince us with facts. Legally, when advertisers make a claim, they must be able to back it up with substantive evidence. But that's often hard to do, especially when making assertions about the quality or effectiveness of a product in comparison to similar merchandise. Therefore, marketing professionals make a living dancing around the truth in ways that imply product superiority, but do not explicitly state it.

The strategy these professionals use employs a highly sophisticated combination of linguistics, images, and emotional tones to communicate implied messages. While some might say this has always been the purpose of advertising, no other medium comes close to the effectiveness of TV. In one study of 174 subjects conducted at Florida State University, students were asked to evaluate the factual quality of four television commercials.[121] The subjects were divided into three groups. The first group only viewed the commercials. The second viewed the commercials and also read transcripts of the messages, without images or background music. The final group only read the transcripts.

While the groups that actually saw the commercials, with and without transcripts, made invalid or unsubstantiated assumptions about the commercials almost 70 percent of the time, those who read only the script were much less likely to believe the ads' implied messages. In other words, reading the transcripts alone without images and music allowed the subjects to better interpret and recognize implied messages as false. But the images inherent in TV advertising cloud that ability.

Television advertisers often target the most vulnerable members of our households: the children. In fact, by age seventeen, the average American child has seen about 350 thousand television commercials, which equates to more than a quarter of the time most children spend in school.[122] Think about that. While children may spend 10 or 20 percent of their school time studying math or science or history, they spend an equivalent of 25 percent of that time learning about consumer products from the television.

A thirteen-country survey of television commercials by Consumer International, a worldwide coalition of more than two hundred consumer groups, found that food advertisements—not commercials for toys, video games, or cartoons—comprised the largest segment of ads aimed at children. More than half of these ads were for sweets, breakfast cereals, and fast food. In fact, 95 percent of all commercials were for foods that were high in fat, sugar, or salt.[123]

The power of child-targeted ads is so strong, several countries regulate commercials aimed at the young. For example, Sweden and Norway ban all advertising directed at children under twelve, and no commercials are allowed during children's programming. Australia prohibits ads during shows for preschool children, and Denmark, Finland, Norway, and Sweden ban commercial sponsorship of children's programming.[124]

Selling Addictions

Adbusters magazine, the publication of the Canadian-based watchdog group Adbusters Media Foundation, calls television "the command center of consumerism."[125] And it is a command center built upon irrational arguments that falsely support the need for an ever-increasing array of products.

The pattern of addiction begins early, with relentless messages designed to capture the widest possible audience—especially kids.

Throughout the 1950s, '60s, and early '70s, for example, television was a key tool in tobacco companies' strategy to hook young people on cigarettes. Tobacco manufacturers were frequent sponsors of family shows during this period and often encouraged the use of tobacco products on air. Television executives gladly complied, sending the not-so-subtle message that smoking was chic, glamorous, and sexy.

The entertainment industry's early success in affiliating smoking with sex opened new vistas of product association. Sex is now used to sell a nearly unimaginable array of products, from feminine hygiene items and automobiles to pasta salad and cleaning supplies.

Since the ban on television cigarette advertising took effect in 1973, the collaboration between tobacco companies and the entertainment industry has become more subtle. Recent movies targeting young audiences routinely feature some of America's most popular stars smoking. One study reported in the *American Journal of Public Health* notes that movie stars appearing in top-grossing films light up three times more frequently than the average American adult. [126]

And although smoking on television took a rapid nosedive once cigarette companies were banned from TV, the 1990s saw a marked upswing in the number of characters on TV who smoke. Interestingly, however, these characters do not exhibit the same addictive behaviors as most real-life smokers. On television, smoking is generally depicted as an occasional indulgence rather than a tenacious and destructive habit. When TV characters smoke, it is usually only to relieve tension during a particularly stressful event. Once the situation is resolved, they apparently have no problem kicking the habit.

TV is also a major purveyor of alcohol. The fast-paced, sexy images used in beer commercials are tailor-made to appeal to television's impressionable viewers. Such messages send a clear message that fun and fellowship are synonymous with alcohol use.

"Adolescents' attitudes are malleable and TV can give teenagers their first real glimpse into the secretive adult world of sex, drugs, and success long before they are able to learn about it firsthand," explains Victor C. Strasburger, who writes on the psychological impact of the media on adolescents. [127]

"Modeling may be a crucial factor in teenagers' decisions about when and how to begin consuming alcohol," adds Strasburger. "For example, sports and rock stars frequently appear in beer and wine ads, and the underlying messages are clear: 'Real men drink beer; beer drinkers have more fun, more friends, and they're sexier; and consuming alcohol is the norm rather than the exception.'"[128]

How well do these ads work? In one study, eight- to twelve-year-olds were able to name more brands of beer than U.S. presidents.[129] Another study by J. Grube and L. Wallack found those fifth and sixth graders who could recall alcohol ads had more positive beliefs about drinking than those who did not recognize brands and slogans.[130] The bottom line: alcohol ads encourage kids to drink.

But beer commercials aren't the only place kids learn positive messages about alcohol. In a 1991 study, Grube and Wallack discovered that prime-time TV programs typically depicted drinking an average of six times per hour. More than half of all prime-time programs routinely feature characters drinking, and up to 80 percent contain references to alcohol.[131] Soap operas—popular after-school fare for teenage girls—are especially adept at portraying alcohol as an effective social enhancement.

Alcohol is now a factor in more than half of all auto accidents and a third of homicides and suicides involving adolescents. Al Gore identified the underlying problem clearly when he pointed out, "We are strip-mining our children's minds and doing it for commercial profit."[132]

Redefining Family Value

Our made-by-TV obsession with consumer goods of all kinds has inadvertently undermined the family by telling adults and children alike what they should have. In the world of television, homes are large and tastefully decorated, no matter what the breadwinners' professions. For example, the show *7th Heaven* warmly depicts the day-to-day challenges of a minister and his family. In real life, with the exception of a few televangelists, most clergy limp along on a fairly slim salary. But in TV land, the *7th Heaven* family lives in a home that in some circles may qualify as a small mansion.

"When TV shows families, they usually tend to be middle class," explains Laura Grindstaff of the Annenberg School of Communication.

"That means other kinds of families are erased."[133] Television rarely depicts working-class or poor families, and when it does so, the results are generally comedic, at the expense of those who are less prosperous. Those who work for a living are generally depicted as poorly educated and profane. The 1993 comedy, *Grace Under Fire*, for example, portrayed nearly all male blue-collar characters as slow-speaking, beer-guzzling louts, unable to maintain a healthy relationship with an independent female.

Grace Under Fire was unusual in one sense, however. Unlike most situation comedies, the show managed to depict the main character, played by a scrappy Brett Butler, both on and off the job. In the drama category, *The Commish* (1991–1995) also stood out for its attempt to integrate the home and family lives of its central character, Police Commissioner Tony Scali, played by Michael Chiklis.

While many dramas focus on career to the exclusion of the characters' family lives, in the world of TV family sitcoms, most jobs are treated as hobbies—momentary diversions rather than full-time obligations. Rarely do TV shows integrate both career and home lives, depicting the challenges of juggling job and family in a realistic way.

Television often creates a fantasy world where everyone is effortlessly affluent. Constant exposure to these images can result in real-life dissatisfaction with a more typical standard of living and career obligations. TV's opulent version of the middle class may compel some families to overextend their financial resources and time commitments to the breaking point—all in an effort to reassure themselves they have not been left behind by the American dream.

Not only does TV create an unrealistic portrayal of prosperity, it also skews our view of family life. Conflict is a key element of both drama and comedy, but television's unique ability to create an alternate reality brings the conflicts it portrays into our homes. In an effort to create entertaining situations, television builds the seemingly perfect family simply to tear it down. Scholars throughout the ages have decried the breakdown of the family and respect for parents, but only in the twentieth century has the popular media been a prime contributor to this breakdown. At no other time has the relentless message that what parents think is outdated become the popular discourse, the narration of greater society and not just its youth.

One recent study points to the notion that the family is more vital than ever in shaping children's values. In the largest study of its type ever, the National Longitudinal Study on Adolescent Health surveyed nearly ninety thousand children, principally teens, on peer pressure, family environment and risky behaviors such as sex, smoking, and alcohol and drug use.[134]

A key portion of the study found that teenagers who reported feeling close to their families were the least likely to engage in risky behaviors. High parental expectation was also important, and having a parent home at key times during the day such as after school and at bedtime also contributed to more responsible teen behaviors. Robert Blum, director of the Adolescent Health program at the University of Minneapolis, notes that researchers may be missing the boat by concentrating most of the efforts on the effects of peer pressure. "What this study is saying," he explains, "is that family environment matters."[135]

Laying the Groundwork

Television's role as the family manager lays the groundwork for its siege on other aspects of the family structure. Its control of the family's "prime real estate"—living rooms, family rooms, and bedrooms—gives it an enormous amount of power to influence family members in a variety of ways. It controls the way families communicate, it defines culture and it even advises us on our love lives. As a communication enhancer, it sets the agenda for our conversations, making it a particularly powerful force in what families view as important. It also helps viewers define their ideas about what constitutes appropriate sexual behavior and which figures act as heroes. Since it is often at the center of family conflicts, it becomes a key tool for family arbitration. And because most families spend the bulk of their free time with this medium, it may appear to be their best friend.

Cultural Narrator

Prior to television, culture was defined and communicated through a complex series of media. A clear cultural identity was vital to maintaining a society's stability as a support system to its members. These individual cultural identities allowed societies to adapt to geographical surroundings, local weather patterns, agricultural conditions, and available natural resources. Simply put, culture was a means to pass down the methodologies that made a given society function effectively.

Early cultures communicated their values, identities, methods of sustenance, family structures, spiritual beliefs, and rituals to offspring by word of mouth. In most oral cultures, select members were tasked with learning the culture's heritage as a means to preserve and communicate it accurately to the society. People in such positions were usually held in high esteem, informally selected early in life for their intellect and communication skills, and then put through a long and arduous apprenticeship.

With the advent of written communication and the printing press, many of the social roles carried out by village elders and the like were transferred to books. Since literacy was still in its infancy, however, other institutions such as religious organizations assisted in the process of culturalizing individual members of a given society.

Within the narrower system of the family, parents and grandparents assumed this role. They were valued for their wisdom and experience, and assumed clearly defined duties meant to help sustain the society through communication of vital cultural information. These roles also laid the groundwork for cultural evolution and technological development. Such information allowed younger members of a society to avoid the pitfalls experienced by previous generations. They could then concentrate their energies on developing technologies and methodologies that built upon the experience of ancestors.

Until the mid-twentieth century, family members, supported and guided by their communities and religious institutions, were the primary links in creating, defining, sustaining, and evolving cultures. They were the vessels by which culture was passed along and refined. They were the cultural narrators.

Since the early 1950s, however, television has increasingly assumed this vital role. The storytellers, sages, and family historians of yesteryear have given way to a steady stream of TV shows that tell us who we are, what we need, how we should speak, what we should believe in, how we should perform our jobs, and even what constitutes a family. How television presents the world becomes our model for how we think the world is to be properly staged. Our reliance upon television as a cultural narrator creates a society that receives its experiences vicariously rather than firsthand. And thus, such experiences can no longer be personalized to any one culture or belief system. The result is a homogenization that omits the depth and importance of race, religion, how we see others, and even how we speak.

Although many studies have provided anecdotal evidence that television is today's primary cultural narrator, little research has been conducted on the society-wide impact of the ubiquitous and varied cultural messages television conveys to society at large.

Our Changing Language

Regional diversity is already losing ground in America. How we speak—our inflections, our use of words—has been changed by the constant presence of television in our lives. Local dialects and accents are becoming diluted or almost non-existant. Television's cultural leaders, such as newscasters and network TV stars, are often chosen for their homogenized accents. And since most television programs are produced in Los Angeles or New York, the rapid-fire and trendy styles of communication found in these areas are quickly becoming America's manner of speech. While it's true that fast, easy modes of transportation are also helping to homogenize language, this natural linguistic evolution is being artificially accelerated by the constant presence of television.

Particularly alarming is the use of profanity in both movies and television, making it appear that America has embraced foul language to a much higher degree than it actually has. A 1999 Parents Television Council survey found that the use of profanity on television had skyrocketed over the course of a single year. Nearly half of all shows on prime-time TV now contain profanity, and on some networks, such as UPN, NBC, and Fox, that number surpases 70 percent. The study noted, for example, that the word "bitch" was used on *Friends*, *Dawson's Creek*, *Buffy the Vampire Slayer*, and *That 70s Show*—all programs targeting teen and young adult audiences.[136]

"Many children assume that if it's OK for characters to speak rudely or use foul language on TV, it must be OK at home and in school," says Allan S. Vann, principal of James H. Boyd Intermediate School, Huntington, New York. "I know I am now hearing third-graders use language that, just five years ago, would not have been spoken by my fifth-graders."[137]

"Frankly we're living in a profane world," says Chris Thompson, producer of the 1999 Fox comedy *Action*. "I don't know anyone out there who says 'frickin' or 'kicked in the hiney' or 'that guy is a real doody-head.'"[138] So *Action* took the "bold" approach of using real expletives which are then bleeped out, rather than substituting poorly disguised euphemisms. Thompson may be right. Relatively few people resort to the kinds of silly words he cites.

But TV executives offer few apologies for the coarse behavior of the characters they create. Fox's entertainment president, Doug Herzog, says it's the responsibility of network TV to be "relevant" and to "keep exploring and experimenting." He adds, "The first priority for Fox was to come up with a half-hour that was funny—something the network hasn't done for a long time.…We think *Action* is funny. And yes, it definitely pushes the line a little bit.…Are we ready to go past that line? Is the audience ready to go there? Are advertisers ready to go there? Our feeling: Yeah, we can get everybody there and make it work."[139]

That statement is especially revealing—an apparent acknowledgement that not everybody is "there" yet, but that it's only a matter of time before shows like *Action*, and others like it, can persuade viewers that there's nothing wrong with crossing the line.

Even products specifically aimed at kids feature profanity. More than half of all PG and PG-13 movies contain offensive language and obscenities. Movies carried on network TV—from G-rated fair to the raciest R-rated films—receive few modifications. Where expletives are deleted or voiced over, most viewers can still discern the original dialogue.

And once we delve into the realm of cable, anything goes. Producers of the animated comedy *South Park*, for example, dismiss claims that it targets kids with profanity, boorish behavior, and gratuitous violence. But it's clear from the child-size official T-shirts and hats available at entertainment-oriented stores that children are a major segment of the audience. The show's reputation has become so widespread, South Park Infants School, Surrey, England, has decided to change its name to avoid the "grotesque and negative" connotations of the name, says a school official.[140]

Television has redefined our language in other ways as well. "Mass communication" requires, to some extent, a standardized linguistic system, and television is particularly adept at creating this national tongue. One need only listen to a conversation between teenagers, or even the first few words of many toddlers, to understand the power of advertising slogans, TV-inspired slang, television's frequent exaggerations of ethnic accents, and the ubiquitous southern California "val-gal" dialects—including the use of "like" several times in every sentence.

This rapid modification of our language changes America's culture. Far from enhancing understanding, the trend may be eroding the ability to communicate at all. One recent study found the written vocabulary of the average American six- to fourteen-year-old has shrunk from twenty-five thousand words to just ten thousand words in less than fifty years.[141]

Professor Lois DeBakey of Baylor University, Texas, decries this trend: "What we are creating is a kind of semiliteracy and breakdown in the way we communicate with one another."[142]

Television's simplification and standardization of language cannot help but restrict our ability to express thoughts and ideas, and will ultimately result in less eloquent and original discourse.

A One-Size-Fits-All World

Have you ever wondered why so many people from other countries appear angry with the United States, even as they wear American jeans and smoke American cigarettes? American television programs may be at least partly to blame for this strange dichotomy.

From reruns of *Bonanza* (1959–1973), *I Love Lucy,* and *Dallas* to newer shows such as *Baywatch* (1989–), *The Simpsons*, *The X-Files* (1993–), and myriad soap operas, some of television's biggest revenues come from exportation of American TV programming—and American culture. In fact, at $50 billion in annual foreign sales, the creative industry—primarily television and movies—is America's third largest export industry.[143]

Television has become so effective at dispersing American pop culture, other countries are almost helpless against the floodtide of messages that threaten to undermine their own unique cultures. Some countries, such as France, have even gone so far as to pass legislation designed to combat the Americanization of their language and other cultural hallmarks.

While the international distribution of American television can be a positive force, spreading ideas of democracy and the potential prosperity of capitalism, this trend also holds the potential to erode the beautifully complex social framework of the world as we know it. Few of us would sacrifice the richness that European art, Latin music, or the cuisine of the Far East adds to our own culture. Without these cultural spices, our own culture would quickly become as bland as oatmeal.

Even more troublesome is America's export of its increasingly violent culture. Nearly half of all TV programs exported to other countries are crime/action shows focusing on violence.[144] One of the biggest reasons for this trend is the ease in which violent scenes are understood by other cultures without translation.

American television also exports another of our culture's most pressing challenges: rampant consumerism. Television is, by far, the most effective marketing tool ever created. And as television programming increasingly becomes a global endeavor, many developing countries now find it difficult to economically support the tastes of their Americanized citizenry.

A fifth of the world's population still lives in poverty. Yet, it's not uncommon to find a TV antenna or satellite dish mounted on the top of even the most rudimentary shack, beaming in a steady diet of American television shows. This programming routinely depicts a culture that consumes ten, twenty, or thirty times the average per capita resources of many foreign viewers.

Television is an instrument of commerce. It is controlled by people whose interests lie not in preserving cultures or natural resources, but rather in introducing other countries to the culture of consumerism. America is the proving ground for the power of this message. It has become increasingly clear that rather than foster a "global village," television's ultimate goal appears to be to create a "global mall." "For the first time in human history, children are born into homes where most of the stories do not come from their parents, schools, churches, communities, and in many places even from their native countries, but from a handful of conglomerates who have something to sell," notes respected media scholar George Gerbner, dean emeritus at the University of Pennsylvania's Annenberg School of Communication.[145]

While simple logic dictates that rational cultures would recognize the value of consuming less, America's new cultural narrator—television—encourages us to consume more. "Buy now!" "Don't wait!" "Call today!" "Operators are standing by..." The messages are relentless. Nearly 30 percent of all broadcast time is now devoted to advertising, and at the current rate of television viewership, average Americans will see more than two million commercials over the course of their lifetime.[146]

Such messages aren't meant to appeal to logic. TV uses gut-level emotions and rapid-fire images to divert viewers from the rational thought process. They're designed to seduce us into buying or threaten us with the notion that we are less sophisticated than our neighbors if we don't possess whatever gadget they happen to be advertising.

As the vanguard of consumerism, television is particularly adept at creating cultural images of affluence, convincing us that the items we once thought of as luxuries—or perhaps couldn't have imagined at all—are now dire necessities. Utilizing ultra-sophisticated market research techniques, television programmers and advertisers conjure a picture of life in America that revolves around "things" rather than relationships.

This jumble of images and ideas has skewed our vision of prosperity. Television tells us that prosperous people have sex more frequently and with more partners. It promotes the idea that profits come before integrity. It convinces us that money frees us from all social constraints and casts a positive light on even the most socially devastating situations.

Under this new vision of prosperity, even the breakup of a family can appear economically beneficial, notes Joe Dominguez, coauthor of *Your Money or Your Life*. On a national level, he points out, an increased divorce rate can appear as an economic upswing. The legal bills, the consumer needs of two separate households, and other results of divorce are reflected as economic growth in America's Gross Domestic Product.[147] Television's message of unrestrained consumerism can put a positive spin on almost anything.

A Monochrome World

The effects of a single cutural narrator not only impact our wallets, but cut to the core of how we relate to our own ancestry and the ethnicity of others. Color TV has been around since the 1950s, but it seems that as the twentieth century closed and a new millennium began, relatively few TV executives understood the power of color in a societal sense.

Of the twenty-six prime-time television series premiering in the fall of 1999, for example, not one featured a minority lead character during initial episodes. Despite inroads in nearly all facets of society, minorities receive relatively little attention on television, and when they are depicted, it's often in a stereotypical or negative way. It seems the long-time network leaders, ABC, NBC, and CBS, have abdicated their responsibilities to depict society in all its multicultural splendor, leaving Fox, UPN, and WB to pick up the pieces.

The reasons for this abdication are less about overt prejudice than sheer economics. Major network execs have caved into advertiser demands to go after large, high-dollar audiences, primarily white, eighteen- to forty-nine-year-old viewers.[148] By gearing programming to demographics and not the viewing audience, however, networks are letting the tail wag the dog, says actor D.L. Hughley. The black star of one of the few "big three" shows with a minority lead, *The Hughleys*, adds, "They stopped writing based on reality. Instead they're writing for advertisers."[149]

TV is particularly adept at telling us who we are. "In general, television dramas portray people in such a simplified and inaccurate way that the characters are often crude stereotypes," explain researchers Leonard D. Eron and L. Rowell Huesmann of the University of Illinois Department of Psychology. "Occupational roles and workers, women, minorities, the aged, single parents, the handicapped, and various ethnic groups are quite commonly presented as stereotypes and given few individual characteristics."[150]

Rather than breaking destructive assumptions about ethnic and racial groups, television too often creates and reinforces popular stereotypes. TV offers up a steady discourse on how particular ethnic groups and races speak and act. Then it classifies these groups into neatly defined socioeconomic categories. Throughout most of television's history, minority actors have usually been cast in low-status jobs such as domestic helpers or blue-collar laborers.

Some of the newest networks, such as UPN and Fox, seem especially intent on depicting the underbelly of America's rich array of subcultures. Instead of portraying blacks or other ethnic or racial groups in a positive light, programs such as *In Living Color* (1990–1994) and *Martin* (1992–1997), for example, offer up exaggerations of cultural and ethnic characteristics or outright stereotypes. Although many of these shows depict characters living in more affluent circumstances than earlier shows featuring minorities, they provide little insight into how these characters actually make a living and frequently dwell on sexual topics that reinforce, rather than dispel, popular stereotypes. "This stereotyping, it hurts because someone sitting behind a desk said, 'This is what I want black people to look like,'" notes comedian and TV star Bill Cosby.[151]

Although African-American women are beginning to capture more diverse roles as attorneys, doctors, police officers, and other professional roles, television historically has portrayed black women in "mammy" roles. Shows such as *Good Times* (1974–1979), *Gimme a Break*

(1981–1987), and *The Jeffersons* (1975–1985), for example, all featured stereotypically large, domineering African-American women in the roles of domestic help and caregivers, although *The Jeffersons* also provided some positive black female role models.

In an equally demeaning twist, TV often falls back on a secondary stereotype of black women: the "Jezebel." In these depictions, usually portrayed by light-skinned black women, African-American females are cast as dangerous and untrustworthy seductresses, perpetuating the hyper-sexualized stereotype of the African-American community.

Studies indicate that African-American families portrayed on television are more likely to be isolated from other families. And the roles members play within these families tend to be in greater conflict with one another. In addition, females tend to be cast in more dominant roles than are depicted in other family-based television situations.[152] Moreover, these shows do little to present an integrated approach to minorities on television. Such shows, for the most part, feature almost exclusively black casts and rarely depict interaction with other racial and ethnic groups, except as a means to point out prejudice and discrimination.

More mainstream networks take a different approach to ethnic diversity. Shows depicting minorities on "the big three" networks frequently Anglicize minority characters in an attempt to capture the widest possible audience. *The Cosby Show* (1984–1992) and *Family Matters* (1989–1998), for example, portrayed fairly positive family values but rarely demonstrated much ethnicity. Although both shows featured black actors, they could have just as easily functioned with white casts. Unlike, say, Eriq La Salle's character, Dr. Peter Benton, on *ER*, who addresses racial issues and often embraces his African-American heritage, many of these shows seem to ignore race altogether.

Fresh Prince of Bel Air (1990–1996) tended to take a different approach. The popular sitcom was set in the trendy Los Angeles suburb of Bel Air and featured an affluent African-American family, replete with a snooty black butler. The show centered around interactions between the main character, a street-wise nephew from West Philadelphia played by Will Smith, and his upscale cousins and their friends. His male cousin, Carlton (Alfonso Ribeiro), was cast as black "preppy" who only embraced his ethnicity with the help and enlightenment of Will Smith's character. The not-so-subtle message was one often communicated in minority-based television programs: successful African-Americans are really just trying to be white. Among the more balanced characters on the show were Smith's aunt and uncle, portrayed as transitional minorities—people with one foot in their inner-city past and another in the world of affluent white America.

While blacks are treated unfairly by television, there is at least some degree of representation. Other minorities still struggle to receive any degree of acknowledgment from the media. Hispanic Americans—the fastest-growing minority population in America—receive almost no attention on prime-time TV, with the exception of a handful of ensemble-cast dramas. While Hispanics represent over 10 percent of the U.S. population, they make up only 2 percent of characters on television.[153]

In early television programming, Hispanics, if depicted at all, generally held ancillary roles as agricultural help. *The Real McCoys* (1957–1963), for example, featured Tony Martinez as Pepino Garcia, a musical farmhand. One of the few Hispanics to go beyond this stereotype was the character Senor Wences (and his talking box), of *The Ed Sullivan Show* (1948–1971). But like nearly all minorities who speak English as a second language, his thick Spanish accent ("S-all right?" "S-all right!") was easy fodder for jokes.

Hispanic males on contemporary television suffer a similar fate to African-American men. Often shown as gang members when they're young, and drug lords when they're more mature, Latino men are frequently stereotyped as criminals of one sort or another. In fact, a national survey of Hispanic Americans found more than 60 percent of respondents felt that Latinos are more likely to be portrayed as being violent on English-language television than on Spanish-language TV.[154] And another study by the Hispanic group National Council of La Raza found that Hispanics on TV were 50 percent more likely to be portrayed as criminals than whites.[155] Moreover, "reality" programs such as *America's Most Wanted* (1988–) and *COPS* (1989–) depict Hispanics as criminals nearly three times as often as national crime statistics indicate.[156] "When positive images of Hispanics are nearly vacant in the national consciousness, our presence becomes minimized and undervalued in the work force," notes actor Jimmy Smits, former costar of *NYPD Blue*.[157]

The one area in which minorities are making increasing inroads is in the area prime-time dramas, such as the highly acclaimed *Homicide: Life on the Streets* (1993–1999) and *NYPD Blue*. These programs feature highly diverse casts, often led by minority officials such as African-Americans Yaphet Kotto as Lt. Al "Gee" Giardello (*Homicide*) and James McDaniel as Lt. Arthur Fancy (*NYPD Blue*).

The real groundbreaker for such diverse casting occurred in 1984 when *Miami Vice* (1984–1989) aired with Latino actor Edward James Olmos playing the grave and gritty Lt. Martin Costillo, and African-American Philip Michael Thomas as Det. Ricardo Tubbs. Supporting roles by Saundra Santiago, Martin Ferrero, and others provided a diverse backdrop that added an air of realism to an otherwise too-cool premise.

These ensemble casts seem to thrive on diversity. Cop shows such as *NYPD Blue* have become adept at depicting minorities in both criminal and crime-fighter roles. Jimmy Smits, who made his network debut in 1986 as attorney Victor Sifuentes on the popular series *LA Law* (1986–1994), went on to become a major TV heartthrob as Det. Bobby Simone on *NYPD Blue*. Smits' success has been augmented by other Hispanic actors such as Nicholas Turturro as Det. James Martinez on the same show, and Benjamin Bratt as Det. Reynaldo Curtis on the popular crime series *Law & Order.*

Although often presented with a certain respect, Asians get little air-time on TV. Early offerings such as *Bonanza*'s Hop Sing, played by Victor Sen Yung, and Mrs. Livingston, played by Miyoshi Umeki, on *The Courtship of Eddie's Father* (1969–1972), cast Asians as deferential domestic help.

The 1972–1975 series *Kung Fu* presented another common role for Asians: the quiet, respectful—and lethal—warrior. In this philosophical Western, David Carradine played the Chinese-American shaven-head Buddhist monk, Kwai Chang Caine. Carradine's usually humble character could almost always be called upon, however, to use his martial arts skills to solve sticky problems with hostile cowboys and Chinese Imperial agents.

In more recent portrayals, Asian characters tend to remain in the background as scientists, computer experts, and other technical personnel. There are two increasing common exceptions to this rule: the Japanese businessman who usually speaks little English and bows frequently, and a new twist on an old theme, the Dragon Lady. Best exemplified by Lucy Liu's character Ling Woo on *Ally McBeal*, the Dragon Lady isn't hard to spot. She's usually sporting seductive clothes and a nasty attitude that borders on the sadomasochistic.

Like Asians, Native Americans are rarely depicted, but when they are, it's often in the vein of the mysterious and philosophical. The 1990 drama *Northern Exposure*, for example, cast Elaine Miles as Marilyn Whirlwind, the stoic and mysterious clinic receptionist. Likewise, Larry Sellers in the Western drama *Dr. Quinn, Medicine Woman* (1993–) creates the stereotypical, if unusually articulate (for TV), and philosophical Native American character Cloud Dancer. He serves as sidekick to Byron Sully, played by Joe Lando, who is a white man seeking the inner peace of the Native American culture—another common theme.

Middle Eastern cultures are almost never depicted on prime-time television except for the occasional convenience store clerk and a smattering of terrorists. Such portrayals are in stark contrast to the growing number and contributions of Americans of Middle Eastern and Indian descent. These ethnic groups apparently remain fair game for nearly any negative stereotype, with little fear of outrage by viewers.

Jewish characters also are likely to be stereotyped on TV. Generally speaking, female Jews are brassy and assertive, i.e., Fran Drescher in *The Nanny* (1993–1999), while males often come off as neurotic and quirky, like Paul Reiser as Paul Buchman on *Mad About You* (1992–1999). Jewish families fare no better, usually portrayed as loud, overbearing and nosey (Jerry Seinfeld's TV family on *Seinfeld*). It seems a fair assumption that while some stereotypes on TV can be attributed to prejudices, often they are simply the result of laziness, allowing writers and producers to rely on easy character crutches for comedies and dramas alike.

The message such stereotypes and omissions send to children is particularly alarming. Only 3 percent of all characters depicted on Saturday morning children's fare were black, and less than 1 percent were Latino. And kids notice! A survey by the advocacy group Children Now of twelve hundred Asian, African-American, Hispanic, and white children between the ages of ten and seventeen found 80 percent felt it's important to see people of their own race on television. And children of all races agreed that the TV news media tend to portray Blacks and Latinos more negatively than whites and Asians. The children reported African-Americans doing "bad things" 35 percent of the time (compared with 9 percent for whites) and doing "good things" only 14 percent of the time (compared with 42 percent for whites).[158]

Rather than celebrating diversity for its ability to enhance culture, today's ethnic programming instead focuses on stereotypes and the differences between races and ethnic communities, or simply ignores ethnicity altogether.

Television advertisements are no better. Despite the fact that minorities represent an increasingly large segment of the consuming population, television commercials rarely depict people of color or ethnic minorities. And when they do, the casts of these commercials are rarely integrated, creating an aura of segregation.

The message we give America's ethnic and immigrant populations—particularly the children—is disturbing on several levels. "For ethnic minority families coming to this country, television becomes a child's social tool and socializing agent," explain researchers Edward Palmer, Taylor Smith, and Kim Strawser. "Beyond the more typical socializing role, television teaches ethnic minority children subtle lessons about themselves and how they are perceived. The portrayals are sparse and almost uniformly negative. Ethnic minorities join women and the elderly as frequently portrayed television victims."[159]

They go on to point out that TV teaches white children that it is a white world. "White characters comprise a large majority of TV roles. Furthermore, whites, especially men, are depicted in highly professional, powerful settings, whereas blacks and other non-whites are pigeonholed into less desirable stereotypical roles....Non-whites, conversely, learn that whites are 'superior' to other groups. The impact is especially potent for non-whites given their heavy reliance on television for information."[160]

Defining Our Spiritual Lives

Consumerism is fast becoming America's deity of choice. And like the Judeo-Christian God, it demands that we worship no other. The traditional

Judeo-Christian concept of God contradicts the deification of consumerism, placing it on a collision course with television. The god of consumerism requires that we sacrifice our time, our families, all that we are, to submit to its will. In return, it promises us prosperity and sexual fulfillment. These are empty promises.

Rather than seeing God as multifaceted, prime-time television creates a watered-down deity that fits neatly into a one-hour time slot. Such depictions lack depth and diversity, and fail to tackle the harder questions that true faith entails.

Dramas such as *Touched by an Angel* and *Promised Land* depict a God who is loving, kind, and all-forgiving. They present moral values, but they also tell us a little bit about ourselves. *New York Times* writer Laurie Goodstein notes that many such shows "feature ministers of ambiguous denominations preaching a Gospel so vague that it still looks as if the television industry is seeking to avoid offense by finding the lowest common denominator."[161]

Most religions practice faith in an unseen God. TV's version requires no such faith. Many characters in television's religious dramas only develop faith after God has sent them a personal message delivered by an angel, replete with special effects and heavenly lighting. In its attempt to capture the widest possible audience, TV offers up a reach-out-and-touch-me God. Scriptwriters create a God who fits equally well into any denomination, homogenizing faith into a single common religion. They create a God for the masses, an easy God, a deity that repairs broken lives in less than an hour.

On *Touched by an Angel*, the angels always reveal themselves. It is typically a highly emotional moment. While such drama may capture the audience's attention, it takes away the mystery, and to some extent, the deity of God. How can the rest of us ever hope to sustain our own faith when we fail to see, in physical form, the angels in our lives?

It is vital that viewers make a clear distinction between the God portrayed on such shows and the God that they worship as individuals and members of a particular faith. The producer of *Touched by an Angel* freely admits that the show is, as she terms it, "the flavor of the month." She also concedes that religious shows are about ratings rather than faith.[162] Yet, how many viewers delve into their beliefs so deeply that they consciously understand the distinction between TV's version of God and their own?

Like television's depiction of universal affluence, the faith born of a TV God creates unrealistic and unfair expectations. It infers that problems should be fixed by angels, requiring little effort on our part. Such programs may make us feel good, but the expectations they create run counter to the traditional Judeo-Christian picture of God—a God who requires a certain degree of responsibility among believers and faith in the unseen.

The drama *Promised Land* depicts a family who travels the country, sharing their faith with others. Its faith is generic and purposely unspecific so as to appeal to a wide audience. The picture it creates of a faithful family represents the fact that 44 percent of Americans now attend church on a weekly basis, and well over half of all Americans say religion is "very important" in their lives."[163]

The entertainment industry is only beginning to understand the depth of America's faith. More than half of all Americans say there is too little religious influence in modern life, rather than too much. Most critics of television's treatment of God and religion are not calling for support of any specific religious doctrine. Rather, they are simply seeking respectful depictions of their beliefs.

In Its Own Image

We are only beginning to understand the ways in which television has impacted our culture. TV is rapidly creating a society in its own image.

Neil Postman notes the danger in allowing television to become America's cultural narrator: "With few exceptions," he explains, "adults on TV do not take their work seriously (if they work at all), they do not nurture children, they have no politics, practice no religion, represent no tradition, have no foresight or serious plans, have no extended conversation, and in no circumstances allude to anything that is not familiar to an eight-year-old person."[164]

A society that lacks the institutional underpinnings of culture, social equality, faith, and a certain level of self-restraint will fall victim to its own selfish desires. Such a culture will make it increasingly difficult to maintain an effective social structure that benefits those who belong to it.

Gender
Mentor

Television isn't the first communication medium to embrace and transmit gender stereotypes, but few media have taken more advantage of such stereotypes than TV. Television's fast-paced format relies heavily on generalizations as a simple shorthand to compact an entire story into a thirty- or sixty-minute time slot.

Stereotypes allow writers to avoid more intricate character development in favor of "personality types" such as the "dumb blonde," the "fiery redhead," the "brawny-but-stupid jock," or the "nerd." Audiences may easily recognize such characters and even feel comfortable with them, since these "types" reinforce some viewers' own beliefs, which may have been formed in part by previous viewing experiences.

Drama often is created out of a need by the characters to "find their place" in life, and often that place has a lot to do with gender identification. Although television can be quite adept at creating and maintaining racial, ethnic, and professional stereotypes, it does some of its most effective work by reinforcing sexual stereotypes. Television rarely speaks more compellingly than when it explains our roles as men and women.

Although many television execs proudly point to TV's progressive views, when it comes to gender roles, the majority of shows remain almost prehistoric in their depictions of men and women. Men are heroes, women are victims; men make money, women spend it; men want sex, women provide it; and while successful men are assertive, successful women are aggressive…or downright evil.

This is not to say that there have been no positive portrayals of men and women in non-traditional gender roles on television. But the numbers clearly indicate that TV leans toward upholding stereotypical gender roles rather than breaking them. When women are depicted, for example, they frequently resort to stereotypical behaviors that reflect the male-dominated entertainment industry.

Even the number of female portrayals tend to mirror the industry's employment statistics. During the 1995–1996 season, women represented only 37 percent of the characters on prime-time television. In the action-adventure genre, the numbers are even more dismal. Women represent only 30 percent of the characters in action-adventure programs.[165] And only about a quarter of Hollywood's writers and 16 percent of its executive producers and directors are women. Overall, women make up only 28 percent of all behind-the-scenes workers in the television industry.[166]

A 1990 report by the National Commission on Working Women notes that the dearth of female influences has another effect beyond gender stereotyping. "The best that isolated women in mid-level positions seem able to accomplish is damage control. They can hold down the gratuitous violence, offensive language, leering camera angles. But they can't take the reins and be the driver."[167]

Rather than providing positive role models that focus on women's intellectual and professional abilities, television continues to churn out a host of female characters that simply fulfill male fantasies. In addition, TV skews all forms of feminism as anti-male, rather than pro-female.

When characters of either sex do break out of stereotypical molds, such as a smart blonde or an intelligent athlete, it is frequently to create conflict. Intelligence in these characters is often manifested as devious and cunning behavior—the plotting cheerleader or the manipulative football star, for example—thus reinforcing viewers' discomfort with those who eschew their assigned roles in life.

TV seems to make a special effort to tell females who and what they should be. Although TV provides a variety of gender roles for both sexes, male characters generally display more positive traits than females.

TV and the Sexes

Much of television is fiction, and fiction is, to a great extent, the product of fantasy. Given that fact, it is no wonder that characters on television often possess characteristics that feed into the fantasies of viewers. What is disturbing, however, is that TV often tends to satiate the fantasies of male viewers while attempting to convince female viewers to live up to these fantasies.

Men on television are more likely to be portrayed as powerful, constructive, and autonomous. Women are typically foils for the actions of men, as opposed to people of action themselves. Boys demonstrate dominant behaviors while girls exhibit more deferential behaviors. Boys typically engage in verbal and physically directive behavior while girls exhibit more gentle touching of people and objects.[168]

Studies of TV ads indicate than men and boys are more likely to engage in executive behaviors that create action. They push, pull, and press buttons more often, and are generally portrayed as more effective and able to make things work. In ads for games, boys also are more likely to win than girls.[169]

Women portrayed on TV often emphasize passivity and sexuality over intelligence and credibility. They're also frequently punished for their achievements. Women are depicted as gentle, even dreamy, and their body language frequently communicates submissiveness. In a study of print advertisements conducted by Erving Goffman, for example, girls were found to exhibit more withdrawal behaviors than boys, including shyness, eye or head aversion, or snuggling and hiding.[170] He found women were portrayed as childlike and represented by their bodies, not their faces.[171]

Another study at the University of Northern Colorado analyzed twelve prime-time television shows appearing over the past thirty years that featured women in major roles for nonverbal content, indicating hegemony over women. Interestingly, the leading ladies of the 1990s scored higher in submissive behaviors than those of any other decade. Characters Ally McBeal (Calista Flockhart), Veronica Chase (Kirstie Alley) of *Veronica's Closet* (1997–), Maya Gallo (Laura San Giacomo) of *Just Shoot Me* (1997–), and Fran Fine (Fran Drescher) of *The Nanny* ranked highest in terms of submissive behaviors and postures, sexist dress and body image, and paralinguistics, making them the most subservient and belittled women in thirty years. When compared to main female characters on shows of the 1980s, such as *Dynasty, Designing Women* (1986–1993), *Cagney & Lacey* (1982–1988), *Roseanne*, and *Murphy Brown*, and the 1970s, including *The Mary Tyler Moore Show* (1970–1977), *Wonder Woman* (1976–1979), and *Charlie's Angels* (1976–1981), top female TV characters of the 1990s showed more cleavage, wore shorter skirts, and generally exhibited more submissive body language. These characters also appeared more distressed over their weight, appearance, and lack of men and sex than their 1970s and '80s predecessors.[172]

Even when television programming or advertisements buck existing stereotypes, it's not always for the better. Often such portrayals highlight the women's assumption of negative, stereotypically male, characteristics such as violence, verbal and physical aggressiveness, destructive competitiveness, anger, and sexual promiscuity. In many ways, female characters appearing on WWF wrestling and on music videos mimic the behaviors of "dominatrix" characters found in pornography and appear to play into such fantasies.

Equally disturbing is the message found in the disproportionate distribution of male and female characters on television. In general, women appear significantly less often on TV than men, and when they do appear, it's often in smaller roles than men. Content analysis reveals a male to female casting ratio of 1.58 males for every female role. Moreover, women appear in only 39 percent of all speaking roles.[173] This dearth of female characters subtly communicates to viewers that what men do is more important and more exciting than women's achievements.

And while men most frequently appear in close-up face shots, women are more often photographed in full-body context. Although research has yet to explore the effect of this format difference, it does suggest that male characters may be presented as more cerebral, while females may be placed in a more sexual context.[174]

The frequency of stereotypical behaviors on TV can have a profound effect on all viewers, but is particularly powerful among young children. A 1974 study in Canada, for example, revealed that children in a rural town with no previous access to television changed their perception of sex roles significantly toward stereotypes within just two years of the introduction of television to the community.[175]

Children recognize stereotypical gender-specific behavior within the first few years of life, and many studies note that children are quickly able to identify such behaviors on television. One study, for example, found that young children—preschool age and below—are able to perceive cartoon characters as exhibiting stereotypical sex-type behaviors.[176]

While research indicates that a child's earliest exposure to what it means to be male or female comes primarily from parents, it seems obvious that the earlier and more frequent a child's exposure to stereotypical roles on television, the more likely the child will be to incorporate those values into his or her own belief system.

Although there are plenty of negative gender role models for boys on television, this early indoctrination into gender expectations may have an even more profound effect on girls, says researcher Mary Pipher. "Many women report that when they were in adolescence, they had someone they could really talk to, who encouraged them to stay true to who they really were....Now, in our more chaotic, fragmented world, fewer girls have that option available."[177] For many girls, therapists have replaced aunts, mothers, and grandmothers as that special "someone." And when "professional listeners" aren't available, girls can turn to television for this affirmation. What they receive, instead, are lessons on sex, manipulation, and brutality.

Given television's power to mold opinions and values, and the decreasing amount of time spent by parents in the home teaching and encouraging young boys and girls, TV is rapidly replacing fathers and mothers as children's primary gender mentors. From Saturday morning cartoons to ever-racier afternoon soaps and talk shows, kids are learning not about their potential as individuals, but about the perceived limitations of their gender.

TV and Manhood

Manhood holds a very special place in most Western cultures. Unlike the phrase "she's a woman," which typically indicates a statement of gender, when we say "he's a man," we're saying something beyond a simple observation of gender identification. That simple statement encompasses a wide array of characteristics: independence and autonomy, physical strength and courage, sexual virility and assertiveness, and a host of other traits. While a "woman-to-woman" chat usually infers intimacy about personal matters, a "man-to-man" talk means getting down to business—and important business at that.

By sheer numbers alone, television provides its most frequent commentaries on what it means to be a man. While dramas tend to emphasize both the heroic and violent aspects of stereotypical manhood, comedies tend to make light of the irresponsibility supposedly inherent in the "typical" male.

The hero character is perhaps the most enduring figure on television, and has been explored in great detail on TV shows ranging from *Combat* (1962–1967) and *Gunsmoke* (1955–1975) to *The A-Team* (1983–1987) and the various iterations of *Star Trek* (original: 1966–1969; *The Next Generation*: 1987–1994; *Deep Space Nine*: 1993–1999; and *Voyager*: 1995–). Even less aggressive programming such as *The Andy Griffith Show* provides cues on what it means to be a "man." Among the most pervasive messages of heroic dramas in particular is that only the fit survive, and fitness is characterized by conforming to the masculine stereotype.

Combat cast Rick Jason and Vic Morrow as Lt. Gil Hanley and Sgt. Chip Saunders respectively, who were leading a World War II U.S. Army platoon across Europe. It provided clear cues about manly authority and camaraderie: that leadership was a lonely business best left to men who could fearlessly bark orders, talk tough and still care for those below them in the pecking order. It also communicated that although friendships may involve little personal intimacy, a true friend protects his buddies, even if it costs him his life.

Gunsmoke provided an equally harsh lesson about leadership: it was lonely at the top and the only way to maintain order was to physically impose it. James Arness as Dodge City, Kansas, Marshal Matt Dillion had few friends, save for "Doc" Adams (Milburn Stone), Chester (Dennis Weaver), Festus (Ken Curtis), and Miss Kitty (Amanda Blake). The rest of the town seemed intent on a daily shootout or fistfight with the marshal. But Marshal Dillion remained steadfast, nonetheless, upholding the law in an otherwise lawless land.

The A Team signaled a new genre of heroes: the misfits who continue to uphold justice while bucking an unjust system. George Peppard as Col. "Hannibal" Smith led a ragtag band of former Vietnam vets on the run from the military and willing to right wrongs for a price. They were a colorful bunch of soldiers of fortune, from the gold-clad Sgt. Bosco (Mr. T) to Capt. "Howling Mad" Murdock (Dwight Schultz). More importantly, they stuck together and took care of each other no matter how wacky their comrades were.

Star Trek, through all of its iterations, made a stab at a more egalitarian system. While females held various positions of authority, the most enduring of its characters remained decidedly masculine, from Capt. James Kirk (William Shatner) to Capt. Jean-Luc Picard (Patrick Stewart). While Kirk provided a jovial, almost campy version of leadership that relied heavily on macho swagger, Picard returned to the stoic, loner version of leadership with a slightly more updated, thoughtful bent.

The ongoing conflict in the original *Star Trek* between Mr. Spock (Leonard Nimoy) and Dr. Leonard McCoy (DeForest Kelley) provided additional insights into the changing nature of manhood as defined by television. While Spock embodied the logical, emotionless male hero, McCoy's crusty appeals for compassion and humanity made the case for the more sensitive male.

The comedy/drama *M*A*S*H* (1972–1983) expanded on this theme, effectively combining the contemporary sensitive male with the very masculine theme of duty, honor, country—all while skewering the concept of war and hawkish extremists in particular. Set during the Korean War, the series followed the 4077 Mobile Army Surgical Hospital and its crew of wacky but effective medical professionals.

Dr. Benjamin Franklin Pierce, a.k.a., Hawkeye, was played by Alan Alda who, as a result of this characterization, became an icon of male sensitivity during the 1980s. Virulently opposed to war, Hawkeye nonetheless performed his duty as a doctor with skill. At the same time, he made a point of decrying the carnage of war and frequently suffered from drunken stupors and the occasional breakdown—all the while cutting the pompous down to size. In between carrying out these duties, he also found time to be a highly proficient womanizer.

Even more benign programs such as *The Andy Griffith Show* made important statements about manhood. Sheriff Andy Taylor (Andy Griffith), though always congenial, provided a certain heroic figure in contrast to the bumbling Barney Fife (Don Knotts), typically protecting Barney and the rest of the community from their own foibles.

Many contemporary depictions of manhood on television increasingly emphasize the most violent aspects of male stereotyping. Such depictions can be especially dangerous when coupled with sexual content. In past decades, portrayals and themes of sexual violence would have been considered pornographic in nature, and would garner strict social and legal sanctions. Although many would argue that today's television is not a pornographic medium, the definition of pornography has changed dramatically over the past few decades.

Boys who watch a steady stream of music videos, in particular, receive a constant diet of messages that real men rarely engage in relationships but frequently engage in sex. Such portrayals communicate the idea that females are simply sex objects and tacitly embrace violence and brutality against women. And numerous studies indicate that materials depicting sexual violence desensitize viewers toward victims of sexual violence and also increase the likelihood that men will engage in sexually violent behaviors. According to the U.S. Surgeon General, violence is now the leading cause of injury in women ages fifteen to forty-four. In fact, one-fifth to one-third of all American women are physically abused during their lifetime.[178] After studying the effects of TV on crime, Brandon Centerwall, an epidemiologist who conducts violence research for the National Centers for Disease Control, Atlanta, suggests that television violence may account for as many as seventy thousand rapes per year.[179]

In one study of Rhode Island teenagers, the subjects were asked to respond to questions about under what circumstances a man "has the right to have sexual intercourse with a woman without her consent." Eighty percent of the respondents said in was acceptable to use force if the couple was married, and 70 percent said it was OK if the couple was planning to marry. More than 50 percent of the teens believed forced sex was justified if the woman had led the man on, and nearly a third said it was acceptable if the man knew the woman had had sex with other men. More than half of the respondents said, "if a woman dresses seductively and walks alone at night, she is asking to be raped."[180]

"We need classes that teach men not to rape and hurt women," says Mary Pipher. "We need workshops that teach men what some of them don't learn: how to be gentle and loving."[181] Unfortunately, most young men receive just the opposite message from America's gender mentor, television.

Those male TV characters who are not overtly violent with women are often portrayed as witless, ineffective slobs who can barely hold down jobs and fail to maintain positive relationships. Comedies such as *Married...With Children*, *Home Improvement*, *The Simpsons*, *The Drew Carey Show* (1995–), *Two Guys and a Girl* (1998–), *King of the Hill* (1997–), and a host of other comedies primarily on Fox, UPN, and WB all play to the notion that men are irresponsible children disguised in adult bodies.

Selling Manhood

Of the roughly twenty-eight hours a week preschoolers spend with television, about five hours are devoted to just commercials. Children receive about 360 thousand commercial messages by the time they graduate high school.[182] Some studies suggest that children pay closer attention to commercials than they do regular programming, perhaps due to ads' fast-paced, compact, and exciting visual messages and the "brightened" sound inherent in many commercials.[183] And, of course, commercials often are repeated several times a day, making them familiar. Children—even very young children—also respond to happy faces...a commercial staple. The messages are simple: products make you happy.

Although not programming, advertisements often give the fullest and most rounded picture of modern stereotypical manhood found on television. Beer ads are particularly adept at tapping into the stereotypical "male psyche" through connections with physical labor, sports, and risk-taking behaviors.[184] The depiction of manhood found on beer commercials usually can be summed up in four words: work hard, play hard.

Beer commercials, although not necessarily directed at young viewers, begin early to communicate myths and values to young boys in particular about men and drinking, as well as sexuality. Some, for example, play on the theme of hard work and pride—and depict a cold beer as an apt reward and a ritual entry into manhood for living up to these values. Other commercials emphasize the idea of masculinity by placing men in bars while young, attractive females wait on them. Bars are depicted as clean, brightly lit places that are both more exciting and wholesome than in real life—no drunks, no haze of cigarette smoke, and no unhappy people.

A new genre of beer commercials is aimed at increasingly younger consumers. These commercials often resemble a college dorm party, prominently displaying young men and women "letting go" and having a good time. The women are often scantily dressed and the scenes frequently appear highly sexualized, appealing to both genders by indicating drinking will free you of inhibitions and make you sexier.

Mixing sexist images with alcohol consumption could create a violent combination, says Arizona State University West researchers Christine C. Iijima Hall and Matthew J. Crum, authors of the study "Women and 'Body-isms' in Television Beer Commercials." "Combining beer and sexy female images may be dangerous considering the increasing alcoholism in America, the increasing connection between alcohol and domestic violence, and the promoting of male aggression."[185] And other researchers note that adults aren't the only ones watching TV beer ads. Some experts estimate that kids may see as many as one hundred thousand beer commercials by the time they turn eighteen.[186]

As a marketing medium, television often strives to make the gender roles it presents to viewers palatable to the widest possible audience, both male and female. Thus, the heroic aspects of manhood as portrayed on TV play to men's fantasies of virility, strength, power, and position. They validate the stereotypical beliefs of male superiority and manifest destiny of men as leaders. To women, heroic male characters satisfy "knight in shining armor" fantasies created by social constructs that dictate the inherent need of women to be rescued.

Even the less flattering portrayals of men—particularly evident in comedies—serve a purpose. Irresponsible male characters may give men permission to act irresponsibly, validating the notion that slovenliness, forgetfulness, excessive use of alcohol, selfishness, and laziness at home are inborn male characteristics. These traits also allow female viewers a sense of validation, telling them that their frustrations with men are common—that they're not alone.

Portrayals at either end of the spectrum do an injustice to manhood, however, engendering both unrealistic expectations and unrealized potential. "Manhood needs to be redefined in a way that allows women equality and men pride," says Pipher. "Our culture desperately needs new ways to teach boys to be men. Via the media and advertising, we are teaching our sons all the wrong lessons. Boys need a model of manhood that is caring and bold, adventurous and gentle. They need ways to be men that don't involve violence, misogyny, and the objectification of women."[187]

Womanhood on TV

If males receive a mixed bag of messages on TV about what it means to be a man, there's little doubt about what women are supposed to be, according to television. Despite a growing number of strong female role models on TV, the overwhelming message remains little changed from the 1950s and 1960s: women are second-class citizens whose primary roles are that of mother and sex object for male characters.

Historically, women have been depicted as secondary characters designed to support male action. Action dramas such as *Hawaiian Eye* (1959–1963), *Surfside Six* (1960–1962), and *77 Sunset Strip* (1958–1964), for example, regularly cast female characters in perky administrative or "sidekick" roles that supported the main male characters or provided a victim for the heroes to rescue. And, of course, there were always plenty of other women in the background to provide ample "eye candy" for male viewers.

When women were cast in more central roles—almost always in comedies—their demeanor changed little. From *Gidget* (1965–1966) with Sally Field to *The Patty Duke Show*, (1963–1966), young women were invariably cast in perky roles with little substance. The overriding message remained that women's greatest power rested in their abilities to manipulate men with flattery and sexual flirtation. Women created "situations" and men fixed them. As Robert Young admonished his daughters Kathy (Lauren Chapin), a.k.a. "Kitten," and Betty (Elinor Donahue), also called "Princess," on *Father Knows Best*, "The worst thing you can do is to try to beat a man at his own game. You just beat the women at theirs."

In a domestic environment, women were frequently seen as helpless objects of circumstance. The 1956–1964 game show *Queen for a Day*, perhaps more than any other show on TV, epitomized this victim role. Hosted by the smarmy Jack Bailey, *Queen for a Day* contestants typically spilled out their most heart-rending stories of martyrdom and victimization. The contestant who suffered the most humiliation in noble silence won a prize designed to ease her burden.

The mid-1960s saw a slight shift in feminine characterizations. Women on programs such as *Bewitched*, *The Flying Nun* (1967–1970), and *I Dream of Jeannie* (1965–1970), were occasionally allowed to succeed with their typically zany plans—as long as they had supernatural powers to assist them. *I Dream of Jeannie* could be especially odious in its depiction of submissiveness and use of feminine wiles to achieve a goal. As Susan Douglas, author of *Where the Girls Are*, points out, Jeannie (Barbara Eden) typically referred to Capt. Tony Nelson (Larry Hagman) as "master." Nelson, in contrast to Jeannie's humble status, served as the ultimate power figure of the 1960s, an astronaut.

A rare exception to the manipulative and dependent characterization of women could be found in Marlo Thomas's Ann Marie character on *That Girl* (1966–1971). Unlike most other female characters of the period, Ann Marie was presented as a purposeful, independent young actress out to conquer the world.

That same era also produced another enduring—but far less positive—image of womanhood: Goldie Hawn as a go-go dancer in a cage on *Rowan and Martin's Laugh-In* (1968–1973). Clad in a bikini and tattoos, Hawn created the ultimate "ditzy-blonde" character whose sole purpose seemed to be as a sexual object of comment for the often lecherous hosts, Dan Rowan and Dick Martin.

By the 1970s, women had moved into the workplace—but primarily as anomalies. The most common of this genre of programs was the female crime fighter. A throwback to the sixties' use of superhuman powers to overcome the perceived handicap of being female, *The Bionic Women* (1976–1978) cast Lindsay Wagner as Jaime Sommers. Sommers was a one-time fiancée of the *The Six Million Dollar Man*'s (1973–1978) lead character, Steve Austin (Lee Majors).

A gender-typical schoolteacher and part-time crime fighter with super-human bionic hearing, Sommers was occasionally teamed up with Austin to fight spies, smugglers, and other international and even extraterrestrial bad guys. However, Sommers had lost the memory of her love for Austin in the skydiving accident that required her rebuilding, so a bionic marriage was not to be.

Although the 1974–1978 drama *Police Woman* broke relatively new ground by casting Angie Dickinson as undercover Los Angeles Police Sgt. Suzanne "Pepper" Anderson, her character frequently utilized sexuality as a means to an end. The typical script called for Dickinson to play a prostitute, gangster girlfriend, or other roles that allowed for low-cut costumes and last-minute rescues by male colleagues.

Charlie's Angels earned the ire of feminists nationwide. The show cast Farrah Fawcett-Majors, Kate Jackson, Jaclyn Smith, and later, Cheryl Ladd, Shelly Hack, and Tanya Roberts, as halter-topped crime-fighters under the direction of the unseen playboy Charlie Townsend (the voice of John Forsythe). David Doyle, played by John Bosley, served as a father figure to the women. Perhaps the most amazing thing about this series was the amount of crime committed in resorts, beaches, and other areas that required skimpy wardrobes. Unfortunately, the show also depicted a vast array of situations where the "angels" were forced to be undressed, trussed up, and otherwise physically accosted.

The 1980s produced one series in particular that provided strong female role models. *Cagney and Lacey* (1982–1988) starred Tyne Daly and Sharon Gless as New York police detectives Mary Beth Lacey and Chris Cagney. Like many cop shows such as *Starsky and Hutch* (1975–1979) before it, *Cagney and Lacey* paired two competent officers willing to risk their lives and use their wits to achieve justice. But the show also showed the personal side of the two women's lives. The characters of Chris Cagney and Mary Beth Lacey presented two strong protagonists—one married, one single—who usually solved their own cases as a team and were rarely in need of rescue by male cops.

The show was not without detractors, however. After the first season, Meg Foster was dropped as Chris Cagney and replaced by a much softer and more traditionally feminine Sharon Gless, breeding a firestorm of protests from feminists. And while Cagney was more attractive and gar-nered more professional status as a sergeant, she also paid a stiff price for eschewing stereotypical feminine roles: she was battling alcoholism—one of television's typical consequences of female success. On the other hand, Lacey was portrayed as more dowdy and at least somewhat submissive to her husband, but she also received less professional success.

Among those shows of the 1980s most likely to offer up stereotypical female roles was *Dynasty*. The nighttime soap opera cast Joan Collins as Alexis Carrington, ex-wife of macho oil magnate Blake Carrington (John Forsythe). Powerful, scheming, and excessive in every way—including eye makeup—Alexis was the ultimate evil vamp. In contrast, Linda Evans played Krystle Jennings-Carrington, the younger working-class current wife. Krystle was usually gentle and sweet—the typical victim. About the only time she could truly toughen up was when she was forced into a cat fight with Alexis.

Like its competing nighttime soap opera, *Dallas*, glamour was the operative word. But *Dynasty* went a step further, becoming the first TV product-licensing venture aimed at upper–middle-class adults—particularly women. The show spawned a variety of upscale products including $150 an ounce "Forever Krystle" perfume.

The 1990s produced a true throwback to the 1960s and 1970s exploita-tion of the female (and for that matter, male) body in the form of *Baywatch*. A sort of video version of the *Sports Illustrated* swimsuit edition, the plots are thin with marginal acting on the part of both genders. About the only thing more predictable is the presence of plenty of bare skin. In 1999, the series celebrated its tenth season by moving from California to Hawaii. It continues to rank among the top shows in terms of popularity—not just in America, but throughout the world. In fact, the show remains the most-watched entertainment program on the entire planet.[188]

A slew of Generation X ensemble shows based upon friendships between twenty-something men and women also decorated the 1990s, but sex was never far from anyone's mind. Series such as *Seinfeld, Friends, Will & Grace* (1998–), and *Jesse* (1998–) provided more face time for female characters and integrated them more fully into the inner circle of main characters. But these shows did little to dispel existing stereotypes.

Most revolved around relationships between the sexes and upheld the notion that men and women could rarely, if ever, be "just friends." Such depictions fly in the face of research, says psychologist William S. Pollack, author of *Real Boys*. "My research reveals that not only are boys capable of forming important platonic friendships with girls, but they are eager to do so and count on these friendships for emotional support and enhancement of their self-esteem."

These shows also featured an assortment of stereotypical characters from Monica's (Courtney Cox Arquette) "house mom" image and Phoebe's (Lisa Kudrow) addled blonde character on *Friends* to the flaky Elaine (Julia Louis-Dreyfus) on *Seinfeld*. And in almost all cases, the central preoccupation for both male and female characters was sex.

Those shows in the 1990s most likely to depict strong, autonomous female characters were among the genre of professional dramas. *ER* featured a variety of strong female characters such as Dr. Kerry Weaver (Laura Innes) and Physician Assistant Jeanie Boulet (Gloria Reuben). *Law & Order*'s feisty Assistant District Attorney Abbie Carmichael (Angie Harmon) and Police Lieutenant Anita Van Buren (S. Epatha Merkerson), lawyers Helen Gamble (Lara Flynn Boyle) and Ellenor Frutt (Camryn Manheim) on *The Practice*, and physician Dr. Sydney Hansen (Melina Kanakaredes) on *Providence* also portray competent professional women. Other roles such as Candice Bergen's main character on *Murphy Brown*, Dr. Michaela Quinn (Jane Seymour) on *Dr. Quinn, Medicine Woman*, and FBI special agent Dana Scully (Gilian Anderson) on *The X-Files* also make a point of showing women as willing to think and act independently, without purely sexual motives.

A key medium for female gender roles throughout much of television's history has been the collection of highly sexualized daytime dramas known as "soap operas." These programs specifically target female viewers and are increasingly aimed at teenage girls—a large part of the afternoon viewing audience. TV viewing remains the number-one after-school activity for most children of both sexes.[189]

The messages communicated by soap operas are particularly alarming: that power and sex are synonymous, and that women's bodies are their most effective weapon in gaining the upper hand. Depictions of women that emphasize the female form over intellectual function continue to send messages to both women and girls that they are, by gender, disadvantaged, and must therefore use their most potent weapon—sex—when competing with men and each other in nearly all realms of life.

The Advantage of Youth

It's a Hollywood maxim that actresses over forty years old often have a difficult time securing romantic roles. An examination of the 1995–1996 season revealed only 29 percent of characters age forty and over were females, and only 40 percent of characters age thirty to thirty-five were women. The only age range in which females outnumbered males was the twenty to twenty-nine group.[190] Overall, 71 percent of the females on television were age thirty-five or younger.[191]

Researchers at Michigan State University and Boston University, after analyzing forty-two hours of programming representing sixty different prime-time shows, concluded that, in general, women on prime-time TV were typically "young, single, independent, and free from family and workplace pressures."[192]

Not only do middle-aged and older women appear less often on television, they're also more prone to negative portrayals. While women over age forty-four represent only one-sixth of all female characters, they make up a third of all female villains. The reverse occurs in men. Although a quarter of all male characters on TV are over forty-five, only a fifth of all male villains fall within that same age range.[193]

Women and Careers

Nowhere on television is the use of sex as a tool of power more evident than on those shows that depict women in the workplace. On TV, women who work outside the home are generally not married, often divorced, younger than their male counterparts and quite attractive, but age quickly. Men tend to be older, in charge, with higher-status positions and appear more capable of combining marriage and career.[194] As stated earlier, powerful women—especially in the workplace—are usually seen as evil.

A 1997 study conducted by Nancy Signorielli, professor of communication at the University of Delaware, Newark, noted that female TV characters tend to be most preoccupied with romance and dating, while men are depicted as most concerned about their careers. Signorielli noted that on television, 41 percent of male characters were depicted while working, while only 28 percent of females were shown in the workplace. Men were also more likely to talk about work (52 percent versus 40 percent), while women talked more about romantic relationships (63 percent versus 49 percent).[195]

Over the past few decades, women have become more likely to be depicted in the workplace, and have achieved higher-status TV jobs. But they are still just as likely to be cast in career roles traditionally assigned to females: secretaries, teachers, social workers, and other non-technical positions. While many medical dramas are beginning to portray more women physicians, for example, females remain much more frequently cast as nurses. Also, when cast in professional roles, women are much more likely to report to men than vice versa. When men do report to women, this arrangement is often used as a source of dramatic conflict, such as when Laura Innes' character on *ER*, Dr. Kerry Weaver, took over the emergency room and supervised several male physicians.

Historically, the media has been reluctant to place women in positions of power or that are seen as requiring higher degrees of intelligence. And often, television and other forms of mass communication have been active participants in communicating "a woman's place."

During the 1950s, for example, the media made a note of the fact that many Russian women were engineers and physicians, but Western media typically portrayed these women as ugly, brutish, and ultra-masculine.

Although the 1950s and 1960s were among the most rapid periods in technological advancements, on TV at least, women were relegated to the periphery, says Susan Douglas. "What film and TV recorded girls doing during these years—teasing our hair, chasing the Beatles, and doing the watusi in bikinis—was silly, mindless, and irrelevant to history....Girls and women come across as the kitsch of the 1960s—flying nuns, witches, genies, twig-thin models, and go-go-boot-clad dancers in cages."[196]

The 1970s saw rapid changes in terms of women's rights and roles within society. In 1972, for example, the U.S. Senate approved the Equal Rights Amendment and sent it to the states for ratification, and the first issue of *Ms.* magazine rolled off the presses. The U.S. Supreme Court in 1973 ruled in Roe v. Wade that women have the constitutional right to abortion. By 1978, the U.S Army integrated women into its ranks, dismantling the "Women's Army Corps," and 1979 became the first year more women than men enrolled in college.

Television made a stab at reflecting some of these trends. *The Mary Tyler Moore Show* was hailed as a breakthrough for women in the workplace. Moore, cast as Associate Producer Mary Richards at WJM-TV News, held a position, at least on paper, as second in command. But even in this portrayal, subtle hints about her status were frequent. Despite her relatively high position, for example, she usually called her boss "Mr. Grant" (Edward Asner), while the men at the station—who held lower-status positions than Richards—called him "Lou." Richards also took dictation, answered Grant's phone, and provided a host of other services a male in the same position would be reluctant to perform.

Grant played a highly paternal role over Richards, and like many shows of the period, the program portrayed most other women on the show as addle-brained or desperately seeking a relationship. Among the few strong female characters on the show, Rhoda Morgenstern, played by Valerie Harper, was punished for that trait by being unable to hook a boyfriend.

On the 1984–1992 comedy *Night Court*, a similar format occurred. Defense attorney Christine Sullivan, played by Markie Post, was far more deferential to court officials than even lower-status male counterparts such as the bailiffs. Harking back to many earlier shows, Post played her character as both perky and lacking self-confidence.

Murphy Brown depicted perhaps the toughest career woman on TV during the late 1980s and early 1990s. Self-confident and professionally competent, she also was seen as abrasive and occasionally even cruel. And like so many of her female TV predecessors, as a recovering alcoholic, she had paid a stiff price for her success. Her antithesis on the show was the perky, image-conscious Corky Sherwood, played by Faith Ford.

By the mid-1990s, many TV comedies turned back to using career as a vehicle for displaying female sexuality and angst. *Veronica's Closet* stars Kirstie Alley as Ronnie Chase, an ex-lingerie model turned entrepreneur. Worried about her weight and fading appearance, Chase embodies the concept of femininity on TV: that maturity naturally makes women frumpy and unattractive, and that a woman truly can't have it all.

In a similar vein, *Just Shoot Me* takes place in the offices of a *Cosmopolitan*-style fashion magazine. Maya Gallo (Laura SanGiacomo), dowdy but sincere, plays off vampish Nina Van Horn (Wendie Malick). While Van Horn seems to learn little beyond the fact that stress causes wrinkles, Gallo usually ends up frustrated by the shallowness of the women's magazine industry and her coworkers.

Among the shows most likely to contain sexist depictions is *Ally McBeal*. McBeal, played by Calista Flockhart, is a twenty-something attorney in a law firm headed by men. In one episode, she becomes furious when a second date doesn't try harder to seduce her. "Why can't he be a man and just paw me a little?" she whines.[197] In a later episode, McBeal is held in contempt of court for wearing a skirt that's too short. A female colleague argues her case on the grounds that such assumptions endorse the myth that sexually attractive women can't be credible. McBeal negates the credibility of any such argument, however, when the judge asks if she has anything to add and she responds, "Only, you know, um, the obvious, your honor." Referring to her sexily coifed colleague, McBeal adds, "I wish I had her hair."

Body Image

The popularity of painfully thin Calista Flockhart also suggests another dangerous trend propagated by television. Few people of either sex can live up to the ideal body shape presented by most television programs and commercials. On TV, thinness is synonymous with being in control and leading "the good life." On the other hand, obesity and, to some extent, even normal body weights are associated with lack of control, poor health, poverty, and other negative stereotypes.

Television portrays overweight women as having a lower socioeconomic status than thin women. In general, obese characters frequently exhibit signs of social deviance. Slender people are generally depicted as more successful, intelligent, and sophisticated.[198]

A 1980 study of TV programs found that teenagers were almost never depicted as obese, and only 7 percent were found to be overweight—this despite the fact that 95 percent of the characters studied were near food or involved in eating or talking about food. Such portrayals negate the extreme sacrifices necessary to achieve the typical level of thinness on TV.[199]

The average model on TV and in other forms of mass media weighs about 23 percent less than the typical American woman, and up to 60 percent of models suffer from eating disorders.[200] Yet, these are the women who represent America's ideal of femininity.

Nearly a quarter of American women are on a diet at any given time, striving desperately to achieve an unrealistic and dangerous image.[201] The constant self-criticism born of modern society's obsession with thinness has resulted in a marked upswing over the past few decades of destructive, self-inflicted maladies such as bulimia and anorexia nervosa.

Susan Douglas says the media impose unrealistic expectations that require women to constantly put themselves under surveillance. "Women learn to turn themselves into objects to be scrutinized; they learn they must continually watch themselves being watched by others," she says.[202]

Advertisements that accompany many female-oriented programs reinforce this notion. "Advertising aimed at women works by lowering our self-esteem," says Naomi Wolf, author of *The Beauty Myth*. "If it flatters our self-esteem, it is not effective."[203]

One study by the University of North Carolina at Chapel Hill suggests that watching even thirty minutes of television programming and advertising can alter a woman's perception of the shape of her body.[204] The experience of women in the tropical nation of Fiji seems to bear this out. Weight used to be a source of pride and beauty in Fiji. But within just a few years of the introduction of television to the main island, the incidence of eating disorders rose significantly and the perception of beauty and thinness changed dramatically. Now many Fijian women view weight as a curse and men's perception of weight and beauty in women is also rapidly being redefined.[205]

While men and boys have not suffered as dramatically as women from unrealistic body image expectations, there is evidence that this may be changing. Cartoon characters and accompanying action figures are becoming increasingly more muscular, to the point that their proportions far exceed that of even the most muscular real-life characters.

Some preliminary research now suggests a tie between these unrealistic body images and the upswing in bodybuilding. These researchers identified a sort of "reverse anorexia," where average or above-average condition young men see themselves as frail and thin. These young men also were more likely to spend inordinate amounts of time working out, bulking up, and even resorting to the use of steroids.[206] And although the standard form of anorexia is typically associated with young women, more than 10 percent of all anorexia cases actually involve males.[207]

Parenthood

Although it seems clear that mothers can have a profound impact on the self-image and self-confidence of young women, their role in bringing up a truly "complete" young man can be equally powerful.

William Pollack notes that mothers are the earliest teachers of masculinity, instructing their sons on how to integrate both components of the split model of masculinity. Mothers, he says, imbue boys with a sense of confidence about their feelings and experiences that add up to being an emotionally balanced and satisfied man.[208]

It seems ironic that so few positive maternal characters exist on television today, when they were such a staple in the early years of the medium. In fact, one of the few positive mothers on television may actually appear on *The Simpsons*. Marge Simpson—the mother—is most often the one character who exhibits a level head...even if it is three feet high and blue. Notes *E!Online* of the beehived Marge: "Great moms have a way of reining-in exuberant youngsters without breaking their spirit."[209]

The father's role in raising children is equally crucial. While mothers usually instill social skills, typical interactions with fathers emphasize independence and autonomy. When fathers are actively involved, boys turn out to be less aggressive, less overly competitive, and better able to express feelings of vulnerability and sadness.[210] Many studies also note that a father's involvement can have a profound effect on daughters' proficiency in critical skills such as mathematics and science.[211] Often, however, dads tend to give attention unevenly, favoring sons over daughters. On weekdays, for example, fathers spend about twenty minutes more a day playing with boys than girls.[212]

Television has done little to promote the idea of males participating in the daily upkeep of the home and care of the children. True, television has depicted male characters such as Uncle Charley (William Demarest) on *My Three Sons* (1960–1972), Charles (Scott Baio) on *Charles in Charge* (1984–1985, 1987–1990), Tony (Tony Danza) on *Who's the Boss* (1984–1992), and Buck (Kevin Meaney) on the short-lived sitcom *Uncle Buck* (1990–1991) who are willing to do housework—often because it was their job. But in almost all cases, the nurturing male is used as a comic device—anomalies rather than the norm. The typical domestic male on TV follows the "fish-out-of-water" theme—a macho guy forced to do "women's work."

Numerous studies indicate that heavy TV viewing can profoundly affect the perceptions of gender roles of both male and female viewers. These studies indicate that in general, the more people watch television, the more likely they are to endorse a traditional division of labor between the sexes.[213]

A survey of 530 fourth- and fifth-graders by Nancy Signorielli and others found, for example, that children who were heavy television viewers held stereotypical attitudes about what household chores should be done by girls and boys.[214] Further studies reveal that heavy viewers believe stereotypical roles portrayed on TV reflect reality.

The results of these traditional beliefs about sex roles and responsibilities can be devastating to women in particular. As a result of the desire to have and be everything to everyone, many career women are working a double shift—the first in the office, and the second at home taking care of the family and house. Women work fifteen more hours a week, and over a year, they have worked an extra month of twenty-four-hour days.[215]

But this division of labor only tells half the story. Men's housework frequently consists of creative or seasonal "projects" such as painting the deck or fixing a broken appliance. Women, on the other hand, are typically relegated to the more odious and repetitive chores of cleaning the kitchen, washing floors, and doing the laundry.[216]

And when it comes to child care, women continue to bear a significantly greater load than men. Even when fathers do participate in child care, their activities tend to be more recreational in nature, such as playing with the children or reading to them, while mothers take care of more mundane responsibilities such as bathing and feeding.[217]

Many studies indicate that the happiest wives are those whose husbands share all facets of household and family responsibilities. But such arrangements also benefit husbands as well. For example, fathers who share household chores equally with their wives generally report a higher degree of satisfaction in the parenting roles as well. They also tend to be more aware of their children's needs and provide a positive example of egalitarianism than those fathers who remain locked into stereotypical roles.[218] And as an added benefit, a large study on dual-income families conducted by Wellesley College found that fathers' positive relationships with their children was the best predictor of the men's physical health.[219]

An involved father not only benefits the kids and mom, dads also get something out of it as well, says Warren Farrell, author of *Why Men Are the Way They Are*. "It helps heal deep wounds they may have from working too much, becoming disconnected from parts of themselves." He adds that being a successful parent can be extremely rewarding for men. "It's like giving a woman in the 1950s some sign of her competence."[220]

Yet, the percentage of American children living apart from their biological fathers has more than doubled to 42 percent, up from 19 percent in 1960, according to the U.S. Census Bureau. Out-of-wedlock births account for 41 percent of all babies born in the U.S., up from 11 percent in 1970.

At least part of the reason can be attributed to the crumbling structure of social mores that direct men toward responsible parenting, says David Popenoe. "Left culturally unregulated, men's sexual behavior can be promiscuous, their paternity casual, their commitment to families weak. In recognition of this, cultures have used sanctions to bind men to their children, and of course, the institution of marriage has been culture's chief vehicle."[221]

Popenoe goes on to point out America's late twentieth-century breakdown of these sanctions—and the accompanying decline of paternal responsibility—has been a major force behind many of the social problems now so prevalent. Although television cannot be assigned full blame for the breakdown of the social mores occurring over the past few decades, it most certainly has helped communicate loosening attitudes toward irresponsible behavior. Moreover, TV, in an effort to create dramatic or comedic situations, often amplifies these attitudes in ways that imply to viewers that they have already become socially accepted.

It seems apparent that like so many functions television assumes from family members, when it acts as a gender mentor, the results can be devastating. As a result, heavy TV viewers of all ages are destined to adopt and repeat the destructive gender behaviors they see on television. By leaving the role of gender mentor to TV, we are effectively perpetuating old, ineffectual, and harmful belief systems, and perhaps even creating new, more harmful gender trends. Rather than learning new tools and coping skills that promote equality and give both sexes permission to experience a full range of emotions and personal and professional possibilities, we are simply continuing to limit individual growth, and ultimately the growth of society as a whole.

Sexual Advisor

From "the talk" by parents and after-date discussions with siblings to the intimate and loving bedroom conversation between husbands and wives, the family has traditionally provided the bulk of information on when and how we manifest our sexual nature.

In the days before television, couples typically learned together about sex, not as a generic act with any individual, but as a very specific and intimate act with one partner. Now, sex often takes on a "recreational" aspect, and part of that "fun" is the variety born of multiple partners. Frequently, the media presents us with an expectation that the average person will have numerous lovers before marriage, and probably several more after marriage. It also tells us that our sexual encounters outside of marriage will be wildly satisfying, and that our love life within marriage is likely to be characterized by infrequent and unsatisfying sexual events.

According to an extensive analysis of television programming conducted by the University of California-Santa Barbara, more than two-thirds of all prime-time television shows deal with sex. And if you happen to be an afternoon television viewer, you'll get an even heavier dose. In fact, more than 85 percent of soap operas contain sexual references and content, and talk shows discuss sex more than three-quarters of the time.[222]

Several studies have concluded that heavy TV viewers—especially those who frequently watch highly sexualized programs—think about sex more often, discuss it with their peers, and assume others are having sex more frequently than they actually do.[223,224] Heavy viewing strengthens the assumption that premarital and extramarital sex is far more satisfying than sex with a spouse.[225]

While research is scarce on the satisfaction levels of contemporary lovers versus those of pre-television society, our modern culture is certainly more inclined to voice opinions on how happy we are with our sex lives. Moreover, the increasing availability of sexual material on TV and in other media allows us to create a model of what constitutes "satisfying" sex, and then compare that model to our own experiences. But is that model an accurate depiction of an average, positive, or even attainable sex life?

Defining Satisfying Sex

Almost all the information required to perform the physical act of sex is revealed on prime-time TV. By offering up this mass-media version of sex, TV creates its own standardized version of the perfect sexual relationship. This version is not based on any particular scientific analysis of humankind, but rather on what the creative community believes will garner the highest ratings. Respected media scholars S. Robert Lichter, Linda Lichter, and Stanley Rothman analyzed 620 prime-time shows produced over the past thirty years, drawn from the most comprehensive collection of television programs—the Library of Congress video archive. In their landmark book, *Prime Time*, which was based on the study, they conclude, "Beyond simply reflecting our changing sexual mores, television has endorsed the changes and...accelerated their acceptance....It has lately played a leading role in questioning traditional moral standards before a vast national audience."[226]

The researchers note that a 1987 Planned Parenthood Federation study found an average of sixty-five thousand sexual references a year are broadcast during the evening and afternoon viewing times. That means that in the 1980s, the average American was exposed to about fourteen thousand sexual references on TV annually.[227] And such exposure hasn't slowed.

A Kaiser Family Foundation–sponsored study found the average "family" show contained 8.5 incidents of sexual behavior, and nearly more than 75 percent of children's programming had some sexual content. In about

13 percent of family programs, teenage girls were involved in sexual activities portrayed as enjoyable and healthy.[228]

Although Lichter, Lichter, and Rothman concede that the television often reflects the loosening sexual mores of a broader society, they maintain TV often draws its moral boundaries from the communities long considered the vanguards of social change, New York and Los Angeles. "Television increasingly transmits Hollywood's perspectives rather than middle America's," they note.[229] Moreover, because of television's omnipresence in Western culture, it becomes harder to determine how much society influences sexual depictions on TV, and how much TV changes society's view of sex.

The sexual act is pleasurable. That's a function of nature's design to encourage intimacy, procreation, and the bonds that create a healthy family life—a fact often ignored by prime-time television. In the sexual environment created by television, sex has little to do with intimacy, commitment, babies, or even sexually transmitted diseases. From a physiological standpoint, the pleasurable aspects of sex are designed to bring two people together. As sex improves with practice, the bond between partners also strengthens. The bottom line: sex is pleasurable to enable intimacy. TV's revision of sex contradicts these purposes. Many media researchers have noted that although television may show a lot of sex, it frequently is not accompanied by the kinds of affection such as touching, hugging, and kissing associated with strong emotions and a permanent relationship.[230] More often, sex is depicted as casual and not necessarily an indication of any long-term commitment.

As America buys into the expectation that everyone can have great sex with anyone else at any time, there's no reason to view sex as a means to bond two people together. Television depicts the relationship between sex and commitment as outdated and an inhibition to sexual freedom.

Separating Sex from Emotion

As sex becomes less an emotional experience and more simply a physical act, humans increasingly view themselves and others as sexual machines. TV portrays the ideal sexual partner as prepared to perform any act any time with no emotional stimulation or expectation of commitment.

The Woody Allen film *Sleeper* depicted a future society that had no need for physical contact to achieve sexual fulfillment. Machines provided sexual stimulation in a safe, sterile environment. We're quickly achieving this prediction via television. But like Allen's tongue-in-cheek version of the future, today's sexual environment ultimately generates little gratification. In the process of attaining this empty nirvana, those human institutions that do provide satisfaction beyond the purely physical—family and monogamous relationships—are being destroyed.

For all its obsession with sex, television creates relatively little passion in the traditional sense. Until the mid-twentieth century, the word "passion" connoted strong emotions. The entertainment industry has redefined this word. Passion is now synonymous with the physical act of having sex rather than its emotional component.

When sex is separated from emotion, it's a fair assumption that viewers' relationships will suffer. As TV creates a society in which sex requires no commitment, real-life committed relationships begin to appear burdensome. Nowhere does this sad fact present itself more potently than in television's depiction of marriage.

The Terminal Marriage

The institution of marriage is facing its biggest challenge ever. With few exceptions, television portrays marriage as stifling, dull, boring, or even dangerous. Wives on TV are frequently depicted as nagging, unattractive, sarcastic shrews. From Peg Bundy on *Married...With Children* and the lead character in *Roseanne*, to Jill on *Home Improvement* and the mother on *Malcolm in the Middle* (1999–), married women on modern television show little respect for their spouses and children. Television husbands don't fare any better. Often, they are portrayed as incompetent, indifferent, and generally fairly dim-witted. Though characters such as Norm on *Cheers* (1982–1993), Tim on *Home Improvement*, and Paul on *Mad About You* may be charming in their lack of finesse, abilities, or desire for their wives, they nonetheless create a picture of husbands as oafish and bungling. While TV may preach equality, it frequently makes a point of creating comedy or drama from the inequity of power, intellect, or capabilities between married people.

In the world of television, sex is something to be enjoyed before marriage, and simply endured, if it occurs at all, after the first few years of marriage. A content analysis of soap operas, for example, reveals that sex in these programs happens twenty-four times more frequently outside of marriage than between married partners. In fact, 94 percent of all sexual encounters on soap operas are between people who aren't married to each other.[231] And rarely do couples over the age of fifty engage in anything akin to intimacy. Affection among seniors is "cute"; senior sex is disgusting.

The series *Get Real* (1999–2000) is a prime example of how TV emphasizes fantasy over a satisfying reality. In a graphic opening sequence, the wife is making passionate love to her cooperative, thoughtful husband. But it is only a dream; she awakes to the disappointing reality of an inattentive, inconsiderate, boring spouse.

For both men and women, marriage is portrayed as something to be escaped. As movie critic Michael Medved points out, "The emphasis on disastrous relationships, and the paucity of positive alternatives, contribute powerfully to the prevailing sense that marriage is an institution under siege; that happy couples are an endangered species; that misery and cruelty are inevitable by-products of the traditional family structure."[232]

The fact is, most viewers long for depictions of marriage that are hopeful and uplifting, that lend credence to their own beliefs that marriage is still a viable and valuable institution. Contrary to TV's depictions, numerous studies show that most people view marriage in a positive light. A Harris poll, for instance, found that 85 percent of all husbands and wives said they would remarry their same spouse if they could do it again.[233] Moreover, mature adults do engage in satisfying sex. An American Association of Retired People survey found, in fact, that at least half of all people age forty-five to fifty-nine have sex at least once a week, and more than two-thirds of couples forty-five and over are "extremely satisfied" or "very satisfied" with their relationship.[234]

Such research demonstrates that most marriages, while imperfect, are fulfilling and generally happy. Nonetheless, television continues to portray singlehood as preferable to the institution of marriage. A disproportionate number of TV shows—*Friends*, *Melrose Place*, and *Seinfeld*, for example—invariably depict lead characters as single or divorced. These characters also appear both happier and more interesting as a result of their single status. While it's true that these shows are meant to appeal to a young, affluent demographic segment, in real life, the actors—particularly the male actors—who star in these shows are often approaching middle age—such as the forty-something Jerry Seinfeld—but their characters still embrace the single life.

Although singlehood is a perfectly acceptable lifestyle, to imply that it is a more satisfying situation than marriage again contradicts statistics. One study by Jacqueline Simenauer and David Carroll, for example, found that more than 60 percent of divorced people still prefer married life to being single and would marry again if they had the opportunity.[235]

Legitimizing Adultery

A key element of television's seeming denunciation of marriage is its incessant depiction of adultery. Television feeds viewers a steady diet of messages that say romance only occurs outside marriage and sexual satisfaction can be achieved only in adulterous relationships—deliciously satisfying in a way only forbidden fruit can offer.

A study by Linda and S. Robert Lichter and Stanley Rothman found that television's attitudes toward extramarital adventures has changed significantly over the past three decades. Before 1970, 38 percent of all shows depicting non-marital sexual situations clearly condemned extramarital sex as morally unacceptable. Contemporary programming is markedly different. Only 7 percent of today's shows portray extramarital sex in a disapproving light, while 41 percent endorsed it without qualification and another 33 percent made no moral judgment.[236] Do these findings accurately present a world inclined to turn away from marriage?

Not exactly. A nationwide poll conducted by the National Opinion Research Center at the University of Chicago found 98 percent of people surveyed claim to have been faithful to their spouses during the past twelve months, with nearly 75 percent saying sex outside marriage is always wrong. Baltimore marriage counselor and psychologist Shirley Glass says the numbers sound reasonable. "Fifty percent of men and a third of women say they have had extramarital affairs, but that's over the lifetime of their marriage, so that could easily work out to 1.5 percent a year," she explains.[237] The bottom line: most people's moral opinions about extramarital sex directly conflict with television.

A Powerful Message

Television's sexual messages are particularly powerful among young viewers. The advice and guidance of parents and older siblings quickly becomes obsolete in the face of television's onslaught of sexual information and risque scenes.

Several polls confirm that television is just behind parents in its power to influence children's values and behavior, and may soon move into the No. 1 position. A survey of ten- to sixteen-year-olds, for example, reveals that up to 62 percent say sex on television influences their peers to have sex prematurely.[238] Yet, the vast majority of American parents continue to allow their children to watch the never-ending parade of sexual escapades that now dominate network TV. These depictions offer a powerful script to children on what is appropriate sexual behavior.

Many in the television industry see little harm in promoting such messages and feel no obligation to promote sexual responsibility. "We're not trying to scare kids and say, 'Don't have sex,'" explains Joss Whedon, creator and executive producer of the teen hit *Buffy the Vampire Slayer*. "Some do, some will, some should, some shouldn't. Still, one of the scariest things is sex. It's going to come up."[239]

Children ages five to twelve are especially affected by sexual content, says Sharon Lamb, assistant professor of psychology at Bryn Mawr College, Bryn Mawr, Pennsylvania. Her research indicates that after watching TV, children are more apt to act out sexual stereotypes and violence, including "play" prostitution, striptease, and rape. "The thing that is worrisome to me is sexual violence may be getting into their play," she says. "I think it's a problem when they rehearse...that stereotype."[240]

Such messages are particularly powerful in the absence of parental guidance. Few parents today understand the importance of having age-appropriate discussions about sex with their children. Unfortunately, because of the prevalence of sexual materials on network TV, preteens often pick up so much sexual information that parental discussions may appear irrelevant.

Many parents simply throw up their hands in frustration after discovering that television has already taught their children more than they feel is appropriate. This sets in motion a cycle that undermines parents' roles as sexual authorities and enhances TV's credibility. Anthropologist Margaret Mead noted that once this phenomenon occurs, children are naturally more inclined to turn to external sources such as television for further information.[241] Television then becomes their sole conduit for sexual advice and guidance.

Irresponsible Sex

Besides offering content that may be inappropriately mature for many viewers, most programs fail to depict characters taking even the simplest precautions, such as use of contraceptives or protection against sexually transmitted diseases. A 1999 study by the Kaiser Family Foundation examined more than thirteen hundred network and cable shows, from soap opera *Days of Our Lives* and talk show *Leeza* to prime-time drama *Melrose Place*. The researchers noted that just 9 percent of programs dealing with sex also dealt with its risks or consequences. Moreover, of the 88 scenes that actually depicted sex or strongly implied it, not one referenced safe sex or contraception—even on teen-oriented shows.[242]

TV characters rarely demonstrate self-control. Rather, the prevailing message is that sex is an act performed with abandon, and that planning is unromantic and ruins spontaneity. Of the fourteen thousand sexual references and behaviors that children witness on American television each year, less than 150 involve birth control or discussions about abstinence or sexually transmitted diseases.[243]

In the world of teen-targeted programs such as *Beverly Hills 90210*, *Melrose Place*, and *Friends*, virginity is a curse to be remedied at the earliest possible opportunity. For the sake of eroticism and drama, innocence and decency are usually only portrayed as attractive when they offer the potential to be destroyed. Numerous shows over the past decade have focused on the loss of virginity including *Doogie Howser, M.D.* (1989–1993), *Felicity* (1998–), and *Blossom* (1991–1995). At times, it seems that the creative community appears to be mired in an adolescent locker room mentality that takes delight in destroying innocence and virtue.

Despite television's onslaught of sexual information, the most vital messages about sex seldom are communicated. The effects of irresponsibly portrayed sex are reflected in the alarming number of unwanted pregnancies and the spread of AIDS and other sexually transmitted diseases. Currently more than 41 percent of first births occurred outside of marriage,[244] and four in ten American girls become pregnant before age twenty.[245] According to the U.S. Centers for Disease Control, young adults ages thirteen to twenty-four are now the fastest-growing population of AIDS victims, accounting for more than half of all new HIV infections.[246] These infections are overwhelmingly the result of increased sexual contact among teens. In the mid-1950s, for example, just over one-quarter of girls under eighteen had had sexual intercourse. By 1995, however, that figure had jumped to nearly 70 percent. And 23 percent of those surveyed had had sex with more than four partners.[247] Another study revealed that, on average, sexually active teenage girls typically engage in unprotected intercourse six months to a year before seeking contraception guidance.[248]

Television's soap operas, which draw thirty million viewers each day,[249] are particularly guilty of portraying even the most casual and irresponsible sexual encounters in a positive light.

A 1996 study by the Henry J. Kaiser Family Foundation evaluated ninety hours of programming from ten nationally televised soap operas. The researchers recorded an average of 6.1 sexual behaviors per hour of programming. Sexual behaviors were defined as kissing, caressing, flirting, or sexual intercourse that was shown, implied, or discussed. Even more alarming, when compared with a study conducted just two years earlier, the 1996 evaluation showed a marked increase in the number of sexual acts depicted rather than simply discussed.

Of the 594 recorded sexual behaviors, only fifty-eight included a discussion or depiction of planning or consequences. "The overwhelming message of sex without consequence is out of synch with reality and not a helpful model, especially for young people," explains Dr. Felicia Stewart, director of reproductive health programs for the Kaiser Foundation. Soap opera sex is almost always portrayed as having a positive effect on a relationship, notes Katherine Heintz-Knowles, author of the Kaiser Family Foundation study.[250]

Even some of the most aggressive sexual acts portrayed on soap operas often have positive consequences. On *All My Children*, for example, several female characters have been transformed by rape from "bad girls" to more kind and considerate characters. And on *One Life to Live*, another character, Todd Manning, leads a gang rape of a female who, he says, "asked for it." Later he is cast as a hero when he rescues the same woman and her children from an auto accident. Perhaps the most notable incidense of soap operas' skewed vision occurred on *General Hospital* (1963–). Luke's rape of Laura during the 1979 season caused quite a stir. But the real fireworks blazed when the two eventually became on-the-run lovers. "Soap opera rape both blames and tames its victims," notes researcher Mary Buhl Dutta, adjunct professor at Mount Ida College, Newton Centre, Massachusetts, who did an extensive survey of soap opera rapes. She adds that rape is often presented as a punishment for bad behavior, and allows the characters to be "redeemed."[251]

Another study, appearing in the journal *Sex Roles*, analyzed twenty-six prime-time soap opera story lines that focused on rapes. The programs were examined for the occurrence of "rape myths," such as "she asked for it," "she wanted it," "she lied about it," and, "she wasn't really hurt by the attack." Such myths occurred more than 130 times, or an average of 5.08 uses per story line. Such myths were opposed in only 38 percent of the programs, and more than 40 percent of shows suggested the victim wanted to be raped. "The over-use of rape myths in prime-time television drama reinforces the belief women are responsible for the rape, not men," says the study's author, Susan Brinson.[252]

A content analysis of soap operas by Bradley Greenberg, distinguished professor of telecommunications at Michigan State University, and Rick Busselle, assistant professor at the Edward R. Murrow School of Communication, Washington State University, also found the incidence of and reference to intercourse occurs between unmarried partners four times as often as between married partners, with sexual behaviors occurring every nine minutes. Furthermore, sexual behaviors occur more than three times as often between unmarried couples compared to married ones.[253]

What is also alarming about these statistics is the fact that television does such a poor job of depicting the realities of parenthood. In fact, other than infants, children are rarely portrayed on soap operas. When married parents are depicted, the children are usually "at grandma's."

And when it comes to the harsh realities of single parenthood, TV most often paints an exceptionally rosy picture of raising kids alone. Soap operas—popular among teen and pre-teen girls in particular—are especially irresponsible in this area and do little to depict sexual responsibility or the consequences of irresponsible sex.

Single mothers on soap operas are usually upper middle class and white with good jobs, well-furnished homes, and stylish wardrobes. They're often depicted as having plenty of help caring for their child, and can frequently bring children to work and social events. The men in their lives, other than their fathers, also seem quite eager to nurture youngsters.[254] And, these women also benefit from being able to venure out without their children any time they choose.

These portrayals have a very real impact on impressionable young viewers. According to a study of 163 junior and senior high students by researcher Mary Strom Larson, soap opera viewers often perceive that single moms have good jobs, are relatively well-educated, and do not live in poverty. They also believe that the offspring of single moms will be as healthy as most children and will receive love and attention from adult male friends.[255]

These perceptions are in stark contrast to reality. In 1992, for example, 45 percent of all female-headed households lived in poverty,[256] and children in single parent households were six times more likely to be poor than those in two-parent families.[257] Children of single parents suffer higher incidents of emotional and crime problems including depression, drug use, neglect, abuse, and adolescent suicide.[258]

Single mothers fair no better. Half of teen mothers will not complete high school,[259] and the average teen mother will realize only 50 percent of the lifetime earnings of those who delay motherhood until age twenty or later.[260]

Scripting Behavior

Due to television's unique power to create realistic images, viewers—adolescents and adults alike—often identify closely with main characters.

In a sense, they step into the fantasy world that TV creates, a world that is difficult to resist when compared to the imperfections of real life.

If there is any doubt about television's power to script or at least influence teens' sexual behavior, one need only to take a look at the statistics. The National Survey of Children, for example, reveals that males who frequently watch TV engage in more sex than any other group. In addition, teens who watch television alone report having intercourse three to six times more frequently than those adolescents who view TV with their families.[261]

Nearly sixty million households receive MTV, which is particularly adept at promoting premarital sex. In one study of seventh to tenth graders, students were exposed to selected rock videos recorded from MTV. After just one hour of exposure, they were more likely to approve of premarital sex than a control group of teens who did not see the videos.[262]

Even more alarming are these programs' depictions with kinky or violent sex. One study by the National Coalition on Television Violence reviewed 750 music videos. The researchers counted, on average, twenty acts of violence per hour—most associated with sexual content.[263] A 1999 study conducted by famed media researchers S. Robert Lichter, Linda S. Lichter, and Dan Amundson found that a single day of music videos shown on MTV contained an average of 446 violent acts.[264] In fact, the researchers found that among television programming, MTV music videos and theatrical movies, the music videos depicted more than twice the incidences of violence as the standard TV and movies. What's truly disturbing is the audience these music videos target.

Dr. Ramon Rojano, director of the Institute for the Hispanic Family, Hartford, Connecticut, calls exposure to TV sex "another form of child abuse." He notes that programs that contain sex and violence lead to promiscuity and encourage boys to "begin at an early age to think of women as objects." He adds, "Children are not getting the message that sex has a spiritual or emotional side."[265]

It's a sad commentary on America's understanding of the problem of teen sex that so many parents allow their children to watch MTV—depicting the most promiscuous and violent sexual images—but then take a puritanical approach to research on the effects of such programming. While the

American Psychological Association reports that more than one thousand studies have focused on the correlation between TV violence and aggressive behavior,[266] none of the studies were designed to test a cause-and-effect hypothesis.

Victor C. Strasburger, chief of adolescent medicine at the University of New Mexico School of Medicine, and Dr. Diane Furno-Lamude proposed a study involving questionnaires that asked teens about the kinds of media they were likely to experience.[267] The survey would also cover risky behavior such as sexual activity, drug use, and violence, as well as questions on sexual knowledge and attitudes. These questions included queries on diverse subjects such as "When is a female most likely to become pregnant?" and "Should only married people have sex?"

The researchers were unable to conduct the study, however, because they lacked the cooperation of local school boards and state departments of education. Most survey opponents feared the questions might be too controversial—even one district that actually allowed distribution of condoms in schools.

The 1999 season of network programs popular among teens are a prime example of highly sexualized content. *Manchester Prep,* for example, depicts a sister checking out her brother's body while he takes a shower, and later shows her apparently masturbating while uttering, "The Bradys never had it so good."

Malcolm in the Middle features a trashy mom who performs her chores sans top and bra and a father who strips naked in the kitchen during breakfast to shave his back. *Shasta McNasty* (1999) focuses on three rappers who sit around concocting schemes to seduce women and features a foul-mouthed, crotch-biting parrot. On shows such as *Friends, Dawson's Creek, Ally McBeal, Melrose Place*, and *Felicity*, sex is often the pivotal plot device around which the entire show is created. These shows also make a point of featuring sexually aggressive female characters who utilize sex to achieve their goals—including revenge.

Although there is plenty of speculation among experts that TV has a profound effect on children's sexuality, scientific studies are desperately needed to confirm these suspicions. Society can no longer turn a blind eye toward how television changes children's views of sex.

Surrogate Lover

Although the actual act of adultery seems to be an increasingly popular theme on television, TV also promotes a different but equally destructive form of unfaithfulness. In a sense, the characters on television become surrogate lovers for many viewers.

Television has become a form of sexual foreplay, and the entertainment industry is particularly adept at creating fantasy lovers whose sexual prowess, financial resources, and physical attractiveness are far beyond reality's ability to compete. Several studies, for example, reveal that sexual material on TV leaves many viewers less satisfied with their partners.[268] TV images of women appear to influence men, in particular, on how they perceive real women in their lives. As early as the 1970s, researchers began to recognize the toll television can take on relationships. For example, a study nearly thirty years ago of male college students who viewed just one episode of *Charlie's Angels* were more harsh in their evaluation of potential dates.[269]

Television creates unrealistic expectations of real-life partners, offering a picture of the opposite sex that is superhuman. As the lines between television fantasy and reality continue to blur, viewers' appetites for this perfection may compel them to seek out more "perfect" partners.

The illusionary sexual images of television characters are virtually unattainable for all but a handful of real-life lovers. The soap opera Don Juan may know just the right words to make a woman's heart pound, but he also has a team of writers to back him up. The made-for-TV vixen's alluring glance has been practiced over and over again. Both are supported by a legion of make-up artists, hairdressers, and wardrobe consultants who cover up imperfections, and lighting technicians and set designers who create a highly sexualized mood. Since few of us actually see these behind-the-scene support systems, however, such depictions instill in viewers the idea that they, too, should be attaining the same level of sexual rapture as their favorite television characters.

Because of its visual nature, television is particularly attuned to the tastes of male viewers—witness *Sports Illustrated*'s show focusing on the photo shoot for the magazine's swimsuit edition. TV creates female surrogate lovers who do not require emotional involvement, love, or tenderness—such relationships are purely sexual in nature. This defeminization of women creates fantasy partners who satisfy male viewers' sexual needs but are otherwise "one of the boys." For men, television reinforces the recurring theme that tenderness and emotional commitment are separate from sex.

This obsession with sex in the absence of emotion has even crept into our dialect. The common definition of "lover" has changed significantly over the past few decades. In earlier times it inferred a romantic relationship. Today, however, it is used almost exclusively to describe sexual partners, from long-term live-ins to one-night stands.

An Appetite for Dysfunction

An absence of emotion and romantic notions opens the door even further to depict relations solely based on sex. Sadomasochist costumes, foul language, and hot tempers are clear TV signals that a character is sexually charged and ready for action. And the glamorization of stripping and prostitution further promotes the notion that promiscuity is harmless and normalizes these endeavors as viable career options.

Sexuality in these portrayals is often manifested in the most mean-spirited, evil, and sadistic ways. Such depictions create an appetite for dysfunction. Unhealthy relationships—ones that destroy self-esteem and team with infidelity—become the most alluring. The message is "evil is enticing, good is boring, and moral is outdated." Popular entertainment not only promotes the idea that we should feed our sexual desires, but that we must give ourselves over completely to the power of our sexuality. Romance holds little sway in the highly sexualized world of TV.

Planting Seeds of Discontent

The sexually charged world of television too often sets up a situation where viewers compare their own love lives with the fantasy of television—a fantasy that because of television's visual and aural power, seems all-too-real.

Although reliable statistics on the relationship of television to promiscuity, marital conflict, infidelity, and divorce are scarce at best, it seems reasonable to assume that the "greener pastures" television infers may have a significant impact on family dynamics that lead to failed relationships.

While today's adults are struggling with the media's flagrant disassociation between sex and emotion, the true victims of TV's sexual propaganda will be future generations. Tomorrow's adults will miss the joy of sex based on strong emotional attachment and a stable family life that such bonds help create.

Hero

Everyone loves a hero. One need only look at ancient cave paintings, hieroglyphics, and other forms of early communication to understand that heroism is a mainstay of human existence.

Heroes have traditionally served as super role models, exemplifying with great clarity the characteristics that we as a society view most precious. Whether real or fictitious, heroes were generally depicted as "larger than life." This is natural, since heroes reflected our personal and cultural aspirations to be more than we are.

Today's heroes generally fall into two categories: the superhero with superpowers and the heroic "everyman"—with a twist. The superhero is not a new phenomenon but has enjoyed an enormous comeback during the last century. Superheroes are, in many ways, a direct throwback to the ancient gods of Greek mythology, possessing superhuman strength, intelligence, and endurance. The "everyman" hero also has been around a very long time. He or she typically was depicted as an ordinary person thrust into extraordinary circumstances.

Until the mid-twentieth century, superheroes and everyman heroes almost universally shared one key trait: honor. Heroes were more than willing to put their own lives on the line for others. Noble thoughts, deeds, and motivations were their stock and trade.

A New Kind of Hero

Over the past few decades, a new kind of hero has emerged. Many of today's heroes are even less honorable than the average person. They are often dark, mean-spirited characters who are reluctant to take risks and only exhibit the most rudimentary heroic traits after being forced to do so. Similar heroes may have occasionally been depicted in earlier entertainment offerings such as the film noir—dark, bleak private eye movies. This genre was, however, only a small part of a much larger and overall brighter stable of heroic characters. Today's good guy is likely to be as crass and obscene as the villain. America is rapidly developing an appetite for the bad-boy protagonist.

Much of the crop of heroes emerging over the past thirty years lack anything akin to idealism. They have no compelling beliefs, no noble motivations, and little, if any, emotion. "The 'good-guys' [on television] are often not much better role models than the villains," notes a report by the U.S. Department of Education. As a consequence, many children are far more familiar with violent, antisocial approaches to problem-solving and conflict resolution than they are with nonviolent and pro-social ones. The problem is not just that children learn inappropriate behavior, but they also tend to adopt the evaluative standards that the programs project.[270]

This is particularly true of the weary cop, pseudo-military, and martial arts genres, with characters such as Det. Andy Sipowicz (Dennis Franz) on *NYPD Blue*, Kung Lao (Paolo Montalbon) on the Nintendo game-based *Mortal Kombat* (1998–), Cordell Walker (former world karate champion Chuck Norris) on *Walker, Texas Ranger* (1993–), and Hercules (Kevin Sorbo) on *Hercules: The Legendary Journeys* (1995–). Two overarching themes on many of such programs are vengeance and a lack of respect for authority. On *7 Days* (1998–), for example, the UPN network billed the lead character, time-traveling "chrononaut" Frank Parker (Jonathan LaPaglia), as "wild, crazy, rude, and wise" and "anything but perfect."[271]

Such characters frequently exhibit personality traits that would in real life brand them as sociopaths—or at least keep them chronically unemployed. They have few relationships and often have trouble communicating and cooperating with others. They simply want to be left alone, but the world won't oblige. Rather than playing the strong silent type, as we saw with John Wayne, these characters are human time bombs ready to explode. The prevalence of such "heroic" characters—alienated by society and unable to function in mainstream situations—sends a clear message to viewers: those who buck the system are more admirable than those who build it.

Shades of Gray

Today's hero no longer wears a white hat. This hero reflects the entertainment industry's apparent conviction that there are no right and wrong answers, only shades of gray. Heroes who battle their own internal demons are considered to be more complex and artistically pleasing than the upright heroes of yesteryear. While a handful of past heroes may have struggled with a dark past, the consistency of their heroic deeds and noble personas provided messages of hope that such difficulties could be overcome.

Present-day heroes, however, typically rely on an occasional grand gesture punctuated by relapses into old habits to establish their hero status, rather than demonstrating a consistent level of integrity. On the show *Angel* (1999–), for example, the title character, played by David Boreanaz, is a vampire who tries to right his past wrongs by fighting other, evil vampires. But the character, when he originally appeared on *Buffy the Vampire Slayer*, had a relapse into his murderous past, and the network continues to hold out the possibility that he will become a killer vampire once again.

Television's definition of the hero seems rooted in the counterculture, rather than the prevailing culture. TV often creates a topsy-turvy world where those who represent apparently positive social institutions are to be mistrusted, while those who do bad deeds, but suffer angst for them, achieve a certain noble status. The series *Lois & Clark: The New Adventures of Superman* (1993–1996), for example, featured one villain who at first appeared benevolent. It was later revealed that this character, who seemed especially pious, was actually intent on taking over the world. His name: "Mr. Church."

The HBO series *The Sopranos* (1999–) often casts its main character, Tony Soprano, in a sympathetic light. A good "family" man, Tony is both husband and father—as well as a violent capo for the mob. Suffering from anxiety attacks and bouts of nostalgia for "the glory days" of organized crime, he sees a psychiatrist to help him overcome job burnout.

Equally disturbing is the glamorization of violent lifestyles and characters. The bleak HBO series *Oz* (1998–), for example, has created a cult hero of fictitious Ozwald Maximum Security Prison inmate Ryan O'Reilly (Dean Winters). The murderous convict has actually won a place in viewer's hearts for his Machiavellian strategies and willingness to do anything to survive. "O'Reilly is smart. He's easily the most dangerous character in Oz," says Dean Winters, who plays the brutal inmate. "I'm amazed at the reaction to the character, especially on the street. They come up to me and profess their undying love for O'Reilly. I mean, you have to wonder about those people."[272]

But apparently that's just the effect HBO's executives were hoping for. "I think there's enough Prozac television—comforting, undisturbing, gentle, huggy, squeezy television," says *Oz* writer and co-executive producer Tom Fontana. "People who like grim television deserve a place to go and be grim."[273]

America's heroes exhibit a general moral ambiguity that mocks the traditional concept of heroics. They are cynical, depressed, angry, hopeless, and out for revenge. The gothic supernatural drama *The Crow: Stairway to Heaven* (1998–) is a prime example. A dark, morose character, murdered rock musician Eric Draven (Marc Dacascos) is back from the grave to exact revenge in a reprise of the 1994 movie *The Crow*. Such television characters exist in a dark and gloomy world where the villains have already won, perhaps reflecting the media's general outlook that real life is a bleak, frightening existence, and things are only destined to get worse.

Portrayals of disturbing heroes battling in a disturbing world appear to have gained an initial foothold in the early days of television during the 1950s and 1960s, when the Cold War cast a dark pallor over a time of otherwise tremendous technological and social advancements. James Dean perhaps best represented this trend. Although primarily thought of as a movie star, the often dark, troubled young actor made several television appearances on dramatic anthology programs such as the *Kraft Television Theatre* (1947–1958), *Schlitz Playhouse of Stars* (1951–1959), *TV*

Soundstage (1953–1954), and *Danger* (1950–1955), as well as dramas such as *Treasury Men in Action* (1950–1955), and even the game show *Beat the Clock* (1950–1974, 1979–1980).

And unlike more mainstream heroic programs of the 1950s such as *The Lone Ranger* (1949–1957), *The Adventures of Superman* (1952–1957), and *The Roy Rogers Show* (1951–1957), the 1960s saw the emergence of high-tech crime fighters battling evil in a bleak world. Comic book characters such as *Batman* (1966–1968) and *The Green Hornet* (1966–1967), for example, were invariably the products of early physical or psychological trauma. Although these characters found their roots in a much earlier, pre–World War II period, the true mass medium of television was much more effective at disseminating their apparent message that evil could never be conquered, only kept at bay. And as our heroes become less heroic, our villains must become even more evil and sadistic to maintain a distinction between the two.

Violence and the Hero

Television over the past few decades has significantly altered its approach to how heroes resolved conflicts. Early heroes such as Superman and Roy Rogers rarely killed their enemies. Although the heroes may have thrown a punch or two, they frequently used superior intellect to outwit their foes. The bad guys were often portrayed as intellectually inferior. Such portrayals carried two important messages: brains win over brawn, and power of any kind carries with it an inherent responsibility.

Such themes may appear innocently simplistic but are no less plausible than today's heroes who kill villains by the score. Any real-life "hero" who used TV's most popular techniques for conflict resolution would spend the rest of their days in a courtroom explaining why it was necessary to destroy millions of dollars in property and obliterate four dozen people to stop one bad guy. In a 1999 study of twenty action shows such as *Hercules*, *Nightman* (1997–1999), *Crow: Stairway to Heaven*, *Xena: Warrior Princess*, *VIP* (1998), and *Stargate SG-1* (1999–), researchers S. Robert Lichter, Linda S. Lichter, and Dan Amundson found an average of twenty-five violent scenes per hour. Some programs evaluated by the researchers had as many as fifty-one scenes per hour—or more than one for every minute of programming. And most of these scenes were of what the researchers termed as "serious" violence—those most likely to lead to death or serious injury.

Today's feminine heroes differ little from their male counterparts and rarely provide positive role models for girls. More often, their main purpose is to satiate male viewers' sexual fantasies. When creating female TV heroes, writers and producers have simply transplanted Arnold Schwarzenegger's brain into a supermodel's body. Characters such as *Buffy the Vampire Slayer*, *Xena: Warrior Princess*, and *VIP*'s cast of lethal female characters led by Pamela Anderson Lee, for example, are simply women on a testosterone high.

When these female characters do act as role models for young women, the results are rarely positive. In fact, an eighteen-year study of 221 girls conducted by L. Rowell Huesmann of the University of Michigan's Institute for Social Research found that girls who frequently watched television shows featuring aggressive heroines during the 1970s grew up to be more aggressive adults. In fact, 59 percent of those subjects who watched an above-average amount of TV violence were involved in an above-average number of aggressive incidents later in life.[274]

A Dangerous Message

Although traditional heroism may have taken a back seat to more earthy protagonists, one thing all of today's heroes seem to have in common is their superhuman ability to withstand physical abuse. And unlike the obviously fake "Pows," "Whams," and "Bangs" of the Batman series, today's television shows depict violence in its most graphic form. Nonetheless, the hero almost always survives. Today's hero can be shot, knifed, beaten, dropped from the top of a building, thrown from a moving car, or otherwise pummeled. He may be bloodied, but rarely does he sustain significant injuries from abuse that would mutilate or kill most human beings. In fact, the Lichter, et al., study of twenty action shows indicated that almost 60 percent of serious acts of violence had no direct harmful effect.[275]

"Much of modern TV violence is highly realistic," says Marcy Kelly, president of the non-profit group Mediascope, which puts on workshops, seminars, and public education campaigns to promote a more accurate depiction of violence on television and in movies. "There are no consequences. You don't see children who've lost their parents, parents who've lost their children, people who can't walk, who've lost their homes because of nine months spent recuperating. You just seen this unbelievable aggression, and then they cut to the hero at a cocktail party!"[276]

Inaccurate depictions of violence communicate the notion that physical abuse has significantly less consequences than medical literature would suggest. The television phenomenon of violence without consequence has become so ingrained in many viewers' psyche that some real-life criminals, when shot or otherwise wounded, have expressed surprise at feeling pain!

"I don't know if you know what it's like to go on a crime scene and see kids gunned down and realize that there is no 'cut, let's get up, make up and do it again,'" says a police officer in a discussion hosted by the Family and Community Critical Viewing Project. "That is what I see. I see reality....It's an ugly reality. Violence on television, sex on television, has an impact on children."[277] The Centers for Disease Control now lists violence as a public health issue that should be treated as an epidemic.[278] And the American Psychological Association notes that while TV violence makes some children more fearful, it desensitizes other children to violent acts and makes them prone to aggressive behavior.[279]

Beyond the ability to withstand an amazing level of physical punishment, today's heroes must also possess a biting, often sadistic sense of humor. Many heroes cannot finish off a villain without uttering a witty remark that demonstrates a lack of compassion or remorse at having to kill another human being. George Gerbner calls ths "happy violence," creating a culture where violence is viewed as pleasurable and even fun. "Happy violence shows no pain or tragic consequences. It is a swift and easy dramatic solution to many problems, employed by good characters as much as bad, and always leading to a happy ending," says Gerbner.[280]

The entertainment industry's penchant for violent resolutions to problems may be exciting, but it also feeds our own anger. In addition, it demonstrates little, if any, creativity on the part of the writers. Rather than depicting resolutions that require intelligence, integrity, or personal sacrifice, many depictions of "heroic" deeds are simply grand opportunities for the special effects department to show off its prowess. The message? A well-placed punch, karate chop, or bullet—or better yet, explosives or incendiary devices—can solve nearly any problem.

Today's heroes demonstrate a level of brutality that goes far beyond that of TV's previous villains. The Lichter, et al., study suggests that almost half of all serious violence on TV is committed for supposedly positive purposes. "We found that a significant majority of violent acts took place in a moral vacuum," said the researchers. "Just as they rarely had direct physical or psychological consequences, most were not judged as right or wrong." In fact, 87 percent of all violence on broadcast TV is unaccompanied by an apparent moral judgment.[281]

Ultimately, these depictions of violence in a heroic context are especially powerful in their ability to desensitize viewers to violent acts. When we surround ourselves with media-generated images of violence, especially violence perpetrated by our heroes, how can we express surprise at our own culture of violence? By creating an imaginary environment in which violence can resolve almost any problem, we normalize violent acts in ways that ultimately transfer to real life.

Some in the entertainment industry argue that the violence depicted in the media is a direct reflection of the violence-laden culture it serves. This runs counter to reality. Several researchers have compared TV violence with real-life crime statistics. Although the gap is closing, the number of violent acts on TV far outnumbers the instances of violence that occur in real life—even in the most decaying and crime-ridden cities.[282]

Trashing Real-Life Heroes

Television is rapidly destroying our ability to identify real-life heroes as well. The professions once respected as heroic have become suspect at best. Police officers, for example, were once portrayed on TV as heroes. In fact, an analysis of shows reveals that prior to 1975, nine out of ten shows affirmed the honor of the justice system. Since then, however, the number has dropped to just half. The researchers note that most positive law enforcers actually work outside the system as private citizens. "These days, TV's police commit crimes as often as everyone else," say researchers S. Robert Lichter, Linda S. Lichter, and Stanley Rothman. "More than ever on prime time, insiders break the law and outsiders enforce it."[283] Moreover, those TV law enforcement officials who do remain in the system are often depicted as have to break—or at least bend—the rules to be effective. The angry superior who must enforce the regulations then becomes an ineffective stuffed shirt.

Police officers are often portrayed as corrupt, alcoholic, overweight, and mean-spirited. In fashioning the dark heroic personas that television's creative community embraces so frequently, series routinely depict police officers as even less deserving of admiration than many of the criminals they pursue. Det. Andy Sipowicz (Dennis Franz) of *NYPD Blue* and Dets. Mick Belker (Bruce Weitz) and Johnny LaRue (Keil Martin) on *Hill Street Blues* (1981–1987), for example, fought a variety of demons, from bouts of alcoholism and relationships with prostitutes, to intense anger and generally antisocial behavior. While the *NYPD Blue* character has evolved to become somewhat more compassionate, he remains cranky and bigoted, often using racial slurs and displaying an "in-your-face" attitude. By its concentration on the "angry cop" both in fiction and in its coverage of real-life news, TV has convinced many viewers that a majority of police officers are violent racists.

Partially as a result of such negative portrayals of public officials, a new trend has emerged, where criminals are viewed as victims rather than perpetrators. This trend is fueled by talk shows that too frequently portray offenders as having been pushed to the breaking point by some outside force or that explore criminals' dysfunctional pasts while essentially ignoring the consequences and real victims of the guests' offenses. Such shows often evoke an undue amount of sympathy for the offender and neglect the inherent responsibility of adulthood. The problem has become so bad, in fact, that criminal jury candidates are frequently asked about their television viewing habits, because, they say, talk show viewers are more likely to distrust the official version of the offense.[284] A study conducted by the University of Alabama apparently confirms this assumption. The researchers found that subjects were less likely to recommend tough punitive punishment for criminal offenses after viewing *Oprah* programs unrelated to the supposed crime, but detailing other criminals' dysfunctional backgrounds.[285]

Evil Business

It is an interesting dichotomy that while television portrays yuppies who struggle to make it to the top often in a heroic light, it almost invariably depicts the top echelon of business as being corrupt and inherently evil. There are few heroic business leaders. In fact, an analysis of television shows by S. Robert Lichter, Linda S. Lichter, and Stanley Rothman found that although business professionals represent about 12 percent of all television characters, they account for 32 percent of all crimes, including 40 percent of murders and 44 percent of vice crimes such as drug trafficking. In fact, nearly half of all businesspeople on TV are portrayed in a negative light.[286]

Such portrayals help generate an intense anger, often misdirected by workers on the lowest rungs of the economic ladder, toward those who are most successful. They create an environment in which success is at once both sought after and viewed as negative.

A New Leadership

Not only have fictional heroes changed their strategies and demeanors, but real-life role models have allowed television to give them makeovers as well. TV's penchant for exciting visuals and its time-compressed nature demand leaders who place image before substance.

Television has significantly changed our political process. The most effective means for pre-TV politicians to earn votes was to rub elbows with common folk, to get out and shake hands and kiss babies, to immerse themselves in society rather than the artificial world of the entertainment industry. This one-on-one campaigning allowed voters to get an up-close and less rehearsed picture of candidates.

By comparison, today's politicians are managed by media experts who conduct numerous focus groups and surveys. This research is then used to determine the combination of words and images—right down to hair styles and tie colors—that will attract the most voters. Candidates are packaged like Hollywood blockbusters. Politics and show business have become one. "Politics is just like show business," noted former president and film star Ronald Reagan.[287] When candidates appear on TV, each word is carefully weighed. If, by some aberration, candidates are forced to speak off-the-cuff, they are surrounded by handlers who provide on-the-spot advice and spokespeople who can "clarify" what candidates "meant to say." Lance Morrow of *Time* magazine points out that presidential elections have become "a series of television visuals and staged events created for TV cameras." He adds, "The issues have become as weightless as clouds of electrons and the candidates mere actors in commercials."[288]

Television also changes the way we define leaders. Leadership is no longer the ability to organize ideas and diverse groups, muster forces, and move the country in the direction it needs to go. Leadership is now defined as image and personality. It is having the charisma, looks, and scriptwriters to create a likable facade. It has little to do with making tough policy decisions and increasingly more to do with deciding which course will gain the most points in public opinion polls.

TV profoundly affects the way our leaders govern. With the technology available to conduct countless polls on every subject imaginable, today's version of leadership is an ongoing popularity contest. From the time our leaders are elected to the time they leave office, they can use television and technology to constantly monitor their favorable standing with the people. More than any other time in history, today's politicians must be acutely aware of their image on a moment-by-moment basis. It is a disturbing but accurate political reality that decisions cannot be made solely on the basis of what's best for the country or its people. Our country's shrinking attention span means long-term national viability must be sacrificed to achieve a positive image in the short term. Moreover, political leaders must be adept at working the media—opening a leak here and plugging one there—in order to place their agenda before the public in its most positive and palatable light.

Television news executives are the new ruling class. They decide which issues are most important, exciting, or newsworthy, and political leaders must then respond. Politics has always included an element of gamesmanship, but in today's environment, leadership must be practiced under a microscope that few politicians can withstand for any length of time.

The *Boston Globe*'s Jeff Jacoby notes that television also has stripped the presidency of its dignity. "Intrusive, melodramatic, confession-hungry, conflict-addicted, TV changed the rules of pop culture—and politicians, chasing popularity, conformed to TV's demands," he says. "Subtly at first, then shamelessly, presidents traded dignity and gravitas for approval ratings."[289]

As mainstream media become more tabloid-oriented, television journalists take increasingly greater delight in assaulting our political leaders as a means of high drama. Whether facts are true or false is not nearly as important as creating compelling entertainment. Such gossip serves both the opposing party and the networks that carry it, providing dramatic sound bites and controversy.

James Fallows, editor of *U.S. News and World Report*, notes that in the age of lightening-fast media, allegations of wrongdoing are frequently reported with little investigation. "We now have a twenty-four-hour-a-day news cycle," he explains. "News gets used up very quickly, and there's a constant hunger for new tidbits." And when reporters do find such claims to be unfounded, vindications are frequently slow to be publicized or buried by other, more juicy stories.[290]

This penchant for dissecting the lives of public figures has another aspect. Television appears to relish as a foundation for drama the ebb and flow of popularity and respect for public figures. It builds its idols up, placing them on higher and higher pedestals, simply to create a bigger bang when these pedestals are knocked down by the very same media that construct them.

While it's no secret that some politicians fail to measure up, the level of scrutiny aimed at our leaders no longer meets the criteria of serving the public good. Instead, it is simply sensationalism meant to grab a larger audience share. Such coverage no longer constitutes credible "news" reporting. Rather, it is simply another avenue for entertainment. Respected TV newsman Walter Cronkite noted in a 1999 speech that market forces have created a vacuum of information. Noting that viewers who rely solely on TV news are "totally uninformed," he called the current state of news coverage "exceedingly dangerous to democracy."[291]

In its quest for ratings, the media is rapidly convincing viewers that it is impossible for anyone—let alone a politician—to maintain a sense of integrity and honesty. It is a sad commentary that a 1991 National Coalition on Television Violence poll found 66 percent of children ages ten to thirteen identified Freddy Krueger as a homicidal maniac in a string of horror movies, but only 36 percent knew Abraham Lincoln as a U.S. president.[292]

Sports and Heroes

Just as politics has collided with and finessed its way into entertainment, the realm of athletics now commands the media. As such, many sports figures now see themselves as entertainers in the same vein as actors, and have therefore shed the burden of having to act as role models. Even the most revered athletic event—the Olympics—has suffered from a variety of drug scandals and incidents of bribery.

Nonetheless, sports figures remain among the most admired personalities within Western culture. "When you reach a certain level of visibility, you are a role model whether you chose to be one or not," notes Cheryl Miller, Olympic Gold Medalist and coach of the Women's Basketball Association's Phoenix Mercury.[293]

Athletics always has spawned a certain number of "bad boys." Babe Ruth, for example, was noted for his drinking and womanizing. But sports was also peopled by men and women of character—notables such as Vince Lombardi, Billie Jean King, and Michael Jordan.

Over the past few decades, however, bad behavior seems to be becoming the norm among athletes who have become household names—and television profiles the deeds that have made these figures both famous and infamous. Moreover, the level of negative activities appears to have sunk to new lows. Sexual assaults, drug charges, murders, and theft accusations have all leapt from recent sports headlines. And a 1996–1997 study of 509 National Football League players found 21 percent were formally charged with a serious crime, including homicide, rape, robbery, assault, burglary, and drug use.[294] "In the end, one conclusion rang true, NFL teams are recruiting a new breed of criminal players, the likes of which should disturb all NFL fans," say researchers Jeff Benedict and Don Yaeger, authors of the book *Pros and Cons*.[295]

Major names such as Mike Tyson, convicted of rape and thrown out of boxing for biting an opponent, O.J. Simpson, accused but never convicted of killing his wife, and Darryl Strawberry, who, fresh from promoting his book about overcoming addiction, was kicked out of the 2000 baseball season for testing positive for cocaine use, are just the tip of the iceberg. During 1999, Kansas City wide receiver Andre Rison was charged with felony theft. The Charlotte Hornets' Eldridge Recasner was accused of assaulting a clerk at a Seattle airport. Carolina Panthers wide receiver Rae Carruth was charged in the murder of his pregnant girlfriend, and North Carolina defensive tackle Brian Norwood was one of ten men accused of gang-raping an eleven-year-old girl.

Such crimes are not just the purview of professional athletes. The culture of violence extends to college-level sports heroes as well. A 1992–1996 analysis of schools with elite basketball and football teams found that while athletes constituted just 3 percent of the student body, they were responsibly for nearly 20 percent of reported sexual assaults. "The fact that popular athletes, society's most recognized male role models, routinely escape accountability for domestic violence, rape, gang rape, and other crimes has dulled public consciousness of their increasing levels of deviance," notes Jeff Benedict in his book *Private Felons: Athletes and Crimes against Women*.[296]

Another survey conducted by the National Institute of Mental Health found athletes participated in about one-third of 862 sexual assaults on U.S. campuses.[297] "Nothing inherent in sports makes athletes especially likely to rape women. Rather, it is the way sports are organized to influence developing masculine identities and male peer groups that leads many male athletes to rape," explain Michael A. Messner and Donald F. Sapo, authors of *Sex, Violence & Power in Sports*.[298]

Although hardly "professional" in nature, professional wrestling is especially guilty of promoting violent, sexually aggressive behaviors both in and out of the ring. This behavior, of course, isn't turning young people away. Youths rountinly flock to WWF events and have turned the "sports" stars into icons and millionaires by snapping up action figures and other WWF paraphernalia. "What the boom-time WWF is, really, is the first pornography to be openly marketed to children," argues *GQ* writer David Kamp.[299] *WWF Smackdown*, for example, routinely depicts simulations of both heterosexual and homosexual sex and offers up subplots fraught with sexual themes.

Never an organization to let teamwork and fair play get in the way of athletics as entertainment, the World Wrestling Federation, during the 1999 Super Bowl, aired a commercial that seems to sum up the state of televised sport. Although downright offensive and disturbing, the commercial made no pretense about the function of professional wrestling. Depicting a typical day at the WWF headquarters, wrestler "Stone Cold" Steve Austin notes in the ad that the WWF offers "a nonviolent form of entertainment" as he slams a passing executive with a folding chair. Other executives are engaged in a brawl, and people are being thrown through windows. "We never use sex to enhance our image," adds female wrestler Sable, as she walks past a woman who has her legs wrapped around a man in a seductive embrace.

Heroes at Home

Heroic acts are not simply the purview of popular media. Although literature and the movies may create some of our most colorful heroes, more mundane but equally heroic deeds occur daily in our homes and families. Home is where children learn some of their most vital lessons—selflessness and sacrifice for the good of others. And it is there where television is so rapidly undermining the traditional role of heroes.

While television heroes may be exciting, they typically offer few positive lessons on how to resolve conflicts. Heroes in the home not only exhibit character and, by example, build character in others, they also teach us to resolve situations in realistic ways, ways that require thought, compromise, and integrity.

Too often, television undermines the idea of heroics as a real-life, daily demonstration of integrity and self-sacrifice. By offering up a steady stream of ultra-violent superheroes and less-than-noble mortal ones, TV destroys our ability to recognize and respect the heroic deeds performed right under our noses.

Television's frequent depiction of trusted figures as villains also undermines today's domestic heroes. A father who quietly perseveres through difficult financial times is now portrayed on TV as a cold, disconnected workaholic. The mother who's up at dawn making breakfast and preparing lunches is depicted as smothering her brood with excessive doting. The football hero big brother or the fresh-faced teenage big sister are now either closet alcoholics and drug abusers, or are plotting to murder their best friends.

If the hero of today represents a lower degree of integrity and character, our culture can expect an even lower level of integrity from society at large. This lack of positive characteristics diminishes society's baseline of what it deems admirable traits, making it easier for us all to attain "hero" status.

By failing to provide credible heroes that exemplify integrity, self-sacrifice, and compassion, we are giving subsequent generations little reason to aspire to anything beyond their own personal success. While such success may satisfy our most immediate needs, it does little to create a long-term sense of self-fulfillment and self-respect. There remains an innate hunger for heroes whose private lives are as admirable as their public personas.

Moreover, by placing selfishness over selflessness, we are undermining the critical foundation of society, which, by definition, requires a commitment to cooperation for the common good.

Arbitrator

onflicts in families are inevitable. Even though family members may share common backgrounds and experiences, they remain individuals, and individuals disagree. The key to maintaining the family structure is to compromise, to create an environment in which members can disagree without dissolving their relationships.

Oftentimes, one or more family members emerge as arbitrators in this process. They are the peacemakers, the people who keep conflict from escalating to a destructive level. They also help others to learn effective problem-solving skills.

The arbitrator role is vital to the stability of the family unit. The mediation and arbitration skills learned through family interaction also aid our relationships with others outside the home. Nearly every facet of our lives—from work to social activities to relationships and parenting—depends on our ability to get along with others. Without arbitration skills, humans typically revert to their most basic animal instincts to resolve contentious situations.

A Poor Example

The role of arbitrator is rapidly being assumed by television as viewers increasingly look to their favorite TV characters for ways to resolve disputes. Unfortunately, television gives us few constructive cues. When viewers rely on the models of television characters for advice on how to solve interpersonal problems, they are placing the fate of their relationships in dubious hands.

In the fantasy world of television, writers may select any means of conflict resolution they wish to use (usually the most dramatic), and be confident that the technique will work within the program's allotted time. Too often, however, viewers fail to recognize the fundamental differences between the resolution of television's fictional dilemmas and real-life conflicts. They assume that what works on TV must also work in real life. Such logic skews our willingness and ability to look for long-term solutions to real-life problems.

Television offers a particularly narrow spectrum of conflict resolution options, mostly limited to witty comebacks, sarcasm, and violence. When we turn to Bart Simpson, Roseanne Barr, or the *Married...With Children* cast for conflict-resolution techniques, we find little advice beyond cynicism, anger, disrespect, and profanity. Such shows, which are meant to portray the American family in a more "honest" and realistic light, do not depict healthy family interaction; instead, they simply normalize conflict as a lifestyle.

Compromising Versus Selling Out

A key element of effective problem solving is the ability to compromise. Television's role models often contradict the idea that compromise is a positive solution. Instead, they communicate the notion that to compromise is to sell out. Those television characters held in highest regard often refuse to give and take, and are immovable in their convictions. Characters such as renegade physician Doug Ross on *ER* and a host of shows featuring cops who refuse to obey orders from superiors are held up as positive, while other characters who play by the rules are too often cast as weak and ineffective.

Effective social systems depend heavily on compromise. It is impossible to gather a large number of people without some disagreements, so dissension must often be subverted for the common good. Without a willingness by the majority to compromise, the social structure of the group quickly erodes.

Violence As an Arbitration Tool

When resolving conflicts, television characters frequently indulge in angry outbursts that few real people could get away with. Television characters are typically more emotional in their resolution of problems than the vast majority of Americans. The outbursts that pepper television interactions are consistent with TV's affinity for the most dramatic and often violent means of conflict resolution.

Violence is, in fact, television's favorite way to resolve disputes. The results of the National Television Violence Study, a three-year effort to assess violence on television, found only 4 percent of violent programs emphasize any kind of anti-violence theme. In fact, the study found very few violent programs that condemn the use of violence or present alternatives to using violence to solve problems.[300]

Most violent programs also fail to portray any negative consequences to violent acts. In fact, nearly half of such programs show no serious harm to victims, and in 58 percent of those programs that depict violence, the victim shows no perceptible pain. Even less frequent is the depiction of any long-term consequences of violence. Very few programs portray long-term negative repercussions of violence such as psychological, financial, or emotional harm.[301]

A 1999 study published in the journal *Communication Research* found a clear impact between entertainment violence and children's value judgments regarding violent acts. In the study, conducted by Marina Kremar of the University of Connecticut and Patti Valkenburg of the Amsterdam School of Communications Research at the University of Amsterdam, 158 children were shown twelve stories in which a character performed either justified or unjustified violent acts. The children were asked how right or wrong they perceived the violence to be. The children who watched more fantasy violence, such as that found in cartoons, were the least likely to judge violent acts as wrong. Those who watched more realistic violence, such as that involving actors or "reality based" programming, judged violent acts as more wrong. In general, children who viewed violent entertainment of any kind were found to utilize less advanced moral reasoning strategies in explaining their judgments.[302]

A 1972 study headed by Aletha Huston-Stein compared children who viewed a steady diet of *Mister Rogers' Neighborhood*, *Batman,* and *Superman* cartoons or "neutral" programs containing neither violence nor prosocial messages. The researchers found the children who watched *Batman* and *Superman* cartoons were more physically active both in the classroom and on the playground. They were also more likely to get into fights with each other, play rough with toys, take toys from others, and be generally more aggressive. The children who watched *Mister Rogers' Neighborhood* were much more likely to play cooperatively, offer help to teachers, and engage in "positive peer counseling," showing concern and sensitivity for others. The "neutral" group was neither more aggressive nor more helpful.[303]

Another study specifically examining the effects of the cartoon *The Mighty Morphin Power Rangers* (1993–) conducted at California State University Fullerton, found a direct link between the program and violent behavior in young viewers. Boys were particularly vulnerable to the effects of this cartoon.[304]

More than one thousand studies over a thirty-year period have found significant links between watching violence on television and in the movies, and acting out real-life aggression.[305] Despite this overwhelming evidence, entertainment industry executives routinely stand before the American public and deny any such correlation. "Television executives, manufacturers and merchandisers…have consistently denied that there is any proved effect of programming on antisocial behavior, although they have never denied an effect on prosocial behavior," notes researchers Leonard D. Eron and L. Rowell Huesmann.[306]

Violence and Children

Particularly alarming is that so many violent programs now target children and teens. These youngsters are especially vulnerable to television's messages as they try to define their own self-images and deal with insecurities.

According to media scholar George Gerbner, more than 90 percent of all programs that appear during children's prime viewing hours feature violence. He calls cartoons "the most controversial and effective demonstrations of power, with humor as the sugar coating pill." Gerbner notes that Saturday morning network programming routinely features more than twenty-five acts of violence per hour.[307] Moreover, researchers at the University of California Los Angeles termed the action found on some of the most popular cartoons as "sinister combat violence," mainly because the story lines typically tend to be centered around violence. It's interesting to note as well that many of these cartoons are rated TVPG DV, indicating the need of parental guidance due to mild violence. Translation: these cartoons may not be appropriate for young children.[308]

More than one thousand studies demonstrate a cause-and-effect relationship between media violence and aggressive behavior in some children.[309] A study by media researcher Wendy Josephson found that although many preschoolers could recognize cartoons as "pretend" or "not real," they were unsure of the definition of "real."[310] Yet other studies suggest that children as young as fourteen months may begin to imitate what they see on TV.[311] One need only watch a group preschoolers kicking and karate-chopping each other after a morning of cartoons to understand the correlation between television and violence.

It seems clear that television is a prime factor in the escalating incidences of violent crime among pre-teens and those in early adolescence. Homicide rates for children fourteen to seventeen years old increased 172 percent between 1985 and 1994,[312] and nearly 40 percent of all homicide victims are under age twenty-four.[313] Recent, highly publicized incidents of violence at school in communities such as Littleton, Colorado; Jonesboro, Arkansas; and Paducah, Kentucky, are really just the tip of the iceberg. National television news now only covers multiple killings, choosing to ignore the daily gun and knife assaults that kill or maim individual teachers and students.

It's difficult to imagine a child of ten or twelve conceiving, without the benefit of television, the level of physical cruelty and perversion we now see so often in real-life crimes perpetrated by kids. "The literature on media violence is compelling and clear," explains researcher Victor C. Strasburger. "Aggression is a learned behavior and young children are particularly vulnerable—although they may not display evidence of being affected until they reach adolescence or young adulthood."[314]

Strasburger goes on to point out that while most adults recognize TV as fantasy and entertainment, children are often not capable of such distinctions. "Therefore, the industry argument that 'no one takes this stuff seriously' may be at least arguable for adults but is completely erroneous when considering young people," he says.[315] There are many examples of children's inability to separate fantasy from reality, such as the five-year-old boy who set his two-year-old sister on fire, killing her. He had just viewed an episode of the cartoon *Beavis and Butthead*, in which the characters were playing with fire.

No other medium provides America's youth such a consistent and steady diet of heinous acts as TV. The average American child will witness two hundred thousand dramatized acts of violence and forty thousand murders by the time they turn eighteen.[316] And on an average day, two hundred seventy thousand children now bring guns to school.[317]

Researchers Eron and Huesmann contend that television creates a downwardly spiraling trend for many children. "The more aggressive child becomes the less popular child and the poorer academic achiever in school. These academic and social failures may become frustrators, instigating more aggressive responses," they explain. "In addition, however, the children who are less successful in school and less popular become the more regular television viewers. Perhaps they can obtain the satisfactions vicariously from television that they are denied in school and in their social life."[318]

Further, Eron and Huesmann's research shows a clear correlation between consuming a steady diet of typical television violence as a child and aggressive behavior later in adult life. The more violent programs children watched at age eight, the more aggressive they became at age nineteen.[319]

Interestingly, viewers who watched TV violence as youngsters are particularly harsh with their own children, Eron and Huesmann explain. And the amount of TV violence parents watched when they were children was an even better predictor of their children's aggression than it was of their own adult hostility.[320] Eron, who tracked 650 New York children from 1960 to the present, also found that those subjects who watched the most violent TV as children were more likely to engage in behaviors such as spousal abuse and drunk driving. And it's not just boys who are susceptible to TV's violent influences. Huesmann's research at the University of Michigan's Aggression Research Group found that girls who watched shows featuring aggressive heroines in the 1970s grew up to be more aggressive adults. They were more likely to be involved in confrontations, shoving matches, choking, and knife fights than women who watched few or no shows featuring aggressive female leads.[321]

Other research has shown that violent depictions in adult-oriented entertainment can be equally destructive and may be responsible for as many as half of all violent criminal acts. According to researcher Victor Strasburger,[322] more than one thousand studies and literature reviews point to media violence as a significant cause of real-life violence.[323]

Another study conducted by the University of Washington's Brandon Centerwall examined the possible correlation between the arrival of television within the cultures of the U.S., Canada, and South Africa and a rise in homicides. He found that homicide rates in these countries climbed rapidly at about ten years after the introduction of TV—when youngsters watching television began to enter into the vulnerable, crime-committing years of adolescence. And at fifteen years after TV began, the murder rates in these countries had doubled.[324]

Centerwall, an epidemiologist who conducted violence research for the National Centers for Disease Control, Atlanta, postulated that if "television technology had never been developed, there would today be ten thousand fewer murders each year in the United States, seventy thousand fewer rapes and seven hundred thousand fewer injurious assaults."[325]

A 1990 Gallop poll found 79 percent of those surveyed were in favor of regulating objectionable content on television, and a 1993 *Times-Mirror* national poll found nearly 60 percent of participants were "personally bothered by violence in entertainment television shows, and 80 percent believed entertainment violence was harmful to society." [326]

TV's Addiction to Violence

Why is television so hooked on violence? Many TV executives say it's what viewers want. In an effort to keep ahead of the pack in terms of excitement, they explain, television's creative community must continually raise the level of violence and corresponding body counts to thwart the competition. TV and movies thus become ever-spiraling cesspools of blood, gore and death.[327] "People choose violence...I don't know what the hell's wrong with us," says media mogul Ted Turner. "You gotta go back and talk to God."[328]

Yet, several surveys dispute the contention that most viewers crave brutality. A 1993 *Mediaweek* poll of one thousand adults, for example, showed nearly two-thirds of Americans find television violence and sex offensive, and nearly half of that majority said they would no longer consider buying products advertised in programs featuring sex and violence.[329]Nielsen ratings reveal that nonviolent programs garnered higher ratings and market shares overall than their violent competitors.[330]

Many entertainment leaders argue that television violence simply reflects today's society. This argument also fails to hold up under scrutiny. Researchers Stanley Rothman, S. Robert Lichter, and Linda Lichter of the University of Illinois reviewed more than six hundred prime-time television shows for violence. They note that television characters are "murdered at a rate 1,000 times higher than real-world victims." A typical night of prime-time network television features more than fifty crimes, including "a dozen murders and fifteen to twenty assorted robberies, rapes, assaults, and other acts of mayhem," add the researchers. Nearly a quarter of all TV crimes are homicides, compared to just 5 percent of all real-life crimes.[331]

Such ubiquitous portrayals of crime create in viewers an impression that the world is a dark, ominous, and threatening place. This is especially true for children. Harvard University developmental psychologist Ronald G. Slaby explains that young viewers often experience what he calls a "victim effect"—they fear they may become casualties of violence. In addition, children may also exhibit a "bystander effect," in which they become increasingly callous toward violence directed at others.[332] George Gerbner has coined the phrase "The Mean World Syndrome."[333]Under this phenomenon, heavy television viewers begin to believe the world is meaner and more threatening than it really is, based upon the depictions they see on TV. Equally apparent, such beliefs naturally result in two possible outcomes: more fearful or more violent viewers. And of course, the combination of fear and violence is perhaps the more volatile of all.

The bottom line is that television violence leaves viewers emotionally impotent, afraid of the world around them and uncaring of others. It hyper-sensitizes viewers to the possibility that they may become victims and desensitizes them to others' suffering. It seems unlikely that such a population can maintain a solid social structure when it is reduced to such low levels of trust and empathy.

Friend

Friendship is a beautiful gift exchanged between two people. As an unspoken promise to "be there" for another and expect nothing in return, it embodies unselfishness. And the foundation of such relationships is trust and loyalty. A key function of the family is to teach children the value of this treasure and how to become an effective friend.

Often our first and most enduring friendships are with siblings. The reasons are both simple and complex. First, siblings usually share a vast pool of common experiences that help forge a sense of camaraderie. They may also share similar senses of humor and other characteristics that enhance communication and friendship.

Even more important for a solid relationship, however, is that friends know one another in intimate ways. "Romantic and career relationships may come and go, but friendships are the interpersonal bond that can exist throughout a lifetime," say Ronald B. Adler, Lawrence B. Rosenfeld, and Neil Towne, authors of *Interplay: The Process of Interpersonal Communication*.[334] With true friendships, the pretenses melt away to reveal the real people underneath. Siblings have a built-in advantage in this department, since they probably already know a great deal about each other.

Friendship also gives the participants a sense of themselves. Friends reflect our interests, what we value and what we hope to attain. Margaret

Mead points out that friendship is based on the "human search for symmetry."[335] By understanding who our friends are, we also help create a clearer definition of who we are, as well.

"Friends react to each other as complete persons, as unique, genuine, irreplaceable individuals," says interpersonal communication expert Joseph DeVito of Hunter College of the City of New York.[336]

A vital function of healthy friendships is their ability to bring out the best in ourselves. Friends encourage us to take reasonable chances, to reach beyond what we are and grasp who we may become. Friends also accept us when we fail and coach us to try again. They give us an external perspective on ourselves and help us to understand how others may perceive us. "A friend encourages your dreams and offers advice," says psychotherapist Doris Wild Helmering, "but when you don't follow it, she still respects and loves you."[337]

This intimate interchange frequently becomes quite apparent to outside observers. Friends who respect and admire one another often begin to take on many of each other's most distinguishable traits. They become mutual role models, pooling resources and exchanging ideas that enhance both parties' lives.

Children learn much of what it means to be a friend from their parents and older siblings. They're especially prone to picking up cues on supportive behaviors from the way mom and dad treat one another. Through these insights, they discover the value of intimate and accepting relationships. They learn forgiveness, tolerance, and respect for conflicting opinions. By witnessing friendships in the home, children learn vital arbitration and negotiation skills necessary to function effectively in later life.

And when family members are involved in active, healthy friendships outside the family unit, children learn the value of trusting others and gain confidence that their own outside friendships will prove worthwhile.

If, on the other hand, family members have few friends, children just as easily learn to live isolated lives devoid of intimacy and trust. Such families frequently produce children who see the world as a threatening place and who view intimate relationship as dangerous to their well-being. Without healthy friendship role models in the home, many children lack the skills required to form viable relationships outside the family. Simply put, families—especially parents—are a gateway to the world of friendships.

A Historical Perspective

Two-income families and working parents are a fact of life in America. Most certainly, World War II was the major turning point in this phenomenon. The advent of the war meant nearly all young and middle-aged men were drafted into military service. Consequently, women were recruited to fill many of the civilian and noncombatant positions left open by the mass exodus of manpower. When the war ended, many women continued to work. Families became dependent upon the prosperity wrought by a double income.

Initially, much of the impact of the two-earner household was softened by the presence of an extended family. Grandparents were a valuable child-care resource. The economy, ease of transportation, and a variety of other factors, however, have meant that the nuclear family now often relocates far from the extended family. Child care is frequently left to strangers. Television has become the ultimate baby-sitter and friend of America's youth.

More than six out of every ten children under the age of six who have yet to enter kindergarten receive some type of care and education on a regular basis from persons other than their parents,[338] and millions of older children come home to empty houses. Most turn on the TV, claiming it eases the loneliness and provides a substitute for the background noise of traditional family life.

Parents who work outside the home often tacitly encourage this artificial friendship with television. In a world that appears increasingly unsafe, they may discourage offspring from going out unsupervised after school. Those children who do spend after-school hours with friends often visit other parentless homes. The result, of course, is an ever-growing population of children left to forge friendships with few healthy role models.

Television fills this void by providing the guidance and companionship inherent in healthy friendships. It does so at a tremendous cost, however, and leaves deep voids that only real friendships can fill. At best, TV offers a counterfeit version of warmth, understanding, and compassion, and for many viewers it provides just enough companionship to keep them from seeking out richer, more enhancing relationships with flesh-and-blood human beings.

Throughout the ages, friendship has been the bedrock upon which society is built. It encompasses shared ideas and values, it provides a support system for its participants, and it is the embodiment of trust. But as children depend more and more on television friends, they begin to perceive that it is safer to run home to watch TV than to deal with the complexities of real-life friendships.

A New Definition of Friendship

As early as 1961, noted historian and scholar Lewis Mumford speculated that human judgment of what is "real" and "important" is shaped more by television than by real-life experiences.[339] Notes Susan B. Landau, coexecutive producer of the 2000 made-for-TV movie *Mary and Rhoda*, about the friendship formed between the two characters on the original sitcom *The Mary Tyler Moore Show*, "In [an age] when people don't have time for friendship, people are interested in the enduring friendship of Mary and Rhoda. People are looking forward to visiting that world again."[340]

More than ever, Mumford's observations appear valid today. How television portrays the concepts of friendship can have a profound effect on how viewers perceive their real-life relationships with others.

Women's relationships on television appear to be particularly dangerous. While some programs are effective at capturing the intimacy and value of feminine friendship, many so-called friends on soap operas, the current crop of teen dramas, and made-for-TV movies tend to be backbiting, cruel, and disloyal. For the sake of continuing drama, the "victims" of this kind of abuse consistently come back for more, creating the impression that traitorous behavior is to be expected among friends.

Depictions of male friendships on television are particularly interesting to study. Early TV westerns such as *The Lone Ranger* (1949–1957), *The Life & Legend of Wyatt Earp*, (1955–1961), and *Gunsmoke*, for example, helped reinforce the notion that men may need each other to achieve an objective, but should never need each other on an emotional level. The westerns of the 1950s and 1960s, in many ways, embodied the idealized, independent, and goal-oriented vision of America. Equally, it reflected the Cold War notion of a clearly defined villain, and the lone hero, courageous enough to single-handedly thwart him.

Early television also insinuated an inherent inequality in friendship. Programs such as *The Honeymooners*, *The Many Loves of Dobie Gillis* (1959–1963), and *The Andy Griffith Show*, for example, all featured a clearly dominant male character and his bumbling sidekick. Often, such shows place the dominant male in a protectorate role, while the subordinate character demonstrates significantly stronger emotions—indicating weakness.

The 1960s, 1970s, and 1980s spawned a number of shows focusing on friendships between men. *Combat*, *Adam* 12 (1968–1975), *Twelve O'Clock High* (1964–1967), *The Wild Wild West* (1965–1969), *The Streets of San Francisco* (1972–1977), *Barney Miller* (1975–1982), *Taxi* (1978–1983), and *Hawaii Five-O* (1968–1980), for example, all featured teams of mostly males who depended heavily upon one another. But again, these shows concentrated more on the achievements of male characters as a means of connection than on the actual emotional bonds between male characters.

Some shows, such as *M*A*S*H*, *Starsky and Hutch*, *Hill Street Blues*, and *thirtysomething* made attempts to at least address the deficit of male-male intimacy, but these shows often concentrated more on the difficulties of "opening up" than the actual positive result of self-disclosure and meaniningful friendships.

With some notable exceptions such as *Sports Night* (1999–) and *The Drew Carey Show*, which feature close friendships based upon trust, and even *Frasier* (1993–), which depicts an intimate friendship between two supportive, if neurotic, brothers, the 1990s and beyond have seen a new twist in TV depictions of friendship. Relatively few dramas depict the loyalty and trust inherent in real friendships, tending to concentrate much more frequently on interpersonal conflicts. More often, friendship is a key premise of situation comedies, where emotional vulnerability can be more fully exploited for the purpose of entertainment value.

Friends as depicted by television often have very little in common. In fact, the typical TV friendship thrives on a diversion of interests among friends as a means to create dramatic or comedic situations. *Seinfeld*, for example, features the unlikely combination of a successful professional comedian (Jerry Seinfeld), a chronically unemployed oddball named Kramer (Michael Richards), Jerry's neurotic boyhood friend George (Jason Alexander), and his thoroughly selfish ex-girlfriend Elaine (Julia Louis-Dreyfus). Although the show was very popular, the only common traits these characters usually seemed to share was an obsession with sex and self-absorption.

Television often seems to take a myopic view of friendship, focusing on the East and West Coasts and ignoring the rich texture of friendships manifest in the variety of situations found outside urban areas. Typical TV friends live in New York and are single, with few marriage values. They often see little value in elders beyond serving as grist for comedic interaction, and tend to be sexually and self-driven, rather than looking outward toward the needs of others. They focus on youth and external image, rather than the sharing of internal values. Commentator George F. Will notes that comedies like *Seinfeld*, *Friends*, and *Ally McBeal* often focus on childlike adults who "loiter on the outskirts of adulthood." He goes on to point out that programs, including cartoons such as *The Simpsons* and *King of the Hill*, that blur the line between adult and childhood entertainment, adversely impact both sets of viewers. "When children are regarded as little adults, adults become childish," he explains.[341]

Often it appears that the only thing most television friends have in common is an overactive sex drive. Unlike real-life friendships, where conversation often centers around an exchange of information about common interests, on television, conversations appear to focus almost exclusively on sex. It wasn't always that way. Although early television often focused primarily on males, utilizing women as a backdrop, several shows were able to depict enduring female friendships. In particular, Lucy Ricardo and Ethel Mertz (Vivian Vance) on *I Love Lucy* often demonstrated both the intimacy of friendship and its challenges. And, as mentioned earlier, *The Mary Tyler Moore Show* featured a strong and supportive friendship between Mary Richards and Rhoda Morgenstern. The 1976–1983 comedy *Laverne & Shirley* remains among the most friendship-centered programs ever offered up by television. Even the theme song, "Making Our Dreams

Come True," focused on teamwork born of a close relationship between the two main characters, Laverne De Fazio (Penny Marshall) and Shirley Feeney (Cindy Williams). This program also depicted a pair of male friends, Lenny Kosnowski (Michael McKean) and Andrew "Squiggy" Squiggman (David L. Lander). While it could be argued that these two characters were dysfunctional at best, they did share common goals and ideas, and equally important, supported one another and even showed compassion for each other when the going got tough.

The 1984–1989 situation comedy *Kate & Allie* demonstrated another important facet of friendship. Characters Kate McArdle (Susan Saint James), a competent working woman, and Allie Lowell (Jane Curtin), an idealized homemaker, shared an apartment in Greenwich Village. While many other shows would typically use such differences as grist for conflict, the two characters on *Kate & Allie* generally complemented one another in their cooperative efforts to survive and thrive following divorce.

In dramatic settings, television tends to utilize conflict to create interesting, if unreal, plots—again emphasizing the lack of commonalties among these friends rather than those interests that bring them together. Ensemble programs such as *Friends*, *Cheers*, and *Beverly Hills 90210* often show friendship in its least positive light by focusing on traitorous friends who take advantage of each other, stealing lovers and taking cheap shots at one another.

The media now spout a steady stream of warnings that admonish us to scrutinize one another carefully. They tell us to watch our neighbors, husbands, wives, children, parents, siblings, leaders, and, most especially, our friends for signs that they may be about to carry out some devious plan. Viewers' concepts of friendship may become twisted as TV depicts friends as covert murderers, con artists, adulterers, and deceptive cheats. The fictitious world they live in creates a picture of friendship as hazardous to one's health, making it unlikely viewers will develop and maintain long-term real-life friendships.

Conversely, shows such as *Friends*, *Cheers*, and *Seinfeld*, as well as a host of other workplace comedies and dramas, frequently eschew depictions of any family interaction in favor of creating a family out of friends and acquaintances. While friendships can be rich and satisfying relationships, in some ways such depictions can create fantasy alternative families composed of mix-and-match components that satisfy specific needs and desires in ways a real-life may be unable to meet.

Viewers ultimately become more isolated and disaffected as television becomes their reality and their friend. But research clearly demonstrates the intense need humans possess for true friendship. And a lack of such relationships often goes hand-in-hand with a variety of social problems including alcohol and drug abuse, violence, and mental illness.

False Intimacy

Friendships require a commitment to intimacy on both sides. The friendship viewers develop with television is purely illusionary and one-sided. The steady parade of people who strip their private lives bare in front of millions of viewers becomes TV's substitute for friendly intimacy.

Marshall McLuhan noted in 1964 that television offers a unique, one-sided relationship that appears so intimate and genuine, viewers often see TV personalities as authentic friends.[342] Joanne Woodward was once asked about the difference between being a movie star and being a television actress. "When I was in movies," she replied, "I heard people say, 'There goes Joanne Woodward.' Now they say, 'There goes somebody I think I know.'"[343]

In the mid 1960s, researcher Jacques Ellul pegged television as the most destructive technical instrument to individual personalities and relationships ever conceived. "Modern man deeply craves friendship, confidence, close personal relationships." he says. Television satisfies those needs by creating a new level of intimacy. As Ellul points out, however, that satisfaction is an illusion, since the relationship is strictly one-sided. "There is no true friendship of any kind between the TV personality and the viewer who feels that personality to be his friend."[344]

Marshall McLuhan[345] and Godfrey Ellis[346] argue that television's format inherently allows for a greater perceived intimacy. They claim that television images are more salient because they are presented more frequently than other role models in radio, print media, and film. Television, they say, presents its images as complete visual symbols that leave little to the imagination.

The MTV program *The Real World* (1992–) took such intimacy to new heights. In this "documentary" series, groups of seven young, photogenic strangers were recruited to live together for periods of twenty weeks. During this time, MTV camera crews basically followed their every move. The subjects often spoke directly to the camera in intimate tones, revealing their "secrets" in a room known as "the confessional." Of course, like many experiments involving direct observation, the presence of the camera and the fact that the subjects were selected for specific, dramatically interesting characteristics, rather than chosen randomly, affected the reality of this "real TV" program.

The CBS debut of *Survivor* (2000–) brought this type of "reality" TV even more into the mainstream. This network program incorporated sixteen people of all ages and backgrounds into a process-of-elimination game show where, along with hidden cameras and microphones, the "players" were encouraged to tell all about themselves and their teammates.

McLuhan argues that TV acting, even aside from "reality" shows like *The Real World* and *Survivor*, is extremely intimate, allowing viewers to become emotionally involved with the characters. Such highly charged emotional states make viewers particularly receptive to the messages contained in the programming. And as individuals become more familiar with specific characters, their images take on the flesh-and-blood qualities of humans.[347]

Despite this perceived intimacy, however, the relationship remains unbalanced. Television opens up every crevice of its fictional but often highly believable characters' lives, creating what appears to be an intimate situation. It then fails to ask of viewers anything beyond their attention. It neither listens to nor cares about viewers' lives, concerns, or personal experiences. TV demands viewers' complete attention but offers no warmth, compassion, or understanding in return.

Like the acquaintance who constantly speaks but never listens, television conveys the message that viewers' lives are uninteresting and unworthy of discussion, that only televised events are significant. Rather than providing the acceptance of a true friend, television criticizes viewers' lives as dull and without merit. It conveys the notion that only when viewers' lives are as twisted and scarred as television characters' lives will the audience be worthy of any reciprocal interest. It then reinforces this message by parading the most outrageous real-life characters across our screens during news programs and talk shows. The underlying message is, "I will listen to you only if your story is more outrageous than mine."

TV talk show hosts are particularly adept at creating fictitious friendships. Speaking in warm, almost conspiratorial tones, they appear to be the viewers' advocate. The fact remains, however, that their job is to stir up controversy for dramatic effect—hardly a friendly aspiration.

A Fast Crowd

As parents, we strive to keep our children from running with a fast crowd. Yet, from the earliest ages, many parents drop their children in front of the television, exposing them to a host of unsavory people and situations. Without parental guidance, these nefarious characters become our children's playmates and role models. "Modeling may be a crucial factor in teenagers' decisions about when and how to begin consuming alcohol, for example," says adolescence researcher Victor C. Strasburger.[348]

Adults also create fictitious friendships with some of the most demeaning, twisted, and dysfunctional elements of society—television characters. In their loneliness, viewers of all ages have begun to run with the proverbial "fast crowd."

Many viewers—young and old alike—spend several hours per day with people who may hold very different values than their own. If these were real, flesh-and-blood friends, could anyone credibly argue that such company would not influence most people's behavior?

Mentor

Even the most benign programming can take its toll on the effectiveness of the family. Children learn to enact social roles through practice during interpersonal interactions with family members. That interaction is reduced or eliminated altogether when TV is used as a baby-sitter. Children must then look to other sources for socialization. Ultimately, we come once again to the same conclusion: television becomes the primary source of role models.

In a sense, television creates a mentoring relationship. It conveys the message that its attitudes, beliefs, and values are more sophisticated and in keeping with the times than its viewers'. It tells viewers that it has nothing to learn from them, and that they have everything to learn from it. TV becomes the ultimate source of social guidance.

We have an unconscious need to emulate those we like and respect. The phenomenon is known as "mirroring,"[349] and is an integral part of humans' learning and interpersonal communication process. Just watch two friends conversing for more than a few minutes. You'll notice that both parties tend to adopt each other's gestures, speech pattern, and posture. The same is true with television. We tend to emulate, at both a conscious and unconscious level, what we see.[350]

When television says everyone is engaged in promiscuous sex or alcohol, tobacco, and drug use, it becomes increasingly difficult for viewers to swim against this perceived tide. On the one hand, television encourages viewers to be individuals, to buck the system. Yet it also creates its own culture that demands conformity. Researcher Godfrey Ellis argues that people acquire social skills from a variety of role models. He adds, however, that television's overwhelming presence and powerful images outweigh nearly all other sources. "Print media and radio are limited to written or auditory symbols and require the reader's or listener's processing to personify the images," he explains. "Television presents its images as completed visual symbols."[351]

When boys watch violent programs or those that sexually demean women, they are ultimately being encouraged to behave in like fashion. Similarly, girls may view the characters appearing on programs such as *Beverly Hills 90210*, *Melrose Place*, or daytime soap operas as role models. What their favorite characters wear, how they act, and the type of men and women they develop relationships with can be strong forces in determining these young viewer's own developing tastes.

Even more alarming, the sexual mores portrayed by such dramas, by virtue of sheer time and exposure, are rapidly becoming the values of the next generation. The constant barrage of teenage promiscuity, extramarital sex, and other aberrations sends a message to viewers—adults and children alike—that lives of peace and morality are dull and unworthy of airtime.

Selling Rebellion

Mary Pipher, in her book *Reviving Ophelia*, points out that teen years are a critical period in child development. "Adolescence is a border between childhood and adulthood. Like life on all borders, it's teaming with energy and fraught with danger. Growth requires courage and hard work on the part of the individual, and it requires the protection and nurturing of the environment."[352] TV robs teens of that protective environment and, in its place, erects a culture in a constant state of rebellion.

Hollywood routinely redefines what it means to be a teenager and how teens should act, dress, speak, date, and otherwise engage in social activities. Television starts early in creating its definition of adolescence. "Most television teenagers have been actors in their twenties, pretending to be seventeen for the amusement of eleven-year-olds," notes journalist Thomas Hine, in the *New York Times*. "'In ten years I'll be twenty-seven,' a character on the UPN series *Clueless* remarks in one episode. 'I'll be almost old enough to play a teenager on television.'"[353]

In marketing jargon, preadolescent fans are known as "aspiring teens." These young viewers spend more time in front of the television than actual teens, because they have more time on their hands than real adolescents. During viewing, many preadolescents actively engage in learning TV's version of typical teenage behavior. "They're actually looking forward to being teenagers," Hine adds, "while those of high school age are inclined to view teenagerhood as a predicament they long to escape."[354]

Preteens are an especially important market for programmers and advertisers, since they represent a significant segment of consumer buying power. Teens and preadolescents spend a large share of the family's disposable income on everything from CDs and clothes to fast food and soft drinks. "With their status as loyal viewers and consumers, young people are probably granted more status and respect on television than in any other arena of American life," Hine notes.[355]

At no other time in human history has disdain for adults been so embraced by the popular media. But the problem goes far beyond a lack of respect for authority figures. Police and judges, for example, are frequently depicted on TV as dishonest or abusive of their power. Social workers and teachers are portrayed as uncaring bureaucrats, and in nearly all instances, government officials are up to no good. An analysis of television programs by S. Robert Lichter, Linda S. Lichter, and Stanley Rothman found that only about half of all shows depict law enforcement officials as honest and effective. Often, those TV officers who are effective must buck the system and break the rules to get the job done.[356] The popular sci-fi drama *The X-Files* is an excellent example. While the two main characters, FBI agents Fox Mulder and Dana Scully, played by David Duchovny and Gillian Anderson, are portrayed as positive characters, they are also depicted as semi-renegade agents battling to uncover government plots to hide the existence of aliens and supernatural forces.

It seems apparent that as at least a partial result of television's low esteem for authority figures, children and adults alike now exhibit less fear of authority. As respect for social boundaries wanes, the cultural pressures that make members of a society conform to its basic tenets are erased.

In their place, authority figures must rely on shear force to maintain order. This may account for the increasingly adversarial relationship between the police and a large segment of American society. Such enmity may also be in part responsible for the recent spate of riots seen at affluent college campuses such as Michigan State University, the University of Connecticut, and Washington State University, and following some major sporting events such as Denver's 1996 Stanley Cup victory and 1999 Super Bowl win.

Confidant

Nearly everyone needs a confidant they can open up to, someone who understands them on an intimate level. It's not hard to identify such people. Often they're someone who has been "through it" and paid the consequences. We learned from their mistakes. We respected their wisdom because it's born of experience.

People play the role of confidant for any number of reasons. Perhaps they keep secrets well or tend to have an open mind. Maybe they're just good listeners or perhaps they possess a level of wisdom that others naturally respect.

Confidants are the people to whom we reveal ourselves. People tell them their deepest, darkest secrets—the things we do not want the rest of the world to know about but feel compelled to share with someone we trust.

In many families, this role has been all but lost. Because we live our lives outside the home, few people may know who we really are. However, that need to open up, to reveal ourselves, to divulge these secret selves has not abated.

For many of us, television has become our new confidant. But it's a poor substitute for flesh-and-blood friends or family members. TV has changed the way we define the role of confidant. Previously, the confidant's purpose was to help us work through difficulties. It wasn't necessarily that our confidants accepted or promoted abnormal behaviors, but rather, they possessed the wisdom to help us overcome our temptations. Often those to whom we confessed actions that deviated from the norm were friends or relatives whose opinions we most respected.

Such confessions fulfill a basic, healthy need to explore ways to cope with or overcome our obsessions, addictions, or other behaviors that run counter to our well-being. In a sense, this need to confess is an internal navigation system leading us back to the social norm.

The confidants of today, however, are not interested in our well-being. They're not concerned with the consequences of behavior outside the norm as much as they are titillated by the potential ratings of a juicy confession. Jerry Springer, Maury Povich, Sally Jesse Raphael, and Ricki Lake are but a few of the friends we turn to with our most disturbing secrets.

Television has become a poor substitute for the family role of confidant. Talk show hosts—and their audiences, which often number in the tens of millions—have now become America's intimate advisors. The sound stage is our confessional. No longer a means of bringing us back toward the norm, these confidants thrive on exposing deviant behavior for its entertainment value. The more outrageous the better. They encourage viewers to revel in degradation and laugh at deviance, and rarely do they deem any behavior unacceptable of coverage.

Guests whose behavior is outside the realm of typical morality and taste are no longer nudged back into the norm. Television encourages us not only to accept what was previously deemed as deviant, but also compels us to embrace it, to become part of the media circus that is the talk show. TV tells us it's OK to perform almost any act without fear of repercussion.

Daytime talk shows are especially prone to depicting antifamily images. In the world of talk shows, the family is the source of all evil, where danger and deviance lurk unrestrained.

Shock value is what talk shows seek, but when outrageous material is presented day after day, it loses its ability to appall viewers. Producers must then seek out even more offensive material to evoke an emotional response from viewers. This cycle results in an ever-increasing level of repugnant and reprehensible behaviors.[357]

America's democratic foundation demands that we value individuality and respect others' right to be different. It is the very basis of our country's greatness. But there are some behaviors that go beyond the parameters of normalcy and delve into the realm of danger and destructiveness. Such behaviors have the potential to weaken or even destroy a society.

Society is, by nature, a structure that creates support systems, norms, and guidelines that allow individual members to thrive. When there are no parameters, however, there is no society. By turning confessions of deviant behavior into mass entertainment, we destroy the natural boundaries that make our society successful and effective.

As America's confidant, television fails to respect its constituents' parameters of acceptable behavior. Rather, in an effort to capture increasingly larger rating shares, the TV industry actively seeks to expand society's boundaries further and further. Eventually, however, the concept of "normal" behavior will encompass such a broad spectrum of lifestyles that the term "normal" will be rendered irrelevant and inapplicable.

A Misguided Cure for Boredom

How often does your child say, "I'm bored"? More importantly, how often is television the cure for that boredom? It's ironic in this age of almost unlimited entertainment resources, a time when so many people are complaining of burnout from too much stress and too many responsibilities, that boredom seems rampant. This complaint obscures a much deeper and more troubling problem. It hides the fact that when children or spouses say, "I'm bored," they may actually be communicating the message, "I'm lonely."

The statistics clearly indicate that television is the No. 1 after-school activity for children.[358] In fact, a study published in the journal *Broadcasting* notes that children spend an average of nearly 20 percent more time watching television after school than they do playing outside.[359] Another study, conducted by the Henry J. Kaiser Family Foundation found kids were five times more likely to watch TV than to read.[360] What those statistics fail to reflect, however, is why television is so popular. Despite the fact that many children may appear perfectly capable of caring for themselves in the afternoon, from a child's perspective, an empty house can be a very lonely and threatening place. Television provides noise and companionship, and gives the illusion to viewers that they are not alone.

While an argument can be made that these individuals would be even more lonely without TV, it seems clear that in most cases television is simply an inadequate substitute for the companionship of real-life family members. Jacques Ellul explains that TV both isolates and insulates viewers. "There is no comparable instrument of isolation," he says. "Television, even more than radio, shuts up the individual in an echoing mechanical universe in which he is alone….In a perpetual monologue by means of which he escapes the anguish of silence and the inconvenience of neighbors, man finds refuge in the lap of technology."[361]

Postman agrees. "TV tends to be an isolating experience," he says, "requiring no conformity to rules of public behavior."[362] This lack of accountability makes television's destructive messages easier to assimilate into the viewer's value system. For many viewers, the TV listings become their social calendar. They arrange their schedules around television programs as if they were planning their week around dates with friends.

Troubling Patterns

The ultimate result of heavy television viewing is often a near-total lack of relationships with others. This in turn can lead to an erosion of social skills, which ultimately results in a steadily increasing pattern of isolation.

Some may argue viewing television helps build conversational skills. This is the equivalent of claiming that simply viewing great art will produce a great artist. Conversational skills require practice, just like any other competence. When the tube is on, studies confirm that conversation stops. As early as 1951, media researcher Eleanor Maccoby suggested that when families view television together, interaction ceases except for occasional exchange during a commercial. Research in the mid-1950s concluded that television viewing decreases family conversation and face-to-face interaction.[363,364]

Heavy television viewers may find conversation with real people increasingly difficult, since TV allows only a one-sided dialogue. The television does the talking; the viewer listens.

It may seem logical to assume, then, that television viewing can at least improve listening skills. Unfortunately, this is even less likely than TV improving conversation skills. TV's rapid-fire images and frequent scene changes erode viewers' ability to concentrate. Viewers receive no more than a few seconds of information on one subject before another topic is presented. The average shot on MTV, for example, is just three seconds, while *Sesame Street*, which has been shown to actually improve children's reading skills, is ten seconds.[365]

While such a jumble of communications may marginally improve viewers' ability to understand cocktail party small talk, it eventually results in significantly shorter attention spans and reduces viewers' ability to follow and participate in more complex conversations. Research conducted by Peter Jensen at the National Institute of Mental Health concludes, "Extensive exposure to television and video games may promote development of brain systems that scan and shift attention at the expense of those that focus attention."[366] Adds psychologist Sidney Segalowitz of Canada's Brock University, the growing visual and aural power of television threatens "a child's ability to control his or her own attentional process."[367]

Psychologist Jane Healy, author of *Endangered Minds: Why Our Children Don't Think and What to Do About It* points to the growing epidemic of attention-deficit disorders and "diminished higher-order thinking skills" as evidence that TV may be harmful to kids' brain functions. Up to 20 percent of students in the United States now suffer from some kind of learning disorder, consuming more than 20 percent of the average community's school budget.[368] "A 'good' brain for learning develops strong and widespread neural highways that can quickly and efficiently assign different aspects of a task to the most efficient system," she says. "A growing suspicion among brain researchers is that excessive television viewing may affect the development of these kinds of connections. It may also induce habits of using the wrong systems for various types of learning."[369]

One of the joys of authentic friendships is their power to intellectually stimulate both parties. Normal conversations frequently exhibit an element of friendly competition as the parties compare information they have gathered on a particular subject. This interchange of ideas increases the knowledge base of all those involved and stimulates abstract and critical thought. Television offers no such interchange, since viewers never have the opportunity to respond. They aren't called upon to contribute anything. Consequently, they may feel less and less compelled to retain information that may be valuable to pass on to others.

A Passive Act

For adults and children alike, real-life friendships give us the opportunity to explore the world around us. From lunch at a new restaurant to exploration of an unfamiliar hiking trail, these forays into new domains encourage us to expand our knowledge of and comfort with the world around us. When television enters the picture, however, many activities cease.

Television naturally squelches children's imaginations because it creates an imaginary world of its own. Young viewers may find their own rudimentary abilities to fantasize lacking when compared to TV's lively, colorful, polished tales. By creating vivid broadcast images, television skews children's imaginary worlds, filling them with pre-packaged fantasies.

While educational shows such as *Sesame Street* and *Teletubbies* can provide many positive messages, when they become a constant, steady diet, they take children away from other activities that require active participation, which can hone eye-hand coordination, verbal skills, and general creativity.[370] "Even programming from as trustworthy a source as the Public Broadcasting System requires careful thought," warn researchers Alvin Poussaint and Susan Linn.[371]

More alarming, many young children watch cartoons designed for older children, or even adult programming that involves issues of sex and violence. TV often conjures a dark, menacing world that stokes children's fears rather than providing a hopeful, positive outlook on the domain they will inherit.

Watching television is a passive behavior leading not only to atrophy of the mind but also the body. When TV becomes a child's primary playmate, young viewers are much more likely to lead passive, sedentary lives. Numerous studies published in respected journals such as the *Archives of Pediatrics and Adolescent Medicine*, the *American Journal of Public Health*, the *Physician and Sports Medicine*, and *Clinician Reviews* all point to TV as a major factor in the epidemic of childhood obesity. A study published in the *Journal of the American Medical Association*, for example, notes that children who watch more than two hours of television per day were much more likely to have higher levels of body fat than those who watched less than one hour of TV per day. The study of 198 third- and fourth-grade youngsters found that children who underwent a six-month classroom curriculum to reduce TV and video game use lost a significant amount of body mass, waist circumference, and tricep skinfold thickness.[372]

A particularly poignant example of this phenomenon appeared in a recent television advertisement for—amazingly—satellite TV. It shows a little boy romping through the woods and meadows, pretending to be a superhero. The boy's father serves as narrator, extolling the joys of satellite television. Following installation of the service, the closing shot depicts father and son prone in front of the TV.

It is ironic that "interactive" is a favorite buzzword in today's entertainment industry. Whether it's a video game or the TV remote control, there's almost nothing "active" about interactive entertainment.

America's youth is rapidly dooming itself to a future of obesity and sedentary lifestyles. The Centers for Disease Control notes that the incidence of childhood obesity has doubled over the past twenty years, placing children at risk for a wide variety of health and emotional problems.[373] And several studies have proven a direct correlation between obesity and the amount of television children watch.

As viewers begin to substitute television events for real-life experiences, activity levels drop off sharply. The American Academy of Pediatrics estimates that 60 percent of childhood obesity can be linked to excessive television viewing.[374]

Thomas Robinson, a pediatrician at the Stanford University School of Medicine, says TV is helping to create a whole new generation of couch potatoes. Citing a San Jose, California, study, he notes that kids who reduced TV viewing also were able to reduce the eating that goes on during watching TV, to reduce exposure to food advertisements, and to promote greater physical activity.[375]

Perhaps a fitting epilogue to the satellite television commercial mentioned earlier would be a scene depicting the son alone in front of the television, clad in the latest MTV-inspired outfit, eyes glazed over and now grossly overweight—a fate increasingly likely for the children of many TV-addicted families.

Video Prozac

More than 60 percent of Americans admit to using television to "unwind."[376] Television most certainly does have the potential to reduce stress and alleviate tension. Frankly, many programs are so inane, they are the visual equivalent of a warm glass of milk. "Viewers remain relaxed while they watch TV because television viewing is so extraordinarily simple to do and because complexity and intellectual challenge have been driven out of most programs precisely because people use television to relax and escape," say the authors of one study examining television addiction.[377] The flip side to that argument, however, is television's penchant for violence and sex. While practicing such escapism, viewers seeking relaxation may find themselves in a higher state of excitement than if they had not watched TV at all.

Many families use television as a means to relax in much the same way earlier cultures turned to the company of friends and family. Such use of television raises some questions, however. For instance, what happens to family relationships when both parents use TV as a buffer from interpersonal demands? Also, what does this trend suggest about society and family life if interaction with family members is perceived as just another task from which to escape in front of the tube?

Part Three:
What The Future Holds

Why Regulation Hasn't Worked

W hile television offers exciting and even sometimes disturbing possibilities, it's also important to understand how outside forces such as the government, consumer groups, and the business community will help shape the medium as we delve into this new century.

The regulatory aspects of television evolved from the government's early attempts to understand and take advantage of broadcast media such as radio. The Communication Act of 1934, for example, was the first major piece of legislation to govern the broadcast industry.[378] It laid the groundwork for much of how television is monitored and controlled today.

Among its provisions, the act established that the airways are public property. At least on paper, that declaration remains in effect. Much like it controls public land, the government, as an extension of the people, holds primary control of the airwaves. The 1934 act also required commercial broadcasters to hold a license to use these public resources, although today's process is significantly different than the original intent of the law.[379]

The 1930s were comparatively innocent times. It's doubtful any legislator could have imagined how broadcast media would be used and abused today. A handful of legislators may have had some inkling, however. They specifically inserted a provision limiting use of public airwaves to broadcasters who served "the public interest, convenience, and necessity."

Unfortunately, they didn't bother to put any teeth into that mandate. Consequently, today's Federal Communications Commission has never bothered to established guidelines for what constitutes "public interest, convenience, and necessity."

Several subsequent attempts to legislate broadcasting were equally ineffective in controlling the budding television industry. During the 1950s, for example, two congressional subcommittees held hearings to examine the issues of children's exposure to violence in adult-oriented shows. Both concluded that a problem existed that required further attention, but no real action was taken.[380]

It wasn't until 1990 that Congress passed what appeared to be truly significant legislation. It took aim at broadcasters' penchant for wooing America's youth. The Children's Television Act (CTA) of 1990 reiterated broadcasters' responsibilities beyond profiteering, laying down a mandate for programming that met the "educational and informational needs of children." It also banned the FCC from renewing broadcasters' licenses if they failed to meet these needs.[381]

This legislation was among the first to acknowledge television's power as an educational tool. Many studies confirm that television can be a highly positive force—a potent teaching tool—in children's lives. The Center for Research on the Influences of Television on Children at the University of Kansas, for instance, confirms television's ability to educate in a positive sense. Their investigations conclude that children who watch *Sesame Street*, for example, know and understand more words, have a better grasp of mathematics, and are more prepared for school than children who only watch cartoons and general programming.[382]

The 1990 CTA seemed poised to change the face of children's television. Like previous legislation, however, it lacked a clear definition of children's needs and failed to outline specific strategies for broadcasters to meet those requirements. Broadcasters rapidly identified and employed such loopholes to get around the legislation's provisions.

For example, network executives frequently point to their own studies that indicate educational programming has increased 100 percent since 1990—more than complying with the act. They fail to explain, however, their definition of educational television.[383]

These executives frequently cite a National Association of Broadcasters study as proof of their compliance with CTA. A closer look at the study reveals that broadcasters typically included programs such as *GI Joe*, *America's Funniest Home Videos*, *The Flintstones*, *The Jetsons*, *Biker Mice from Mars*, *Teenage Mutant Ninja Turtles*, and *60 Minutes* in their "educational" lineup.[384] At one point, ABC even tried to push *Tales from the Cryptkeeper*, based on cable network HBO's adult horror series, as a way to teach children "a wonder-filled morality lesson."[385] Furthermore, the FCC acceded to the broadcasters by implying that cable stations that cater to kids and the availability of children's fare at local video stores could also be counted on to provide educational programming.[386]

True educational television hasn't expanded at all, reports researcher Dale Kunkel. "Reliance on the unregulated marketplace produces virtually no educational children's programming on commercial broadcast television," he claims.[387]

Children's programming such as *Sesame Street*, *Barney*, *Mister Rogers' Neighborhood*, *Wishbone*, and a handful of other bona fide educational programs generally air on public television. However, they must compete with commercial powerhouses such as *Mighty Morphin Power Rangers*, a program the University of California at Los Angeles Center for Communication cited as a prime example of "sinister combat violence." The center went on to note that each episode of *Power Rangers* "had a very similar look and feel, always conveying the same underlying message: violence is not really horrible, and no one is really hurt by it."[388]

The lackluster performance of the Children's Television Act hasn't dissuaded children's advocates from continuing their crusade against irresponsible broadcast practices—and hasn't kept broadcasters from trying to appease sponsors and viewers without changing their programming habits.

The Ratings System

The television rating system is similar to the movie rating system and features six age-based categories preceded by the prefix "TV":

TV-MA is for mature audiences only. These programs are designed for adults and are usually unsuitable for kids under seventeen. They feature mature themes, profane language, graphic violence, and explicit sexual content. Consumers should be aware there is a high probability the television industry will use the TV-MA designation as an excuse to broadcast increasingly explicit materials. It's a good bet the industry will argue that a TV-MA rating gives parents sufficient warning and discharges television's responsibility to maintain a level of decency.

TV-14 strongly cautions viewers that the program probably contains material some parents will find unsuitable for children under fourteen. Under the industry guidelines, parents are urged to exercise care in monitoring such programs and cautioned against letting children under fourteen view these shows unattended. TV-14 programs include what the TV industry calls "sophisticated themes, sexual content, strong language, and more intense violence."

TV-PG means parental guidance is suggested. These programs feature materials some parents will find unsuitable for younger children. Parents should watch TV-PG programs with their children since themes may call for guidance. TV-PG programs may contain "infrequent coarse language, limited violence, and some suggestive sexual dialogue and situations."

TV-G programs are ostensibly suitable for all ages. They contain little or no violence as defined by the television industry, no strong language, and little or no sexual dialogue or situations.

TV-Y7 programming is designed for ages seven and above. These programs may contain "mild physical or comedic violence," says the television industry, or may frighten children under seven.

TV-Y shows target very young children—ages two to six—and should not contain any frightening content.

Many ratings are followed by a one- or two-letter designation that describes why the program has earned its age-based rating. Ratings in the TV-Y7 category, for example, may include a designation of "FV" for fantasy violence. *Mighty Morphin Power Rangers* and many animated action shows often fall into this category. In the TV-PG and TV-14 categories, a program may also earn a "V" for violence, "S" for sexual situations, "L" for use of course language, or "D" for suggestive dialogue.[389]

Program distributors determine the ratings based on criteria originally hammered out by Jack Valenti, president of the Motion Picture Association of America. Federal Communications Commission Chairman Reed Hundt notes that it is the first time television has ever carried any consistent content labeling. "Practically every product in America is labeled and described by the people who make it and sell it," he explained during a 1996 National Town Hall Meeting. "You just go down the grocery store aisle and every product you see there you can look at the back or the top and there will be some kind of warning or some kind of discussion about the content. Until [1996], television was practically the only product in this country that did not label itself or describe itself so that people know what they're getting."[390]

A key weapon in most recent battles has been the controversial v-chip. The v-chip is a computer chip installed in most new televisions that allows parents to program their televisions to block certain undesirable programs. The chip "reads" ratings embedded in programs and then only allows shows identified by the user—such as a parent—as "acceptable" to be viewed. Parents may block all programs with a "TV-14" rating, for example. A password allows users to bypass the system.

The v-chip and corresponding rating system is an integral part of the Telecommunications Act of 1996, which garnered nearly unanimous support from the Clinton Administration and Congress. Vice President Al Gore called its passage a "historic event that will change forever the way every American lives, works, learns, and communicates."[391] In addition to the v-chip, the 1996 act called for broadcasters to air a minimum of three hours of children's educational programming per week. The FCC quickly concurred.[392]

Surprisingly, the act was even embraced by top TV executives such as Rupert Murdoch, who founded the Fox network, producer and distributor of *Mighty Morphin Power Rangers*. Murdoch also owns more TV news outlets than any other person on the planet. To understand why broadcasters were so quick to jump on the ratings bandwagon, one must delve into the cloudy world of politics, high-level deal-making, and the ultra-sophisticated psychology of television programming. Although supporting the rating system may outwardly appear to be an act of social responsibility, a closer look reveals that it's simply good economics.

First and foremost, the act gave television broadcasters what they wanted: more broadcast spectrum. Complying with v-chip technology and ratings was a small payment for the allocation of six additional megahertz of spectrum, effectively doubling the airwaves for broadcasters.[393]

What made the deal especially sweet was the price. While the FCC sells the same kind of spectrum to other industries such as cellular telephone companies for billions of dollars, broadcasters got the additional spectrum for free. Some experts now value the broadcasters' total spectrum at nearly $150 billion.[394]

Secondly, the definition of what constitutes "educational TV" remains unclear. It's uncertain whether the three hours of educational programming broadcasters are obligated to air will consist of *Sesame Street* or *The Oprah Winfrey Show*. Even more alarming, the act lays the groundwork for a "safe harbor." Television executives are hoping their compliance will result in fewer government controls over the remaining 165 hours per week of broadcast time.[395] With fewer restrictions, broadcasters may be tempted to produce non-educational TV that's even racier and more violent than their current lineups. As an added bonus, TV executives hope the v-chip, ratings system, and agreement to air three hours per week of children's educational programming might even quell further debates on children's educational television.[396]

Perhaps most telling, however, is that many insiders see the television rating system as just another savvy marketing tool. Most experts predict that few parents will actually use the v-chip, and a survey by the Kaiser Family Foundation found that although 65 percent of parents with children ages ten to seventeen said they would use the system, nearly 70 percent said they did not plan to buy a TV with the system in the near future.[397] A 1999 Gallup/CNN/*USA Today* poll found only 4 percent of American households actually use v-chip technology.[398]

Many industry experts predict that programming and reprogramming the TV to prevent children from viewing some programs while allowing adults in the household to view others will be too complicated for most parents to bother.[399] The entertainment industry is banking on the assumption that the American public quickly will grow tired of such a seemingly cumbersom device.

That leaves the rating system. Although the rating system may help responsible parents limit the violence and sex that comes into their home via TV, it also will pit parents against the prevailing culture—a culture developed, refined, and communicated by commercial television.[400] Parents who insist upon limiting their children's viewing to TV-G rated programs, for example, will be cast in the same light as those who only let their kids see animated movies—overprotective and ultraconservative.

More importantly, the TV rating system suffers from the same paradox of censorship experienced by the movie industry. A study commissioned by the cable television industry reports that 53 percent of boys age ten to fourteen would voluntarily watch a movie with an R rating without even knowing its content. Not one of the boys surveyed would voluntarily chose a G-rated movie.[401] Like the proverbial "forbidden fruit," TV ratings reflecting violence or sex simply will whet the appetite of children for prohibited programming. Humorist Dave Barry characterized the TV ratings scheme as "a system for rating TV shows for sex and violence so that young people looking for these things will not have to waste valuable time channel-surfing."[402] He may be right. A Mediascope, Inc., study commissioned by the cable television industry found more than a quarter of surveyed children ages ten to seventeen turned off shows simply because they felt the ratings indicated the content was too immature.[403]

It's a nearly perfect deal for broadcasters. They gain additional spectrum and increase viewership of what television sells best—sex and violence—all while appearing civic-minded. In essence, the v-chip and associated rating system allow programmers to argue that it's no longer their fault if children are exposed to inappropriate materials on television. They can wash their hands of all responsibility, placing it squarely on the shoulders of beleaguered parents.

A Look Down the Road

Compared to many other forms of communication, television as a technology is still in its infancy—a mere sixty years old. Until the advent of computers and the Internet, it was, in many ways, the baby of the communication technology family. Some futurists have made a career out of predicting what the mature medium will become. The limitation of such predictions is that they rely on current, known technologies. Sixty years ago, humankind hadn't even envisioned transistors, let alone microchips and the related technologies they have enabled. It's likely that our predictions too will fall short of reality in, say, the year 2050.

As the influences of these technologies increase, the stage is set for expanding exponentially all the cultural, social, educational, and family problems now inherent in today's television programming.

No salient discussion of television can avoid the inevitable convergence of TV with computer technologies. This marriage is on the horizon, and if even half of what technology futurists predict actually occurs, our lives, our social structure, and our ways of communicating will be forever altered.

In the near future, many people will find it difficult to sort out what constitutes television and what is computer technology. The federal government already has mandated the conversion of television to digital technology.[404] Although TV fans tout five hundred–channel capabilities and razor-sharp images, the real fallout will be the ability to truly merge television and computer into one seamless, yet-to-be-named product.

Digital technology will make current televisions obsolete. They will be replaced by interactive devices that connect users to a highly sophisticated offspring of the Internet. While a cruise down today's information highway may be akin to traveling a two-lane road strewn with billboards, tomorrow's version promises to place you smack in the middle of those colorful beer commercials where everyone is having a good time. It's still commercialism, but it will be infinitely more irresistible.

In the short term—five to ten years—what most likely will emerge will be a hybrid that functions as both a TV and computer. The system will be incorporated with your stereo system for even more realistic sound and will feature a digital screen that produces extremely high-definition pictures comparable to today's computer screens. The system will be highly interactive, capable of performing typical computer functions while consumers participate in interactive entertainment products.[405,406]

Whether users browse the Web in the traditional sense or watch a hybrid interactive version of television, consumers most likely will be exposed to even more advertising than traditional TV. In addition, the lines between programming production organizations and advertisers will blur even further. In the new world order, those boundaries may be almost nonexistent. Consumers may participate in programs produced and directed by a Microsoft subsidiary on a device manufactured by a Microsoft partner while they watch Microsoft ads flash across the top of their screen.[407]

Unlike today's television, which requires little physical and/or mental participation, hybrid computer/TVs will call upon participants to actually join in the programming. The commercial merits of such a strategy are no doubt already being assessed. Consumer participation inevitably will result in a much higher level of buy-in and loyalty, making participants an easier sale for sponsoring products.

Some futurists predict that computer/TV content will be based on a "virtual community."[408] Such a community will replace the sense of real community lost as a result of increasing amounts of time spent in front of the screen. A virtual version of the popular TV program *Cheers*, for example, may place viewers at the bar of a congenial pub, surrounded by their favorite characters.

Another twist on this concept would be the virtual chat room. "Customers" could move around a virtual bar making screen-to-screen contact with the images of other users. Of course, that beer sitting in front of the viewer would be the sponsor's brand. In essence, the viewer would already be the advertiser's virtual customer—just a small step away from the real thing. Savvy marketers will create environments that appeal to a wide variety of users, from mom and dad to the youngest child. Imagine— a virtual Playboy mansion for dad and a virtual Romper Room for little Jimmy!

Interactive talk shows may become standard daytime fare. These programs will allow an even more personal relationship to emerge with broadcast personalities. Viewers will be able to speak face-to-face with even the most outrageous guests. The emotional bonds created by such an exchange will further normalize behaviors now deemed unacceptable.

The content of computerized television may have another edge over traditional TV beyond interactivity. Since it will circumvent broadcast networks by using the Internet, cable TV, or satellites, it may not be subject to the same controls as today's television.

The government has been reluctant to delve into the complex issue of Internet regulation, and its few forays mostly have been dismal failures. Provisions in the Communications Decency Act of 1996, for example, originally required Internet companies to take "good faith" effective actions to prohibit access by minors to adult-oriented sites. They also required organizations to restrict such access by demanding forms of age proof such as a verified credit card or adult identification number.[409]

The Supreme Court struck down the act's provisions that barred "indecent transmission" and "patently offensive display" on the Internet, saying they violated the First Amendment's guarantee of free speech. The court described the provisions as "overbroad" and added that they also violated the Fifth Amendment because they were vague. Regulators, as usual, were caught in a catch-22. More specific guidelines could not hope to cover the vast possibilities of future Internet use, and broader rules against indecency were pegged as violating Internet companies' constitutional rights.[410]

The court even struck down arguments that imposed the most rudimentary regulations now proscribed upon the broadcast industry. "The special factors recognized in some of the Court's cases as justifying regulation of the broadcast media—the history of extensive government regulation of broadcasting...the scarcity of available frequencies at its inception...and its 'invasive' nature—are not present in cyberspace," the court said.[411] In essence, the justices maintained that the lack of previous regulation of the Internet and the fact that computers require a higher level of interactivity on the part of consumers makes cyberspace less needy of regulation.

The convergence of TV and computer is only the beginning. New products involving cable, satellite, and other technologies emerge almost daily. Future technologies will combine televisions and computers with phones, email, pagers and other devices yet to be discovered. Information, personal communication, and entertainment eventually will merge into a single technology.

While manufacturers will tout the sophistication of such technologies and their ability to enhance our lives, current trends appear to suggest otherwise. In essence, we are handing over our value system, our ability to communicate with one another, our sense of community, and all that we are to companies whose primary purpose is to make money.

Such a change in the power structure could reap global repercussions. As entertainment, communication, commerce, and economics merge, the very idea of what constitutes a culture or even a nation may become blurred. Today, distant countries such as China are deeply concerned that new technologies will allow American programming to invade and freely impact their cultures.

George Orwell's book *1984* frightened readers with the prospect of unprecedented government control. But what if control eventually ends up in the hands of the business community? Beyond the simple lack of privacy, organizations easily could learn to use information such as our favorite Internet sites, shopping habits, or obsessions to make their products, services, and ideas even more irresistible. Most of us already have a grocery store card, for example, which tells the merchants' computers what we buy and how often, and this is only the most basic use of such technologies.

It has been financially beneficial for broadcasters to assume the roles of individual family members. It seems unlikely future technology leaders will reverse this trend. In all likelihood, new technologies will allow programmers to take over even more of the family's key responsibilities. Consequently, we will further lose the social skills necessary to interact with the real world around us.

Without these skills, the real world becomes uncomfortable and hostile. There is an increasing probability that much of society ultimately will exist in a "virtual world" created by our own abdication of key family responsibilities and our failure to learn and practice the social skills necessary to function in a tangible human society.

Take Back Control

Taking back control of the roles television has assumed from family members is more complicated than just hiding the remote. It means getting involved in your family's lives, your community, and even, in America's political process. Television wields a powerful influence on many families. We must be willing to exert an equally powerful effort to put TV back in its place as an occasional entertainment or information technology, rather than the center of our lives.

First, we must be more vigilant and selective about the programs our families watch. America's living rooms are on the front lines of this battle. They are ultimately where the war for our families will be won or lost.

The challenge also will involve government policies and political action groups composed of citizens, educators, and responsible members of the media. And just as important, educational institutions and watchdog groups must develop media literacy curricula that enhance critical viewing skills.

"In the twenty-first century, the century our children will live in, the century they will, in fact, shape, media literacy will not be a luxury, it will be a necessity," says Linda Ellerbee, host of *The American Family and Television: A National Town Hall Meeting*.[412] The bottom line: parents can't do it alone. As families, communities, and a nation, we must grow future citizens capable of understanding the role of the media in society.

Understand Television's Power

Conscientious viewers must realize they are in a war. Like any good strategist, they must understand their enemy if they are to devise effective tactics to overcome their family's addiction to television.

TV executives already know the power they wield. They use this knowledge to manipulate audiences and attract advertisers. Why would any sponsor invest millions of dollars in television ads if they didn't believe TV influences viewers?

The same people who promote television as an effective advertising medium argue that violence and sex on TV has little or no effect on the audience. Don't fall for this argument. "Until we can use the most powerful communications medium in the world to benefit all children, rather than to exploit them, all the other efforts we make on their behalf will be incomplete," explain Newton Minow and Craig Lamay in their book *Abandoned in the Wasteland*. "In a nation where, increasingly, children spend more time with television than doing anything else, it is unacceptable that that time should be taken up principally by salesmen, animated assault artists, and leering talk-show hosts."[413]

Start at Home

The first step in reducing TV's influence on your family is to be available as an influence yourself. You cannot force-feed positive values. Your family must be motivated to make changes, not pummeled into submission. That means spending time with your kids, communicating with them, and building relationships that result in respect for your opinions, morals, and values. It means engaging in conversations with your spouse that go beyond, "What's for dinner?"

It's not going to be easy. Families who allow TV to fulfill their internal roles must be committed to change and willing to initially suffer for it. Television is an addiction, and like other addicts, those who depend on TV are never really "cured." They must always be on guard against returning to old habits.

The majority of viewers now recognize TV as a "negative influence" on society, but many seem unable to break their addiction to it. A 1999 survey of 1,179 Americans conducted by the Pew Research Center for the People & the Press found that 70 percent of those polled think television contains too much violence. The same poll indicated that 89 percent were "very" (64 percent) or "somewhat" (25 percent) concerned about what children see on TV.[414] A 1999 Harris poll of 1,006 people reveals that nearly two-thirds of adults think television contributes "a lot" to violence.[415]

"Although we may be powerless in the face of the abstract machine that modern society has become, we can still assert our wills in the face of that real and tangible machine in our homes, the TV set," says psychologist Marie Winn, author of *The Plug-In Drug*. "We can learn to control it so that it does not control us."[416]

Media expert George Comstock concurs, adding that parents must hold final authority over TV use. "Television viewing is largely within the province of the authority of the child," he says. It needs to become "largely within the province of the authority of the family."[417]

Turning off the TV means standing up to children's complaints and badgering. Ignore the heat. Your children, perhaps even your spouse, will use the excuse that everyone watches television. You must be committed to the idea that this is not true, and that most families who watch little or no TV are actually stronger and better able to carry out the purpose of the family unit. And when conflict arises regarding television, make the solution the "off" button.

Organize "No-TV" Weeks

Although most children and, surprisingly, many adults may believe otherwise, turning off the TV isn't the end of the world. In fact, doing so may open doors to new vistas of entertainment, discovery, and family unity. Just vowing to turn off the tube probably won't result in much change, however. Television is an addiction, and in some ways the best method for kicking the habit is going "cold turkey."

Ladies Home Journal Managing Editor Mary Mohler decided to unhook her TV for a month after noticing a distinctly insolent trend in her three children's communication patterns. "There was a feeling that conversation was no longer even a genuine interaction, but a kind of scripted reaction," she explains in an article chronicling the experience.[418]

Mohler notes that her children adjusted amazingly well and actually found numerous activities—from reading to playing games—to keep them occupied. She adds that her kids demanded more attention as a result of turning off the tube, which resulted in more time spent together.[419]

In addition, Mohler found their time together more gratifying than the time she used to spend watching TV with her children. "I see now that [television viewing is] a phony kind of togetherness—we're each in our own world, thinking different thoughts, not talking, not sharing, together only in body," she explains. It's "a kind of narcotic....In fact, there is no more potent drug in our lives than this TV set, and if I speak honestly, that's how I use it. Kids acting crazy? Give them some of mommy's little helper."[420]

Mohler offers several suggestions for making a "No-TV" week a positive experience. First, pick a workable start date. Decide when the television gets unplugged, then stick to it—no exceptions. Also, discuss the plan with your children well in advance. Give them a chance to accept and participate in the scheme before imposing it on them. Also, Mohler says, don't congratulate your family on how well they're doing or tell them you're so pleased with the situation that you may continue it indefinitely.[421]

Most importantly, be prepared. Have a plan chock full of other activities. Know what's happening in your community and make outside activities a priority. Finally, play fair: no turning on the TV after the kids go to bed. Turning off the tube is an exercise designed to benefit the whole family, mom and dad included.

If you're not prepared to go it alone, consider starting a community-wide "No-TV" week. Andover, Connecticut, resident Dianne Grenier organized such a week after neighbors asked how she managed to work full-time, serve on several committees, and volunteer at two soup kitchens. "People kept saying, 'Wow! How do you do all that?' I said: 'Simple, I don't watch television.'"[422] Grenier then challenged her community of twenty-five hundred to turn off their televisions for one week. An organizing committee printed up pamphlets listing alternate activities from nature walks and puppet shows to stargazing and model rocketing.[423]

"My son Eric found toys he didn't even know he had," says participant Corrine Ackerman. "The toys were all up on the shelf collecting dust, and as soon as the TV went off, down they came."[424]

Organizer Grenier says most people discovered a variety of new ways to occupy their time. Relatively few found the experience negative. "A few couch potatoes developed signs of fatigue due to moderate activity," she says, "but there were no fatalities."[425]

Keep a TV Diary

The first step in understanding television's power is to discover how TV affects you and your family. This requires close scrutiny of individual and household viewing habits over a period of about a month.

Over the first two weeks, keep a log of what shows you and your family view, when they are on, and who's watching them. If you're unsure of the value of such information, keep in mind that the A.C. Nielsen Company has made millions on both written and electronic versions of such diaries. This information is used specifically to determine which shows stay on the air and which shows are cancelled. Advertisers gamble billions of dollars based on the information such TV diaries yield. It makes sense that you should be armed with similar information.

Using a ledger-ruled notebook, keep a record of every hour your television is on. Your TV diary should include the time and duration of the program, its name, channel, major sponsors, TV rating, which family members are present, and perhaps even a four- or five-word synopsis of the plot to help jog your memory later. You may even consider noting particular scenes of dialogue that you find offensive or that run counter to your value system. If you have more than one television in the house, keep a separate diary in each viewing area.

Maintaining such a diary requires effort. It may mean monitoring closely what younger children view and even engaging the help of older kids. If possible, make a game of it. At the very least, make it a mandatory requirement for the use of any television over the course of your two-week survey.

Analyze What Your Family Watches

It's vital to assess how often your family depends on TV to entertain, inform, or occupy leisure time. At the end of the two-week survey period, tally up the number of hours the TV is on and the amount of time each family member spends watching television. Also, note the types of programs individual members watch, and look for trends in sponsorship. Some companies may be prone to sponsoring specific genres of programs that you find offensive. Let those sponsors know!

Most families who perform the diary exercise are shocked at how much TV they actually watch. Once you grasp the amount of time your family spends with television, it becomes equally vital to understand what they're watching and analyze the possible effects of these viewing habits. Make a list for each member of their ten most frequently viewed programs—probably their favorites.

Over the subsequent two weeks, watch at least one episode of each show, preferably with the person or people who most frequently view the programs. This exercise may mean you have to give up some of your own favorite programs or activities and may even require that you to videotape some programs for viewing at a more convenient hour.

During viewing, keep notes on scenes or dialogue that attack the family, marriage, spouses, genders, and ethnic groups, or scenes that conflict with your values in other ways. Note the number of sex scenes or references to sex in dialogue as well as depictions of violence. It's important to annotate the context of violence. While most TV violence can affect viewers negatively, some forms are particularly destructive. An old rerun of *The Three Stooges* probably has more instances of violence than many of today's police dramas, but the dramas may be far more graphic and disturbing.

Talk about What You See

Viewers learn from television. That's a fact both experts and TV executives understand. This learning experience does not, however, have to be a passive one. Research indicates that frequent discussions of programs and the values they present can reduce the influence of negative content on children. Frequent parent/child interaction regarding TV helps kids become more discerning viewers. It's important to explain to children that people interpret what they view on television in a variety of ways. What some people find funny may be offensive or insulting to others.

As you and your family watch TV, make a point of discussing content and themes. Ask them how they would feel if a real-life person came into your home and behaved in a similar fashion. Would they find the language offensive, or would they be uncomfortable if a stranger discussed equally sensitive topics? Understand and help your children grasp that television programs are created for very specific purposes—to inform, to titillate, to sway viewers, and simply to entertain—but not all purposes are in the best interest of the viewer.

Help your family understand that TV's influences are glacial in nature—slow but deep. Like advertising, the messages communicated by television programs are cumulative. Few sponsors expect one airing of their commercial to yield significant results. They realize that advertising messages must be communicated over and over again until they're engraved on consumers' brains. Television sells sex and violence in a similar fashion.

Explain how ideas of right and wrong, morality, and the way we treat fellow human beings are being shaped by the media. We may not see fundamental changes in society's behavior immediately, but over decades, these changes become increasingly obvious. Help your child compare and contrast TV characters' behaviors from real-life people and ask them how they would react in a similar situation. Also, point out that most TV situations are scripted and directed by people behind the scenes, and actors may have little in common with the characters they play. Such discourse helps children think independently from the influences of television.

In both dramas and comedies, be aware of subtle manipulation tools. Make a game of counting laugh tracks or musical cues that suggest emotionally intense moments, and correlate them to what's happening on screen. Look for patterns that suggest how these tools manipulate viewers' feelings and ideas.

Discuss how families are depicted on television. It may come as a surprise to many children—and adults, as well—that not all families bicker or take cheap shots at one another. Without frequent discussion and analysis of TV, some viewers may conclude that the majority of American families are wealthy and riddled with conflict. Explain to children that the middle class is still in the majority, and most households remain peaceful, loving sanctuaries where members thrive. Note that family members can disagree without personally attacking one another or dissolving the family unit.

Spend time with your children analyzing television programs by paying extra attention to the commercials that air during certain programs. Discuss TV's function as a marketing tool and examine how advertisers may sponsor specific programs based on their potential audience or messages the shows communicate. Note that action-packed programs may be more likely to feature beer commercials, for example, while soap operas are usually supported by women's products. Also, make a game of looking for product placements and discuss why certain merchandise may be associated with a particular character or show.

Point out instances of tobacco or alcohol use on television. Explain how advertisers use images to create an idea that may not be accurate. Point out, for instance, that smokers have more wrinkles and less pliable skin than nonsmokers. Therefore, the image of smoking as something "beautiful people" do is inaccurate.

One of the real challenges of being a discerning viewer is that eroticism is a key element of many programs' marketing strategy. Even viewers who choose to watch the most benign and morally upright programs find themselves exposed to steamy sexual content in the ads for other, less-wholesome programs. Make a point of discussing how networks use such promotional spots and why they may choose to place such advertisements in less erotic fare.

Encourage children to watch for stereotypes or biased depictions of men and women or ethnic groups. Identify real-life figures who defy the ethnic, racial, and gender stereotypes presented by the media. Ensure that family members understand why stereotypes exist and how they can be inaccurate.

Listen for new speech patterns that appear on television and help your family understand how the "mass media" aspects of television can influence how they speak. Discuss the language used in programs and encourage children to look for new words and phrases that appear in common use as a result of programs or commercials.

Be aware of your children's response, or lack of reaction, to offensive or disturbing scenes. Kids know what they need. Listen for signs that your children may be distressed by what they're viewing. If you notice a problem, make sure you discuss it in a comforting enviornment.

Make Viewing Inconvenient

Most American homes are set up for the primary purpose of watching television. Look around. Chances are your living room or family room is arranged around the "entertainment center." The dining room table, if used frequently, may be positioned so that most family members have a clear view of the TV. You may have a television on the kitchen counter and one or two in the bedrooms. These "sleeping quarters" are probably arranged for comfortable viewing. The average American household has 2.25 television sets and nearly 14 percent of homes have four or more TVs.[426] It's a fact that many Americans organize their lives around television.

The key to taking your family life back is to wrest it away from television, and the best way to accomplish that is to eliminate the competition. Some families refuse to own any TVs at all. While this may seem extreme, it's a highly effective way to spur family interaction and end TV's dictatorship over your life. But it's probably not practical for most families.

A more palatable arrangement may be to limit your household to one television—preferably the smallest. Restricting your family to one TV encourages members to be accountable to each other and often forces parents to watch what their children are viewing. With only one television, couples are also more likely to reveal their true viewing habits, exposing ways TV may be affecting their relationship.

Another tactic for reviving family interaction is to place the television in an inconvenient location. A drafty unfinished basement or a room with particularly uncomfortable furniture forces viewers to make television an active choice rather than a passive experience. As a minimum, place the TV in a corner that doesn't allow family members to lie on the sofa or get too comfortable while viewing. Few homemakers arrange their living rooms around a set of encyclopedias or a bookcase. Relegating television to an inconvenient location puts TV back in its place as just another information resource.

Hiding the remote also can help achieve this goal. Two-thirds of Americans admit to channel surfing.[427] Forcing family members to get up and change the channel manually encourages them to take an extra second or two to consider what they're watching.

Finally, never watch television during dinner. "Dinnertime is often the only time of the day when there's an opportunity for the whole family to be together and feel a real sense of connection," notes William J. Doherty, Ph.D., author of *The Intentional Family: How to Build Family Ties in Our Modern World*. He adds that without frequent reinforcement—reinforcements such as family meals—the connection can be lost and children will start to feel isolated.[428]

The idea behind many of these strategies is to make television a less pleasurable experience, and make interaction a more enjoyable one. Making television inconvenient compels viewers to ask themselves if the program they intend to watch is worth the effort and discomfort. Frequently the answer will be no.

Create a TV Schedule

Sit down with your family and go through the television program guide. Mark out shows that are strictly forbidden and identify those that communicate values you respect. Unfamiliar programs should be viewed with a critical eye.

Establish group-defined, realistic limits on the number of hours each member may watch TV. The American Academy of Pediatrics recommends that children watch no more than one or two hours of TV per day.[429] Also, establish quiet times for alternative family activities. Line out TV programs that conflict with these activities—no exceptions.

Remember, you and your family may already live by a schedule imposed by television. Taking back control means creating your own schedule—and sticking to it. Turn the television on only to watch specific, previously planned programs. Then turn it off immediately following those shows. Television networks study their program lineups carefully to ensure viewers make a smooth, almost unconscious transition to the next show. Programming is marketed as a "whole package." Viewers eventually cease to watch specific programs and begin to view TV in blocks of several hours.

Consider videotaping favorite programs for later viewing. Then ensure the VCR is set up to only record one show and not a whole evening's worth of entertainment. That way, you and your family aren't sucked into a programming lineup specifically designed to lead you from one show to the next, and you can watch the program around your schedule.

Afternoons are especially hazardous to children. Networks and local stations create afternoon lineups designed to keep young viewers' attention right up until the evening news. Although networks may observe family viewing hours, late-evening programs sometimes air as reruns in the afternoon or early evening—prime viewing times for teens and children.

Be sure to make a point of knowing what your children are watching. Create a specific list of programs that are acceptable, and those that aren't, and also place realistic limitations on the amount of time spent on afternoon viewing.

Make TV a Family Activity

The only way to keep tabs on what your family is consuming is to be there with them when they consume it. Watch television with your children and your spouse. Know what they're watching and admit to what you view. If anyone feels embarrassed, that's a pretty good cue the program may not be particularly healthy for your family life. Few parents or spouses read pornography in the open or visit strip clubs together, yet many people erroneously rationalize that similar entertainment on TV is harmless.

Watching television with your family opens up opportunities for discussions on how TV may affect viewers' values. It also allows children to ask questions about topics they may not understand. This gives you the opportunity to decide how much or little information is appropriate for your child, rather than leaving it in the hands of television.

And never use TV as a reward or punishment. Granting or taking away television privileges places undue value on the medium and conveys a subtle message that TV is an enjoyable and positive experience.

Ban Television from the Boudoir

Some spouses argue that watching an evening talk show helps them unwind, making them more relaxed and ready for intimacy. But when there's a television in the bedroom, it's a good bet someone is going to feel ignored. By banning TV from the boudoir, couples can begin to refocus their attention on what should be their first priority—each other.

Removing TV from children's bedrooms is also important. More than 40 percent of children ages six to eleven and a quarter of kids younger than six now have a television in their room.[430] Removing the TV from children's bedrooms forces them to watch television in a more conspicuous location where you can better monitor viewing activities. It also enhances children's concentration on other activities such as hobbies or homework by removing America's No. 1 diversion. Homework should be done in a quiet, isolated area with few distractions. That usually means the bedroom. Although most children won't admit it, TV's rapid-fire images require a high degree of attention. Few kids can study effectively in such an environment.

In addition, children who fall asleep by the television usually stay up later and experience less restful sleep than those in homes with a clearly defined "lights out" policy. Banning TV from sleeping quarters returns the bedroom to its former and most important role as a resting place.

Understand TV Ratings

The television rating system can be a powerful tool in helping your family decide which programs are appropriate for viewing and what shows should be banned. In fact, a survey conducted by the Kaiser Family Foundation found nearly all parents who have ever used the TV ratings found them useful, and 54 percent of parents with children ages ten to seventeen use the system to help guide their children's viewing.[431] But TV ratings also have some serious drawbacks that must be understood to use the system effectively.

First, it's important to realize that relying solely on the rating system means that you're putting your trust in a host of faceless writers, producers, and directors. TV executives, however well-meaning, may not embrace the values you hold dear. While most early childhood programs offer fairly universal values of right and wrong, they also may subtly and inadvertently communicate ancillary values held by the programming staff. More than half of all parents who have used the rating system found they occasionally disagree with some program ratings.

Also, keep in mind that ratings are determined by program distributors. These organizations may have a vested interest in rating a program for a particular age group. Aged-based ratings have become a powerful marketing tool in the movie industry. Distributors know that a "G" rating will pretty much send teen viewers running for cover, while mature audience classifications can attract a surprising number of unsupervised children of all ages. This is probably true of television as well. Some distributors may rate programs based on potential audiences rather than content. In addition, television producers may manipulate language or violent scenes to gain valuable market shares.

Even more important, viewers who base program selections solely on ratings rely on the values of those who determine the ratings—TV industry representatives who often have very different views of right and wrong than many viewers.

Keep in mind, as well, that sports and news programs—including many news magazines—are exempt from the rating system. That means professional wrestling or graphic TV magazine accounts of a mass murder will not receive any rating at all.

Television ratings appear in the upper left-hand corner of the screen for fifteen seconds at the beginning of each program or each half hour. That makes it difficult to flip to another channel and find out the rating of a second or third program choice. One study indicated that two-thirds of parents were unable to catch program ratings even when they made a specific effort to look for them.[432] Consider encouraging your local newspaper to publish TV ratings in their program guide as a public service. This allows parents and viewers to make informed choices before turning on the tube.

Televisions with v-chips can be programmed to block out specific combinations of ratings, but many experts believe relatively few families will use the feature, and astute kids quickly will find ways to circumvent the system. It's vital that you, as a parent, read the instructions for your television and utilize the v-chip properly. This is especially true if you're unable to monitor your children's viewing habits on a regular basis.

As new technologies come into your home, make a point of learning to understand and use them to your family's advantage. Interactive television, for instance, will result in immediate feedback to the companies that produce and sponsor program content. This means you may be able to provide real-time responses to programs you find objectionable. Parents also must make their voices heard by television and computer manufacturers, and demand more user-friendly and effective tools to lock children out of undesirable content.

Plan Alternate Activities

Once you decide to reduce or even eliminate the influences of television in your home, you must be prepared to fill up that extra time with other, more meaningful activities. Talking, playing board games, going for walks, eating meals as a family, or participating in athletic activities together can go a long way toward reestablishing the family's influence in individual family members' lives. Make a list of things your family likes to do together. Each week, ask one member of the family to choose activities from that list.

Also, make outside cultural activities a priority. Doing so helps more mature members of the family recapture the role of cultural narrator. Visit the art or natural history museum, the zoo, or concerts. Most communities offer several low-cost concerts or free admission days. Call ahead to find out, then incorporate these activities into your schedule.

Encourage children to ask questions about homework and let them know you're available to help. Also, keep a stash of books available for all ages to pull out when family members complain of boredom. Make a game of finding interesting plants and insects in your yard to help kids rediscover the world beyond TV. You may be surprised to find out how much time your family has spent watching TV and how many other activities they could have been participating in if you had simply turned off the tube.

Seek Other Sources of Information

Are newspapers piling up in your garage unread? Is the bookshelf a bit dusty with disuse? If you're like many families, television has become your main or even sole conduit for information. By relying on television alone, families invite TV to take over several key family roles. Remember that television doesn't have all the answers and may not even care about the same questions you do.

By searching out a wide variety of information sources, you can help your family make better decisions on nearly all aspects of their lives, from career aspirations and political decisions to moral values and spiritual beliefs.

During political campaigns, for example, spend more time reading about and less time watching the candidates. Remember that most candidate images you see on TV are produced and directed by teams of media experts who know how to manipulate viewer's perceptions. Make a point of researching candidates' credentials beyond those presented by television. Look for specific voting patterns, and be sure to go back far enough that you can get a sense of who the candidates were and what they stood for before "media handlers" and image consultants got hold of them. Often, written materials will delve significantly deeper into a candidate's background than most television programs.

It's also important to talk to your kids about political choices. A 1998 survey found more than 26 percent of college freshmen had little or no interest in the political system.[433] This lack of involvement results in an increased concentration of authority in a smaller pool of politicians—men and women who may seek such power not for the common good, but for personal gain.

If you hold specific religious beliefs, consider joining a church or synagogue, and make participation a priority. It's important that you understand the full doctrine of your chosen faith and explain your beliefs to your children. Also, look for ways you can incorporate the values of your faith into everyday activities. If your family watches programs that depict God, make sure they understand it's fiction and may conflict with your personal beliefs. In addition, such programs may reflect the religious views of the writers and producers, or may simply be designed as a tool to pluck at your heartstrings.

Write Letters

Television is a commercial activity. It's designed to make money. If network executives and advertisers discover the programs they offer cause viewers to turn off the TV or otherwise jeopardize their ability to make money, they'll sit up and take notice.

During the 1997 Super Bowl, for example, Holiday Inn debuted a new commercial touting its $1 billion makeover. The advertisement depicted a former male student showing up at his class reunion following a sex change. This "personal overhaul" was used as a metaphor for the hotel chain's makeover. Many viewers took offense and let the advertiser know. Despite investing millions of dollars in production costs and air time during the industry's premier advertising event, Holiday Inn pulled the ad within forty-eight hours.[434] The viewers spoke; the advertiser listened.

What's ironic about television's penchant for sex and violence is that study after study by respected sources indicate TV executives could expect substantial profit growth if they catered to more family-oriented values. Top-rated shows such as *Touched By an Angel*, *Promised Land*, and *7th Heaven* bear this contention out.

If you find a particular program or episode offensive, write a letter to the network (see the "Resources and Key Addresses" section), your local station, or, better yet, advertisers. Also write to the Federal Communications Commission, your congressional representatives and local newspapers. Note that the offending program "fails to service the public interest." It's a phrase that makes TV executives' blood run cold, since that's their mandate as defined by the government. If a station frequently airs offensive programming, write the FCC recommending that the station's license not be renewed.

Become an Activist

Viewers must be willing to tell the entertainment industry that enough is enough, that as a society we crave some limitations, and that open-mindedness is not a viable solution to every problem. TV executives must understand what most viewers already know: that a solid social structure and parameters are necessary for the well-being of humankind; that even though viewers may enjoy sex or derive some excitement from violence, they're willing to forego these pleasures on television to maintain the social structure.

Although some television programs are targeted at adult audiences, television is easily accessible to a wide range of viewers. Therefore, the entertainment community has a responsibility to create programs that do no harm to young viewers. "Children are the most sensitive and vulnerable component of the family, so it is their interests that are typically considered, rather than families as a whole, in the formulation of broadcast policy," explains Bryant Jennings in his book, *Television and the American Family*.[435]

Viewers must possess a sense of passion for their beliefs. The television industry may insinuate that such passion constitutes a "radical right" bent, yet the entertainment community holds equally passionate views on its self-proclaimed "right" to air whatever it deems appropriate. "We are in the midst of a cultural war," says Michael Hudson, executive vice president of the Hollywood-funded lobbying group People for the American Way. "The extremist right-wing political movement no longer has the evil of communism to fight, so they look to other fields including putting on economic pressure to boycott television programming."[436]

The entertainment industry can no longer dismiss those who call for responsibility in the media as right-wing fanatics, however. Viewers of all political persuasions are beginning to sense that something is amiss in their family life. The truth is, the call for media responsibility has risen up from nearly every quarter of mainstream society, Democrat and Republican, liberal and conservative. Calling for responsibility in the media isn't an attack on the First Amendment. It is simply a request by consumers that manufacturers create products that meet the needs of its customers. Because television program purchases occur in our homes rather than in a store, it may appear that TV is different than most businesses. It isn't. Make no mistake, you and I pay for the product known as television each time we purchase something from a company that advertises on TV. Those purchases gives viewers the right to demand products that meet their needs and are safe to use.

The first step toward becoming an activist is to get involved. Join your local Parent-Teacher Association. Media expert Neil Postman argues that in one form or another and no matter how diluted the effort, the school will stand as the last defense against the disappearance of childhood wrought by television.[437]

Your local PTA is a direct funnel to an even more powerful organization: the National PTA (see the "Resources and Key Addresses" section). When the television rating system was first introduced by the TV industry in 1996, is was purely age-based, much like the movie rating system. The

National PTA was among the first organization to go head-to-head with television executives. Teaming up with other organizations such as the American Academy of Child & Adolescent Psychiatry, the National PTA demanded and eventually won additional rating designations such as "V" for violence or "S" for sexual situations—designations that help parents make better-informed decisions about their children's viewing habits.

Parents who are both educated on the entertainment industry and involved in their school systems and communities can send a strong signal to advertisers. By organizing and participating in sponsor boycotts, refusing to watch specific programs, and making a conscious effort to direct their time and dollars toward other media that promote the values they seek, parents have the power to turn the tide.

"One of the important instruments for gaining the attention of the entertainment establishment is the threat of sponsor boycotts," advises media critic Michael Medved. "Nowhere in the Constitution is it written that TV viewers must sit quietly on their couches and passively accept whatever the industry chooses to place on the air. The right to protest degrading material is not limited to those favored few who are asked to report their viewing on a Nielson box."[438]

The Parents Television Council, part of the Media Research Center, asked sponsors in 1999 to become active participants in the programming process by looking more closely at the shows they sponsor. "The heads of these companies are fine people," noted comedian Steve Allen, honorary chairman of the council. "Many are parents and grandparents. The trouble is they have been letting their ad agencies and others decide which programs to sponsor and they are unaware of the harm they are doing. We can really get them to stop sponsoring the TV that is so harmful to our children and our country. All it takes is for enough of us to make our voices heard."[439]

As organizations that depend on the goodwill of their customers, and as consumers themselves, sponsors are beginning to respond to the groundswell of opinion regarding the current state of television. In 1999, companies such as Procter & Gamble, General Motors, IBM, Johnson & Johnson, AT&T, Pfizer, and Wendy's International banned together to pay Hollywood to write cleaner shows. The group of sponsors is footing the bill to develop up to eight "family-friendly" pilot scripts designed to air on Time Warner's WB network.[440]

Such efforts don't have to raise the specter of censorship or manipulation by commercial forces. "We're not going to be involved in the content," says Robert Wehling, global marketing officer for Proctor & Gamble. "We're asking that in general the shows be ones that it would be reasonable to assume a multigenerational household unit could get together and watch without embarrassment." The alliance is the result of a meeting of nearly thirty of the country's largest advertisers to explore ways to induce networks to air prime-time shows with less sex and violence.[441]

Parents must also demand a higher quality of children's programming. They must force networks to devote the same level of resources used to create successful commercial programming and advertisements to children's programs that present truly positive messages.

The television industry generally views children's educational programming as unproductive money pits, but shows such as *Sesame Street* and more recent additions such as *Wishbone*, which depicts a literature-loving dog, prove this assumption wrong. Both programs appear on PBS but have earned significant corporate sponsorship not only because many companies wish to show their community-mindedness, but also because they want to be associated with popular quality programming.

Finally, television must own up to its own foibles and be willing to help viewers understand how to use TV in positive ways. The 1990s saw consumers and the government force tobacco companies to reveal internal studies on the effects of their products. A similar revelation and accompanying warnings must also occur in the television industry. TV executives spend millions of dollars researching television's ability to persuade consumers to buy products. Since this research is probably the most well-funded of all investigations into television's power, it can and should be used to analyze how TV affects viewers in other ways.

Many networks now feature public service spots on responsible viewing. If properly produced, they can help persuade viewers to develop more positive viewing habits. A similar campaign targeting drug use demonstrated that public service advertising can be effective. In a study published in the American Journal of Diseases of Children polling nearly one thousand students ages eleven to nineteen, more than 80 percent recalled exposure to anti-drug ads. In addition, half the students who had tried drugs reported that the ads convinced them to decrease or stop using drugs.[442]

Children can be quite astute, however. If an actor with a reputation for playing violent or highly sexualized characters appears on a public service announcement warning about the dangers of violence or irresponsible sex, children will quickly pick up on the contradiction.

Viewers also can make a difference on a community level. Encourage local schools to invite guest speakers on topics that may not be properly addressed by TV. Direct exposure to teen mothers, smokers dying of cancer, or recovering alcoholics can help kids understand the real-life consequences of behaviors depicted on television.

Make Family Life a Priority

The most important tactic in taking back control of family roles has relatively little to do with television. The fact is, many families have almost eagerly handed over much of their responsibilities to TV. It comes from having too much to do. It stems from the fact that many of today's parents and even grandparents were raised on television themselves. These TV generations may have little insight into how healthy families can and should function. Most of all, it comes from making other things besides family higher priorities.

We can condemn the entertainment industry for its irresponsibility, and we may even be right. But as parents, as brothers and sisters, as families and communities, and as a nation, the ultimate responsibility—the responsibility to instill values—remains our own. Humankind has not developed in isolation. To a great extent we become what we surround ourselves with. If we immerse ourselves in television, no matter how positive and uplifting the programming, we will eventually become like TV.

As consumers, we have every right to be incensed by the poor quality of television programming. But as individuals we should be upset at ourselves for surrounding our families with TV, for succumbing to its powers. We don't let physicians and pharmacists off the hook if they become addicted to drugs simply because they have easy access to these substances. We expect them to exercise self-control. So, too, must we exercise self-control with television. We cannot excuse our addiction to TV simply because we have easy access to the medium.

Television is what it is—a marketing tool. Although it's true that television can be improved, no matter how good TV gets, it's still TV. Certainly the television industry must be held accountable. But we as parents, as spouses, and as individuals, also must be held accountable for our well-being. That means we must be willing to turn off the TV, to turn back to our families, and to spend time with them engaged in activities beyond watching television.

We can impose rules about TV. But in the absence of loving relationships, rules aren't worth much. Almost anyone, young or old, can figure out how to break them.

Our task, then, is to create a loving family environment where healthy roles thrive—an environment of trust with clearly defined expectations for all members. This means we must recognize the value and purpose of each role we perform. It means standing up as parents and spouses to shoulder the mantle of responsibility as the family managers. It means identifying members of the household who may have an interest in the arts or social sciences, and recognizing and encouraging their roles as cultural narrators. It means creating gender models that do not rely on stereotypes and outdated thinking. It means defining for ourselves what it means to be a spouse and understanding the questions our children may have about their own sexuality. It means identifying heroic members of our families and communities. It means learning to compromise and arbitrate disputes in a dignified and fair manner. And, it means creating friendships among family members and outside the home.

Little exercises can go a long way toward achieving this goal. Encourage your children in the arts. Spend an evening as a family identifying heroic qualities in other family members. Make a list of why you love your spouse—even little things count. Then communicate these traits before or during an intimate moment so that emotion, rather than appearance, becomes the primary stimulus.

Discuss conflicts thoroughly. Even more important, listen. Part of developing strong arbitration skills among family members is the ability to understand not only your own position, but others' as well.

Most importantly, leave the door open. Be willing to talk—with your kids, with your spouse—about anything that concerns them. That's the essence of friendship. That doesn't mean accepting every behavior. Boundaries are important. But it does mean you must be willing to discuss topics openly and honestly without letting emotion cloud good judgment.

We have the ability to reclaim control of our lives from television. But it requires dedication and it takes commitment to change, even if it means giving up some things that may be pleasurable but are also destructive. By putting our family's well-being before our own immediate gratification, we can change not only the course of our family's lives, but also impact the future of our society as a whole.

The family remains the foundation of society and humankind. It is too vital to simply hand over that responsibility to an inanimate box. Make your family the center of your household, rather than the TV. It will take some work, but the rewards will be a stronger marriage, children who contribute to society rather than destroy it, and a community that embraces the family as its centerpiece.

Resources & Key Addresses

ABC, 77 West 66th Street, New York, NY 10023, (212) 456-7777, www.abc.com

Accuracy in Media, Inc., 4455 Connecticut Avenue NW, #330, Washington, DC 20008, (202) 364-4401, (202) 364-4098 (fax), www.aim.org

Adbusters, 1243 W. Seventh Ave., Vancouver, British Columbia V6H 1B7, Canada, (604) 736-9401, (800) 663-1243, www.adbusters.org

Alliance for Children and Television, 1002, 60 St. Clair Avenue East, Suite 1002, Toronto, Ontario M4T 1N5, Canada, (416) 515-0466, (416) 515-0467 (fax), www.act-canada.com

American Center for Children's Television, Central Educational Network, 1400 East Touhy Avenue, Suite 260, Des Plaines, IL 60018-3305, (847) 390-8700, (847) 390-9435 (fax)

American Family Association, Inc. PO Drawer 2440, Tupelo, MS 38803, (662) 844-5036, (662) 842-7798 (fax), www.afa.net

Asian American Journalists Association, 1182 Market Street, Suite 320, San Francisco, CA 94102, (415) 346-2051, (415) 346-6343 (fax), aaja1@aol.com (e-mail)

Association for Media Literacy, 2204-1 Aberfoyle, Etobicoke, MXB 2X8, Canada, (416) 696-7144, ami@interlog.com (e-mail)

CBS, 51 W. 57th Street, New York, NY 10019, (212) 975-4321, www.cbs.com

The Center for Educational Priorities, 72025 Hill Road, Covelo, CA 95428, (707) 983-8374, www.cep.org

Center for Media Education, *2120 L Street. NW, Suite 200, Washington, DC 20037, (202) 331-7833, www.cme.org*

Center for Media Literacy, 4727 Wilshire Blvd., Suite 403, Los Angeles, CA 90010, (323) 931-4177, (800) 226-9494, (323) 931-4474 (fax), www.medialit.org

Children Now/Kaiser Family Foundation, 2400 Sand Hill Rd., Menlo Park, CA 94025, (800) 656-4533, (650) 854-9400, (650) 854-4800 (fax), www.kff.org

Christian Action Network, P.O. Box 606, Forest, VA 24551, (800) 835-5795, (804) 525-0191, (804) 525-0243 (fax), www.christianaction.org

The Christian Coalition, 1501-L Sara Drive, Chesapeake, VA 23320, (757) 424-2630, (757) 424-9068 (fax), www.cc.org

Christian Voice, 208 N. Patrick Street, Alexandria, VA 22314, (703) 548-1421, (703) 548-1424 (fax), jmconsult2@aol.com (e-mail)

Citizens for Media Literacy, Wally Bowen, 34 Wall Street, Suite 407, Ashville, NC 28801, cml@main.nc.us (e-mail)

Columbia Journalism Review, Journalism Building, 2950 Broadway, Columbia University, New York, NY 10027, (212) 854-3958, www.cjr.org

Communications Consortium, 1333 H Street NW, Suite 700, Washington, DC 20005, (202) 682-1270 (fax)

Creating Critical Viewers, Great Plains National Library, University of Nebraska, P.O. Box 80669, Lincoln, NE 68501, (800) 228-4630, (800) 306-2330 (fax), gpn@unl.edu (e-mail), www.gpn.unl.edu

Developing Capable People, Capabilities Inc., P.O. Box 1926, Oren, UT 84059, (800) 222-1494, www.capabilitiesinc.com

FAIR (Fairness & Accuracy in Reporting), 130 W. 25th Street, New York, NY 10001, (212) 633-6700, (212) 727-7668 (fax), fair@fair.org (e-mail) www.fair.org

Family Support America, 20 N. Wacker Dr., Suite 1100, Chicago, IL 60606, (312) 338-0900, www.frca.org

Federal Communications Commission, Complaints and Investigations, 445 12th Street SW, Washington DC 20554, (888) 835-5322, www.fcc.gov

Federal Trade Commission, 600 Pennsylvania Ave. NW, Washington, DC 20580, (202) 326-2180, (202) 326-3366, www.ftc.gov

Fox Television, Fox Entertainment Co., P.O. Box 900, Beverly Hills, CA 90213, (877) 983-2645, www.fox.com

Institute for Media Analysis, 145 W 4th Street, New York, NY 10012, (212) 254-1061.

KIDSNET, 6856 Eastern Avenue NW, Suite 208, Washington, DC 20012, (202) 291-1400, (202) 882-7315 (fax), www.kidsnet.org

Media Education Foundation, 26 Center Street, Northampton, MA 01060, (413) 586-4170, (800) 897-0089, (413) 586-8398 (fax), (800) 659-6882 (fax), www.mediaed.org

Media Network, 2565 Broadway, Suite 101, New York, NY 10025, (212) 501-3841

Media Research Center, 325 Patrick Street, Alexandria, VA 22314, (703) 683-9733, (703) 683-9736 (fax), www.mediaresearch.org

Media Studies Center, Daughters of St. Paul, 50 St. Paul's Avenue, Boston, MA 02130-3491, (617) 522-8911, (617) 522-4811 (fax), www.pauline.org

Media Watch, P.O. Box 618, Santa Cruz, CA 95061-0618, (831)423-6355, (800) 631-6355, www.mediawatch.com

Media Watch, 517 Wellington St. West, Suite 204, Toronto, Ontario, Canada M5V 1G1, (416) 408-2065, (416) 408-2069 (fax), www.mediawatch.ca

MTV, 1515 Broadway, New York, NY 10036, (212) 258-8000, www.mtv.com

The Advertising Council, 261 Madison Ave., New York, NY 10016, (212) 984-1939, (212) 922-1676 (fax), www.adcouncil.org

National Advertising Review Board, 845 Third Ave., New York, NY 10022

National Alliance for Media Arts and Culture (NAMAC), 346 Ninth Street, San Francisco, CA 94103, (415) 431-1391, (415) 431-1392 (fax), www.namac.org

National Asian American Telecommunications Association, 346 Ninth St., 2nd Floor, San Francisco, CA 94103, (415) 863-0814, (415) 863-7428 (fax), www.naatanet.org

National Association of Broadcasters, 1771 N Street NW, Washington, DC 20036, (202) 429-5300, (202) 775-3520 (fax), www.nab.org.

National Black Media Coalition, 1738 Elton Road, Suite 314, Silver Spring, MD 20903, (301) 445-2600, (301) 445-1693 (fax)

National Cable Television Association, 1724 Massachusetts Avenue NW, Washington, DC 20036, (202) 775-3669, www.ncta.com

National Commission on Working Women, 815 15th Street NW, Washington, DC 20090, (202) 638-3143

National Education Association, 1201 16th Street NW, Washington, DC 20036, (202) 833-4000, www.nea.org

The National Institute on Media and the Family, 606 24th Avenue S., Suite 606, Minneapolis, MN 55454, (888) 672-5437, (612) 672-4113 (fax), www.mediaandthefamily.org

National Parenting Association, 51 West 74th Street, Suite 1B, New

York, NY 10023-2495, (212) 362-7575, (212) 362–1916 (fax), www.parentsunite.org

National PTA Headquarters, 330 N. Wabash Avenue, Suite 2100, Chicago, IL 60611, (312) 670-6782, info@pta.org (e-mail), www.pta.org

National Telemedia Council, 120 E. Wilson Street, Madison, WI 53703, (608) 257-7712, (608) 257-7714 (fax), ntelemedia@aol.com (e-mail)

NBC, 30 Rockefeller Plaza, New York, NY 10112, (212) 664-4444, www.nbc.com

PBS, 1320 Braddock Place, Alexandria, VA 22314, (703) 739-5000 , www.pbs.org

The President of the United States, The White House, Washington, DC 20500, (202) 456-1414, (202) 456-2461 (fax)

Radio-Television News Directors Association, 1000 Connecticut Avenue NW #615, Washington, DC 20036, (202) 659-6510, (202) 223-4007 (fax), www.rtnda.org

Sojourners, 2401 15th Street NW, Washington, DC 20009, (202) 328-8842, (800) 714-7474 (202) 328.8757 (fax), www.sojourners.com

U.S. House of Representatives, Washington, DC 20515, (202) 225-3121

U.S. Senate, Washington, DC 20510, (202) 224-3121

UPN, 11800 Wilshire Blvd., Los Angeles, CA 90025, (310) 575-7000, www.upn.com

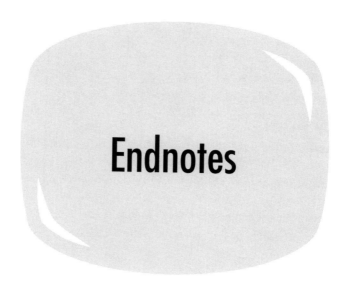

Endnotes

Electronic Family

1. G. J. Ellis, "Television and the Family," *Journal of Family Issues* 4, no. 2 (June 1983): 276.

2. N. Postman, *The Disappearance of Childhood* (New York: Delacorte Press, 1982).

3. J. Meyrowitz, *No Sense of Place* (New York: Oxford University Press, 1985): 241.

4. G. J. Ellis, "Television and the Family," *Journal of Family Issues* 4, no. 2 (June 1983): 276.

5. G. J. Ellis, S. K. Streeter, and J. D. Engelbricht, "Television Characters as Significant Others and the Process of Vicarious Role Taking," *Journal of Family Issues* 4, no. 2 (June 1983): 367-384.

6. N. N. Minow, and C.L. LaMay, *Abandoned in the Wasteland: Children, Television, and the First Amendment* (New York: Hill and Wang, 1995): 82.

7. J. Bryant, *Television and the American Family* (New Jersey: Hillsdale, 1990): 22-24.

8. E. Medrick, "Constant Television: A Background to Family Life," *Journal of Communication* 29, no. 2 (1979).

9. E. Palmer, T. Smith, and K. Strawser. "Rubik's Tube—Developing a Child's Television Worldview." In *Children and TV*, eds. Gordon Berry and Joy Keiko Asamen (Newbury Park, Calif., Sage Publications, 1993).

A Brief History of the Media

10. N. Postman, *The Disappearance of Childhood* (New York: Delacorte Press, 1982): 28.

11. N. Postman, *Teaching as a Conserving Activity* (New York: Dell Publishing, 1979): 74.

12. N. Postman, *Technopoly: The Surrender of Culture to Technology* (New York: Vintage Books, 1992): 124.

13. N. Postman, *Technopoly: The Surrender of Culture to Technology* (New York: Vintage Books, 1992): 124.

14. N. Postman, *Technopoly: The Surrender of Culture to Technology* (New York: Vintage Books, 1992): 15.

15. N. Postman, Class Lecture, New York University, 1994.

16. N. Postman, *Teaching as a Conserving Activity* (New York: Dell Publishing, 1979): 74.

17. N. Postman, *Conscientious Objections: Sturring Up Trouble About Language, Technology, and Education* (New York: Alfred A. Knopf, 1988): 160-161.

18. N. Postman, *Teaching as a Conserving Activity* (New York: Dell Publishing, 1979): 39.

19. E. L. Eisenstein, *The Printing Press as an Agent of Change* (New York: Cambridge University Press, 1979): 429.

20. E. L. Eisenstein, *The Printing Press as an Agent of Change* (New York: Cambridge University Press, 1979): 429.

21. P. Ariés, *Centuries of Childhood: A Social History of Family Life* (New York: Vintage Books, 1962): 403.

22. P. Ariés, *Centuries of Childhood: A Social History of Family Life* (New York: Vintage Books, 1962): 405.

23. N. Postman, *Technopoly: The Surrender of Culture to Technology* (New York: Vintage Books, 1992): 76.

24. E. L. Eisenstein, *The Printing Press as an Agent of Change* (New York: Cambridge University Press, 1979): 424.

25. E. L. Eisenstein, *The Printing Press as an Agent of Change* (New York: Cambridge University Press, 1979): 415.

26. N. Postman, *Teaching as a Conserving Activity* (New York: Dell Publishing, 1979): 74.

27. M. Winn, *The Plug-in Drug: Children and the Family* (New York: Viking Press, 1977): 12.

28. J. Meyrowitz, *No Sense of Place* (New York: Oxford University Press, 1985): 151.

29. J. Meyrowitz, *No Sense of Place* (New York: Oxford University Press, 1985): 237.

Ozzie and Harriet vs. The Simpsons

30. G. H. Mead, *Mind, Self and Society* (Chicago: University of Chicago Press, 1934).

Endnotes

31. U. Bronfenbrenner, and M. Mahoney (eds.), *The Origins of Alienation: Influences on Human Development* (Hinsdale, IL: Dryden, 1975).

32. E. Shorter, *The Making of the Modern Family* (New York: Basic Books, 1977).

33. C. Nystrom, Class Lecture, New York University, 1999.

34. E. Medrick, and N. Waxler, *Interaction in Families* (New York: John Wiley, 1968).

35. E. Medrick, "Constant Television: A Background to Family Life," *Journal of Communication* 29, n2 (1979): 171-176.

36. E. Taylor, "From the Nelsons to the Huxtables: Genre and Family Imagery in American Network Television," *Qualitative Sociology* 12, n1 (Spring 1989): 13-27.

37. E. Taylor, "From the Nelsons to the Huxtables: Genre and Family Imagery in American Network Television," *Qualitative Sociology* 12, n1 (Spring 1989): 13-27.

38. T. Skill, and J.D. Robinson, "Four Decades of Families on Television: A Demographic Profile, 1950–1989," *Journal of Broadcasting and Electronic Media* (Fall 1994): 449-464.

39. T. Skill, and J.D. Robinson, "Four Decades of Families on Television: A Demographic Profile, 1950–1989," *Journal of Broadcasting and Electronic Media* (Fall 1994): 449-464.

40. T. Skill, and J.D. Robinson, "Four Decades of Families on Television: A Demographic Profile, 1950–1989," *Journal of Broadcasting and Electronic Media* (Fall 1994): 449-464.

41. D. Quayle, Speech to the Commonwealth Club of San Francisco, May 19, 1992.

42. R. DeWolf, "Group: Women and Work/Family Issues Shorted on TV." *The Denver Post*, June 28, 1998: 8J.

43. Writers Guild of America, West, Inc., v. Federal Communications Commission, et al., U.S. District Court for the Central District of California, Nov. 4, 1976.

44. T. Mauro, "National Trending Toward Do-it-yourself Censorship," The Freedom Forum First Amendment Center, 1997.

45. J. Meyrowitz, *No Sense of Place* (New York: Oxford University Press, 1985): 153.

46. M. Mead, *Culture and Commitment: A Study of the Generation Gap* (Garden City, N.Y.: Doubleday & Co., 1970).

47. M. Mead, *Culture and Commitment: A Study of the Generation Gap* (Garden City, N.Y.: Doubleday & Co., 1970).

48. M. Mead, *Culture and Commitment: A Study of the Generation Gap* (Garden City, N.Y.: Doubleday & Co., 1970).

49. W. Douglas, "The Fall From Grace? The Modern Family on Television," *Communication Research* 23, n6 (December 1996): 675-702.

50. J. Comstock, and K. Strzyewski, "Interpersonal Interactions on Television: Family Conflict and Jealousy on Primetime," *Journal of Broadcasting & Electronic Media* 34, n3 (Summer 1990): 263:282.

51. W. Douglas, and B. Olson, "Subversion of the American Family? An Examination of Children and Parents in Television Families," *Communication Research* 23, n1 (February 1996): 73-99.

52. S. R. Lichter, L. S. Lichter, and S. Rothman, *Prime Time* (Washington: Regnery Publishing, Inc., 1994): 87.

53. M. Morgan, S. Leggett, and J. Shanahan, "Television and Family Values: Was Dan Quayle Right?" *Mass Communication & Society* 2 (Winter/Spring 1999): 47-63.

54. M. Medved, *Hollywood vs. America* (New York: HarperPerennial, 1993): 96.

55. W. Douglas, and Olson, B, "Subversion of the American Family? An Examination of Children and Parents in Television Families," *Communication Research* 23, n1 (February 1996): 73-99.

56. E. Medrick,"Constant Television: A Background to Family Life," *Journal of Communication* 29, n2 (1979): 171-176.

57. K. Heintz-Knowles, "Balancing Acts: Work/Family Issues on Prime-Time TV," National Partnership for Women & Families, 1998.

58. W. Douglas, "The Fall from Grace? The Modern Family on Television," *Communication Research* 23, n6 (December 1996): 675-702.

59. W. Douglas, "The Fall from Grace? The Modern Family on Television." *Communication Research* 23, n6 (December 1996): 675-702.

Family Manager

60. B. Cutler, "Where Does the Free Time Go?" *American Demographics* (Nov. 1990): 36-39.

61. J. P. Robinson, "I Love My TV," *American Demographics* (Sept. 1990): 24-27.

62. F. C. Lawrence, G. E. Tasker, C. T. Daly, A. L. Orhiel, and P. H. Wozniak, "Adolescents' Time Spent Viewing Television," *Adolescence* 21, n82 (Summer 1986).

63. A. C. Huston, C. Wright, J. Marquis, and S. B. Green, "How Young Children Spend their Time: Television and Other Activities," *Developmental Psychology* 35, n4 (July 1999): 912(1).

64. A. C. Huston, C. Wright, J. Marquis, and S. B. Green, "How Young Children Spend their Time: Television and Other Activities," *Developmental Psychology* 35, n4 (July 1999): 912(1).

65. C. M. Koolstra, and T. H. Van Der Voort, "Longitudinal Effects of Television on Children's Leisure-time Reading: A Test of Three Explanatory Models," *Human Communication Research* 23, n1 (Sept. 1996): 4(32).

66. K. Zinsmeister, "TV-free: Real Families Describe Life Without the Tube," *The American Enterprise* 8, n5 (Sept.-Oct. 1997): 63(9).

67. K. Zinsmeister, "TV-free: Real Families Describe Life Without the Tube," *The American Enterprise* 8, n5 (Sept.-Oct. 1997): 63(9).

Endnotes

68. B. Cutler, "Where Does the Free Time Go?" *American Demographics* (Nov. 1990): 36-39.

69. J. P. Robinson, "I Love My TV," *American Demographics* (Sept. 1990): 24-27.

70. A. C. Huston, C. Wright, J. Marquis, and S. B. Green, "How Young Children Spend their Time: Television and Other Activities," *Developmental Psychology* 35, n4 (July 1999): 912(1).

71. G. B. Armstrong, and B. S. Greenberg, "Background Television as an Inhibitor of Cognitive Processing," *Human Communication Research* 16, n3 (Spring 1990): 355-385.

72. P. S. Jensen, D. Mrazek, P. K. Knapp, L. Steinberg, C. Pfeffer, J. Schowalter, and T. Shapiro, "Evolution and Revolution in Child Psychiatry: ADHD as a Disorder of Adaptation." *Journal of the American Academy of Child and Adolescent Psychiatry* 36, n12: (December, 1997): 1672-1679.

73. K. Moody, *Growing Up on Television: The TV Effect* (New York: Times Books, 1980): 53.

74. K. Moody, *Growing Up on Television: The TV Effect* (New York: Times Books, 1980): 53.

75. K. Moody, *Growing Up on Television: The TV Effect* (New York: Times Books, 1980): 67.

76. K. Moody, *Growing Up on Television: The TV Effect* (New York: Times Books, 1980): 5.

77. J. Ostrow, "It's 'Teletubbies' Time," *The Denver Post*, January 18, 1998: 1H, 12H.

78. "Television and the Preparation of the Mind for Learning: Critical Questions on the Effects of TV on the Developing Brains of Young Children," Conference sponsored by the Division of Children and Families of the U.S. Department of Health and Human Services, Oct. 2, 1996, Washington, D.C.

79. "Television and the Preparation of the Mind for Learning: Critical Questions on the Effects of TV on the Developing Brains of Young Children," Conference sponsored by the Division of Children and Families of the U.S. Department of Health and Human Services, Oct. 2, 1996, Washington, D.C.

80. "Television and the Preparation of the Mind for Learning: Critical Questions on the Effects of TV on the Developing Brains of Young Children," Conference sponsored by the Division of Children and Families of the U.S. Department of Health and Human Services, Oct. 2, 1996, Washington, D.C.

81. J. P. Robinson, "I Love My TV," *American Demographics* (Sept. 1990): 24-27.

82. J. Brown, K. Childers, K. Bauman, and G. Koch, "The Influence of New Media and Family Structure on Young Adolescents' Television and Radio Use," *Communication Research* 17, n1 (Feb. 1990): 65-82.

83. M. Winn, *The Plug-in Drug: Children and the Family* (New York: Viking Press, 1977): 24.

84. L. Wright, "Television and American Parents," *The World & I* (May 1990): 573.

85. R. W. Kubey, "Television Use in Everyday Life: Coping with Unstructured Time," *Journal of Communication* (Summer 1986): 109-123.

86. R. W. Kubey, "Television and the Quality of Family Life," *Communication Quarterly* 38, n4 (Fall 1990): 312-324.

87. R. W. Kubey, "Television Use in Everyday Life: Coping with Unstructured Time," *Journal of Communication* (Summer 1986): 120.

88. P. Wilson, and E. S. Christopher, "The Home-Television Environment: Implications for Families," *Journal of Home Economics* (Winter, 1992): 29.

89. U. Bronfenbrenner, *The Ecology of Human Development: Experiments of Nature and Design* (Cambridge, MA: Harvard University Press, 1979): 242.

90. J. Walters, and V. Stone, "Television and Family Communication," *Journal of Broadcasting* 15, n4 (Fall 1971): 409-414.

91. E. Maccoby, "Television: Its Impact on School Children," *Public Opinion Quarterly* 15 (Fall 1951): 421-444.

92. R. W. Kubey, "Television and the Quality of Family Life," *Communication Quarterly* 38, n4 (Fall 1990): 312.

93. G. Brody, Z. Stoneman, and A. Sanders, "Effects of Television Viewing on Family Interactions: An Observational Study," *Family Relations* (April 1980): 216-220.

94. A. Dickinson, "Must-See TV? Too Much Media—Television Especially—Can be an Isolating Experience. Get It Under Control," *Time* 154, i22 (Nov. 29, 1999): 114.

95. M. St. Peters, M. Fitch, A. Huston, J.C. Wright, and D. Eskins, "Television and Families: What Do Young Children Watch with Their Parents?" *Child Development* 62, n6 (Dec. 1, 1999): 1409-1423.

96. P. Albinlak, "Beat it Kid, I'm Watching TV," *Broadcasting & Cable* 128, n30 (July 20, 1998): 19.

97. J. Lull, "The Social Uses of Television," In *Inter/Media—Interpersonal Communication in a Media World*, eds. G. Gumpert and R. Cathcart (New York: Oxford University Press, 1982): 566-579.

98. F. A. J. Ianni, "Home, School and Community in Adolescent Education," *Clearinghouses on Urban Education* (1983): 84.

99. E. Katz, and D. Faulkes, "On the Use of Mass Media as 'Escape,'" *Public Opinion Quarterly* 4 (1962): 377-388.

100. Kaiser Family Foundation, New National Surveys of Parents and Children on TV Rating System, Press Release (May 27, 1998).

101. P. C. Rosenblatt, and M. R. Cunningham, "Television Watching and Family Tensions," *Journal of Marriage and Family* 38, i2 (1976): 105-111.

102. I. F. Goodman, "Television's Role in Family Interaction: A Family Systems Perspective," *Journal of Family Issues* 4, i2 (June 1983): 416.

Endnotes

103. I. F. Goodman, "Television's Role in Family Interaction: A Family Systems Perspective," *Journal of Family Issues* 4, i2 (June 1983): 415.

104. M. Bowen, *Family Theory in Clinical Practice* (New York: Jason Aronson, 1985).

105. J. Stossel, P. Fleming, and R. Schlenker, "TV Sports Junkies." *20/20* (New York: ABC News, Nov. 8, 1996).

106. J. Stossel, P. Fleming, and R. Schlenker, "TV Sports Junkies." *20/20* (New York: ABC News, Nov. 8, 1996).

107. W. Pollack, *Real Boys* (New York: Henry Holt and Company, 1998): 276.

108. J. Stossel, P. Fleming, and R. Schlenker, "TV Sports Junkies." *20/20* (New York: ABC News, Nov. 8, 1996).

109. "Boys to Men: Messages About Masculinity. A National Poll of Children, Focus Groups and Content Analysis of Sports Programs and Commercials," *Children Now* (Sept. 1999).

110. "Sports Fans Get Testosterone Rush," *Kaleidoscope Interactive News & Features* (May 19, 1998).

111. J. Stossel, P. Fleming, and R. Schlenker, "TV Sports Junkies." *20/20* (New York: ABC News, Nov. 8, 1996).

112. "Sports Fans Get Testosterone Rush," *Kaleidoscope Interactive News & Features* (May 19, 1998).

113. W. Pollack, *Real Boys* (New York: Henry Holt and Company, 1998).

114. J. Stossel, P. Fleming, and R. Schlenker, "TV Sports Junkies." *20/20* (New York: ABC News, Nov. 8, 1996).

115. P. J. Mohr, "Parental Guidance of Children's Viewing of Evening Television Programs," *Journal of Broadcasting* 23, n2 (1972): 213-218.

116. E. Palmer, T. Smith, and K. Strawser, "Rubik's Tube—Developing a Child's Television Worldview," In Children and TV, eds. Gordon Berry and Joy Keiko Asamen (Newbury Park, Calif.: Sage Publications, 1993).

117. J. Meyrowitz, *No Sense of Place* (New York: Oxford University Press, 1985): 151.

118. "America's Smallest School: The Family," Educational Testing Service, 1992.

119. N. Postman, *The Disappearance of Childhood* (New York: Delacorte Press, 1982).

120. D. Langrehr, "A Critical Reading of Television Commercials." Unpublished manuscript. Florida State University, Department of Education Theory and Practice, 1999.

121. D. Langrehr, "A Critical Reading of Television Commercials." Unpublished manuscript. Florida State University, Department of Education Theory and Practice, 1999.

122. D. Langrehr, "A Critical Reading of Television Commercials." Unpublished manuscript. Florida State University, Department of Education Theory and Practice, 1999.

123. "A Spoonful of Sugar—Television Food Advertising Aimed at Children: An International Comparative Survey," *Consumer International* (1996).

124. "A Spoonful of Sugar—Television Food Advertising Aimed at Children: An International Comparative Survey," *Consumer International* (1996).

125. S. Simons, "Affluenza," PBS (September 15, 1997).

126. A. R. Hazan, H. L. Lipton, and S. A. Glanz, "Popular Films do not Reflect Current Tobacco Use," *American Journal of Public Health* 84: 998-1000.

127. V. C. Strasburger, *Adolescents and the Media: Medical and Psychological Impact* (Thousand Oaks, CA: Sage Publications, Inc. 1995).

128. V. C. Strasburger, *Adolescents and the Media: Medical and Psychological Impact* (Thousand Oaks, CA: Sage Publications, Inc. 1995).

129. V. C. Strasburger, *Adolescents and the Media: Medical and Psychological Impact* (Thousand Oaks, CA: Sage Publications, Inc. 1995).

130. J. W. Grube, and L. Wallack. "Television Beer Advertising and Drinking Knowledge, Beliefs, and Intentions Among School Children," *American Journal of Public Health* 84 (1994): 254-259.

131. J. W. Grube, and L. Wallack. "Television Beer Advertising and Drinking Knowledge, Beliefs, and Intentions Among School Children," *American Journal of Public Health* 84 (1994): 254-259.

132. *The Problem with Kids' TV*, The Center for Educational Priorities (1997).

133. R. DeWolf, "Group: Women and Work/Family Issues Shorted on TV," *The Denver Post*, June 28, 1998: 8J.

134. S. Gilbert, "Study Stresses Family Role: Home May Be as Vital as Peers to Teenagers," *Denver Post*, September 19, 1997: 15A.

135. S. Gilbert, "Study Stresses Family Role: Home May Be as Vital as Peers to Teenagers," *Denver Post*, September 19, 1997: 15A.

Cultural Narrator

136. "The Family Hour: Worse than Ever and Headed for New Lows," Parents Television Council Special Report, August 31, 1999.

137. A. S. Vann, "Kids, Media, and Family Values" *The Education Digest* (March 1996): 23-25.

138. J. Ostrow, "'Action' Risqué but Realistic," *The Denver Post Online*, August 24, 1999.

139. J. Ostrow, "'Action' Risqué but Realistic," *The Denver Post Online*, August 24, 1999.

140. "School Changes Name from 'South Park' After Movie Release," *Associated Press*, August 30, 1999.

141. *The Problem with Kids' TV,* The Center for Educational Priorities (1997).

142. *The Problem with Kids' TV,* The Center for Educational Priorities (1997).

143. J. Stuller, "Uniquely American," *The American Legion Magazine* (September, 1998).

144. G. Gerbner, "Television Violence and the Art of Asking the Wrong Question," *The World & I: A Chronicle of Our Changing Era* (July 1994).

145. G. Gerbner, "Study Guide: Crisis of the Cultural Environment," Media Education Foundation, 1998.

146. "Television Statistics and Sources," TV-Free America (1999).

147. S. Simons, "Affluenza," PBS, September 15, 1997.

148. J. Flint, "Fade to White," *Entertainment Weekly* (April 23, 1999): 8-9.

149. J. Flint, "Fade to White," *Entertainment Weekly* (April 23, 1999): 8-9.

150. L. D. Eron, and L. R. Huesmann, "Television as a Source of Maltreatment of Children," *School Psychology Review* 16, n2 (1987): 195-202.

151. "Bill Cosby Blasts Hollywood's Portrayal of Blacks on Television," *Jet* 95, n19 (April 12, 1999): 12.

152. G. L. Berry, and J. K. Asamen, *Children and Television: Images in a Changing Sociocultural World* (Newbury Park, Calif.: Sage Publications, 1993): 180.

153. S. R. Lichter, and D. R. Amundson, "Don't Blink: Hispanics in Television Entertainment," for the National Council of La Raza, April 1996.

154. "Latinos Talk Back to TV Through a National Survey," *La Prensa San Diego* 22, n39 (October 2, 1998).

155. S. R. Lichter, and D. R. Amundson, "Don't Blink: Hispanics in Television Entertainment," for the National Council of La Raza, April 1996.

156. S. R. Lichter, and D. R. Amundson, "Don't Blink: Hispanics in Television Entertainment," for the National Council of La Raza, April 1996.

157. "Latinos Talk Back to TV Through a National Survey," *La Prensa San Diego* 22, n39 (October 2, 1998).

158. M. Gardner, "Children Say Television Distors its Portrayals of Minorities," *The Christian Science Monitor* (May 14, 1998): 13.

159. E. Palmer, T. Smith, and K. Strawser, "Rubik's Tube—Developing a Child's Television Worldview," in *Children and TV*, eds. Gordon Berry and Joy Keiko Asamen (Newbury Park, Calif., Sage Publications, 1993).

160. E. Palmer, T. Smith, and K. Strawser, "Rubik's Tube—Developing a Child's Television Worldview," in *Children and TV*, eds. Gordon Berry and Joy Keiko Asamen (Newbury Park, Calif., Sage Publications, 1993).

161. L. Goodstein, "Has Television Found Religion? Not Exactly," *The New York Times*, November 30, 1997: 37, 43.

162. L. Goodstein, "Has Television Found Religion? Not Exactly," *The New York Times*, November 30, 1997: 37, 43.

163. "Study of Worldwide Rates of Religiosity, Church Attendance," University of Michigan News and Information Service 17 (December 10, 1997).

164. N. Postman, *The Disappearance of Childhood,* (New York: Delacorte Press, 1982): 126.

Gender Mentor

165. M. M. Lauzen, and D. M. Dozier, "Making a Difference in Prime Time: Women On Screen and Behind the Scenes in the 1995–1996 Television Season," *Journal of Broadcasting & Electronic Media* 43, n1(Winter 1999): 1–19.

166. M. M. Lauzen, and D. M. Dozier, "Making a Difference in Prime Time: Women On Screen and Behind the Scenes in the 1995–1996 Television Season," *Journal of Broadcasting & Electronic Media* 43, n1(Winter 1999): 1–19.

167. S. Steenland, *What's Wrong With This Picture: The Status of Women on Screen and Behind the Camera in Entertainment TV* (Washington, D.C.: National Commission on Working Women on Wider Opportunities for Women, 1990): 63.

168. B. Browne, "Gender Stereotypes in Advertising on Children's Television in the 1990s: A Cross-national Analysis," *Journal of Advertising* 27, n1 (Spring 1998): 83-96.

169. B. Browne, "Gender Stereotypes in Advertising on Children's Television in the 1990s: A Cross-national Analysis," *Journal of Advertising* 27, n1 (Spring 1998): 83-96.

170. E. Goffman, *Gender Advertisements* (Cambridge, MA: Howard University Press, 1979).

171. P. Velknap, and W. M. Leonard II, "A Conceptual Replication and Extension of Erving Goffman's Study of Gender Advertisements," *Sex Roles* 25, n3/4 (1991): 103-188.

172. J. Liebelt, "You've Come a Long Way Baby: Or Have You? An Examination of Hegemony for Women Nonverbal Communication on Television," Unpublished Thesis, University of Northern Colorado, 1999.

173. M. Elasmar, H. Kazumi, and M. Brain, "The Portrayal of Women in U.S. Prime Time Television," *Journal of Broadcasting & Electronic Media* 44, n1 (Winter 1999): 20-34.

174. F. J. Fejes, "Masculinity as Fact," *Past Study on Men and the Media*, Part I: 11.

175. W. Cordellan, "Television and Children: Towards the Millennium." *Communication Research Trends* 10, n3 (1990).

176. S. L. Mayes, and K. B. Valentine, "Sex Roles Stereotyping in Saturday Morning Cartoon Shows," *Journal of Broadcasting* 23, n1 (1979): 41-50.

177. M. Pipher, *Reviving Ophelia* (New York: Ballantine Books, 1994).

178. Uniform Crime Reports, Federal Bureau of Investigation, 1991.

179. D. Grossman, and G. DeGaetano, *Stop Teaching Our Kids to Kill* (New York: Crown Publishers, 1999): 31–32.

180. M. Pipher, *Reviving Ophelia* (New York: Ballantine Books, 1994).

181. M. Pipher, *Reviving Ophelia* (New York: Ballantine Books, 1994).

182. "Television Statistics and Sources," TV-Free America. 1999.

183. N. Postman, C. Nystrom, L. Strate, and C. Weingartner, *Myths, Men & Beer: An Analysis of Beer Commercials on Broadcast Television* (Washington, D.C.: AAA Foundation for Traffic Safety, 1987).

184. N. Postman, C. Nystrom, L. Strate, and C. Weingartner, *Myths, Men & Beer: An Analysis of Beer Commercials on Broadcast Television* (Washington, D.C.: AAA Foundation for Traffic Safety, 1987).

185. C. C. Iijima Hall, and M. J. Crum, "Women and 'Body-isms' in Television Beer Commercials," *Sex Roles* 31, n5/6 (1994): 329-337.

186. C. C. Iijima Hall, and M. J. Crum, "Women and 'Body-isms' in Television Beer Commercials," *Sex Roles* 31, n5/6 (1994): 329-337.

187. M. Pipher, *Reviving Ophelia* (New York: Ballantine Books, 1994).

188. D. Johnson, "Europe Still Hot for U.S. Shows: Although Prime Time Slots are Scarce, Hits Still Find a Home," *Broadcasting & Cable* 127, n2 (Jan. 13, 1997): 92(2).

189. "TV Viewing Top After-school Activity for Children," *Broadcasting* (Jan 11, 1988).

190. M. M. Lauzen, and D. M. Dozier, "Making a Difference in Prime Time: Women On Screen and Behind the Scenes in the 1995–1996 Television Season," *Journal of Broadcasting & Electronic Media* 43, n1 (Winter 1999): 1–19.

191. B. S. Greenberg, and L. Collette, "The Changing Face on TV: A Demographic Analysis of Network Television's New Seasons, 1966–1992," *Journal of Broadcasting & Electronic Media* 41 (Winter 1997): 1-13.

192. M. Elasmar, H. Kazumi, and M. Brain, "The Portrayal of Women in U.S. Prime Time Television," *Journal of Broadcasting & Electronic Media* 44, n1 (Winter 1999): 20-34.

193. G. Gerbner, "A Look at the Characters on Prime time and Daytime Television from 1994–1997," *The 1998 Screen Actors Guild Report: Casting the American Scene Fairness and Diversity in Television: Update and Trends since the 1993 Screen Actors Guild Report Women and Minorities on Television*, 1998.

194. M. M. Lauzen, and D. M. Dozier, "Making a Difference in Prime Time: Women On Screen and Behind the Scenes in the 1995–1996 Television Season," *Journal of Broadcasting & Electronic Media* 43, n1 (Winter 1999): 1–19.

195. N. Signorielli, "Reflections of Girls in the Media: A Content Analysis Across Six Media and a National Survey of Children."Kaiser Family Foundation, *Children NOW* (#1260) (April 1997).

196. S. Douglas, *Where the Girls Are* (New York: Times Books, 1994).

197. S. Fields, "Harriet's Back in Feminist Form," *Insight on the News* 14, n17 (May 11, 1998): 48(1).

198. D. M. Garner, P. E. Garfinkel, D. Schwartz, and M. Thompson, "Cultural Expectations of Thinness in Women," *Psychological Report* 47 (1980): 483-491.

199. L. Kaufman, "Prime Time Nutrition," *Journal of Communications* 30, n3 (1980): 37-46.

200. N. Wolf, *The Beauty Myth* (New York, William Morrow, 1991): 184.

201. N. Wolf, *The Beauty Myth* (New York, William Morrow, 1991).

202. S. Douglas, *Where the Girls Are* (New York: Times Books, 1994).

203. N. Wolf, *The Beauty Myth* (New York, William Morrow, 1991).

204. P. N. Myers, and F. A. Biocca, "The Elastic Body Image: The Effect of Television Advertising and Programming on Body Image Distortions in Young Women," *Journal of Communication* 42, n3 (Summer 1992): 108-133.

205. "Getting the Skinny on TV," *Discover*: 34.

206. U. L. McFarling, "Muscle-Minded Boys Look Up to GI-ant Joes," *The Denver Post*, May 19, 1999: 2A.

207. F. Romeo, "Adolescent Boys and Anorexia Nervosa," *Adolescence* 29, n 115 (Fall 1994).

208. W. Pollack, *Real Boys* (New York: Henry Holt and Company, 1998): 82.

209. D. Eicher, "Evolution of the Television Mom: Attitudes Change, Realistic Families of '90s Disappear," *The Denver Post*, May 9, 1999: G1(2).

210. D. Popenoe, *Life Without Father* (New York: The Free Press, 1996).

211. D. Popenoe, *Life Without Father* (New York: The Free Press, 1996).

212. M. Elias, "Fathers Focus Increased Care on Boys," *USA Today*, June 14, 1999: 6D.

213. N. Signorielli, "Television's Contribution to Sex-Role Socialization," Paper presented to the Seventh Annual Telecommunications Policy Research Conference, Skytop, PA, April 1979.

214. N. Signorielli, and M. Lears, "Children, Television, and Conceptions about Chores: Attitudes and Behaviors," *Sex Roles* 27, n3/4 (1992): 157-170.

215. A. Hochschild, "The Second Shift: Employed Women are Putting In Another Day of Work," *UTNE Reader* 190 (March/April 1990): 66-73.

216. A. Hochschild, "The Second Shift: Employed Women are Putting In Another Day of Work," *UTNE Reader* 190 (March/April 1990): 66-73.

217. B. A .McBride, and G. Mills, "A Comparison of Mother and Father Involvement with their Preschool-age Children," *Early Childhood Research Quarterly* 8 (1993): 457-477.

218. L. Haaf, "Role-Sharing Couples," in *Marriage and Family in a Changing Society,* J.M. Henslin (ed.) (New York: MacMillian): 333-343.

219. W. Pollack, *Real Boys* (New York: Henry Holt and Company, 1998).

220. W. Farrell, *Why Men Are the Way They Are* (New York: Berkley Publishing Group, 1990).

Endnotes

221. D. Popenoe, *Life Without Father* (New York: The Free Press, 1996).

Sexual Advisor

222. G. E. Veith, "Not Suitable for TV," *World* 27, n8 (Feb. 27, 1999).

223. D. Kunkel, K. M. Cope, and E. Biely, "Sexual Message of Television: Comparing Findings from Three Studies," *The Journal of Sex Research* 36, n3 (August 1999): 230-236.

224. V. C. Strasburger, *Adolescents and the Media: Medical and Psychological Impact* (Thousand Oaks, CA: Sage Publications, Inc. 1995): 52.

225. M. Ward, and R. Rivadeneyra, "Contributions of Entertainment Television to Adolescents' Sexual Attitudes and Expectations: The Role of Viewing Amount Versus Viewer Involvement," *The Journal of Sex Research* 36, n3 (August 1999): 237-249.

226. S. R. Lichter, L. S. Lichter, and S. Rothman, *Prime Time* (Washington: Regnery Publishing, Inc., 1994).

227. "Sexuality, Contraception, and the Media" (RE9505), *Pediatrics* 95, n2 (February 1995): 298-300.

228. Kaiser Family Foundation, "So-called 'Family TV Hour' Pretty Racy." Media Report to Women (Winter, 1997): 1-3.

229. S. R. Lichter, L. S. Lichter, and S. Rothman, *Prime Time* (Washington: Regnery Publishing, Inc., 1994): 80.

230. B. S. Sapolsky, and J. O. Tabarlet, "Sex in Prime-time Television: 1979 Versus 1989," *Journal of Broadcasting & Electronic Media* 35, n4 (Fall 1991): 505-516.

231. V. C. Strasburger, *Adolescents and the Media: Medical and Psychological Impact* (Thousand Oaks, CA: Sage Publications, Inc. 1995): 52.

232. M. Medved, *Hollywood vs. America* (New York: HarperPerennial, 1993).

233. L. Harris, *Inside America* (New York: Vintage, 1987): 87-90.

234. S. Jacoby, "Great Sex: What's Age Got to do With It?" *Modern Maturity* (September/October 1999).

235. J. Semenauer, and D. Carroll, *Singles: The New Americans* (New York: Simon and Schuster, 1982): 351.

236. S. R. Lichter, L. S. Lichter, and S. Rothman, *Prime Time* (Washington: Regnery Publishing, Inc., 1994): 87.

237. "Married People Claim They're Faithful," *San Francisco Chronicle*, June 29, 1991: A7.

238. V. C. Strasburger, *Adolescents and the Media: Medical and Psychological Impact* (Thousand Oaks, CA: Sage Publications, Inc. 1995): 49.

239. T. Hine, "Buffy Saves the World, but She's Still a Teen," *The Denver Post*, Nov. 16, 1997: 9I-10I.

240. S. Lamb, Bryn Mawr College, Bryn Mawr, PA. As quoted in the *Denver Post*, Aug. 26, 1995.

241. M. Mead, *Culture and Commitment: A Study of the Generation Gap* (Garden City, N.Y.: Doubleday & Co., 1970).

242. Kaiser Family Foundation, *Sex on TV: Content and Context: A Biennial Report to the Kaiser Family Foundation,* 1999.

243. Kaiser Family Foundation, *Sex on TV: Content and Context: A Biennial Report to the Kaiser Family Foundation,* 1999.

244. R. Rubin, "Pregnancy No Longer Pushes Women to Wed," *USA Today*, Nov. 9, 1999: D1.

245. E. Zwingle, "Women and Population," *National Geographic* (October 1998): 50.

246. Illinois Department of Public Health, 1998.

247. "HIV/AIDS Among Adolescents & Teens." *Why We Should Care: The 1997 World AIDS Day Resource Booklet*, 1997.

248. V. C. Strasburger, *Adolescents and the Media: Medical and Psychological Impact* (Thousand Oaks, CA: Sage Publications, Inc. 1995): 52.

249. B. S. Greenberg, and R. W. Busselle, "Soap Operas and Sexual Activities: A Decade Later," *Journal of Communication* 46, n4 (1996).

250. The *Denver Post,* Sept. 8, 1996.

251. M. B. Dutta, "Taming the Victim: Rape in Soap Opera," *Journal of Popular Film and Television* 27 (Spring 1999): 34(6)

252. S. L. Brinson, "The Use and Opposition of Rape Myths in Prime-time Television Dramas," *Sex Roles* 27, n7/8 (1992).

253. B. S. Greenberg, and R. W. Busselle, "Soap Operas and Sexual Activities: A Decade Later," *Journal of Communication* 46, n4 (1996).

254. M. Larson, "Sex Roles and Soap Operas: What Adolescents Learn About Single Motherhood," *Sex Roles: A Journal of Research* 35, n1-2 (July 1996).

255. M. Larson, "Sex Roles and Soap Operas: What Adolescents Learn About Single Motherhood," *Sex Roles: A Journal of Research* 35, n1-2 (July 1996).

256. National Commission on Working Women, *Women, Work and Family: Working Mothers Overview* (Washington, D.C.: Fall/Winter, 1992).

257. B. Whitehead, "Dan Quayle was Right," *The Atlantic Monthly* (1993): 47(19).

258. R. Kotulak, "Youngsters Lose Way in Maze of Family Instability," *Chicago Tribune*, Dec. 14, 1986: 6-1(3).

259. B. Kantrowitz, "High School Homeroom," *Newsweek* (June 1990): 50-54.

260. A. Lewis, "Helping Young Urban Parents Educate Themselves and Their Children," *ERIC/CUE Digest,* n85 (Dec. 1992).

Endnotes

261. J. L. Peterson, K. A. Moore, and F. F. Furstenberg, Jr., "Television Viewing and Early Initiation of Sexual Intercourse: Is there a Link?" *Journal of Homosexuality* 21 (1991): 93-188.

262. V. C. Strasburger, *Adolescence and the Media: Medical and Psychological Impact* (Thousand Oaks, Calif.: Sage Publications, 1995).

263. V. C. Strasburger, *Adolescence and the Media: Medical and Psychological Impact* (Thousand Oaks, Calif.: Sage Publications, 1995).

264. S. R. Lichter, Lichter, L. S., and D. Amundson, "Merchandising Mayhem: Violence in Popular Cult.

265. R. Rojano, Institute for the Hispanic Family, Hartford, CT. As quoted in the *Dever Post*, Aug. 26, 1995.

266. J. Tepperman, "Toxic Lessons: What Do Children Learn from Media Violence?" *Children's Advocate* (January/February 1997).

267. V. C. Strasburger, "Tuning in to Teenagers," *Newsweek* (May 19, 1997).

268. D. T. Kenrick, and S. E. Gutierres. "Contrast Effects and Judgments of Physical Attractiveness: When Beauty Becomes a Social Problem," *Journal of Personality and Social Psychology* 38, n131 (1980).

269. V. C. Strasburger, "Adolescent Sexuality and the Media," *Pediatric Clinics of North America* 36, n3 (June 1989): 747-773.

Hero

270. "TV Viewing and Parental Guidance," *Office of Research Education Consumer Guide* 10 (U.S. Department of Education, October 1994).

271. "New Season: UPN Wednesdays," www.upn.com, 1999.

272. P. Scwartz, "Behind the Curtain and Into the Brutal Land of Oz," *New York Times*, July 12, 1998.

273. "International Fans," (Interview with Tom Fontana), *Crime Magazine*, 1999. www.crimemagazine.com.

274. "Children and Television Violence" American Psychological Association Statement, 1997.

275. S. R. Lichter, L. S. Lichter, and D. Amundson, "Merchandising Mayhem: Violence in Popular Culture" (Washington: Center for Media and Public Affairs, September 1999).

276. C. Clark, "TV Violence," *CQ Researcher* 3, n12 (March 26, 1993): 267.

277. L. Ellerbee, moderator, *The American Family and Television: A National Town Hall Meeting*, Lucky Duck Productions, 1997.

278. L. Ellerbee, moderator, *The American Family and Television: A National Town Hall Meeting*, Lucky Duck Productions, 1997.

279. "Children and Television Violence," *American Psychological Association Statement*, 1997.

280. C. Clark, "TV Violence," *CQ Researcher* 3, n12 (March 26, 1993): 267.

281. S. R. Lichter, L. S. Lichter, and D. Amundson, "Merchandising Mayhem: Violence in Popular Culture" (Washington: Center for Media and Public Affairs, September 1999).

282. "Television Statistics and Sources," TV-Free America, 1999.

283. M. Medved, *Hollywood vs. America* (New York: HarperPerennial, 1993): 222.

284. J. R. Hill, and D. Zillmann, "The Oprahization of America: Sympathetic Crime Talk and Leniency," *Journal of Broadcasting & Electronic Media* 43, n1 (Winter, 1999): 67-82.

285. J. R. Hill, and D. Zillmann, "The Oprahization of America: Sympathetic Crime Talk and Leniency," *Journal of Broadcasting & Electronic Media* 43, n1 (Winter, 1999): 67-82.

286. S. R. Lichter, L. S. Lichter, and S. Rothman, *Prime Time* (Washington: Regnery Publishing, Inc., 1994): 211.

287. E. Drew, *Portrait of an Election: The 1980 Presidential Campaign* (New York: Simon and Schuster, 1981): 263.

288. "The Problem with Kids' TV," Center for Educational Priorities, 1997.

289. J. Jacoby, "You Never Saw Harry Truman in Jogging Shorts," *The Boston Globe*, January 13, 1998.

290. J. Vorman, "Media Frenzy over Clinton Case Draws Criticism," *Reuters* (January 28, 1998).

291. M. Crissey, "Cronkite, Moyers Speak at Newspaper's Centennial." *Associated Press*, Oct. 1, 1999.

292. L. Corpus, "Violence: The Mainstreaming of Mayhem," *Unholy Hollywood*, 1991.

293. S. Globus, "Athletes as Role Models," *Current Health 2* 24, n6 (February 1998): 25(3).

294. J. Benedict, and D. Yaeger, *Pros and Cons* (New York: Warner Books, 1998): xi.

295. J. Benedict, and D. Yaeger, *Pros and Cons* (New York: Warner Books, 1998): xii

296. J. Benedict, "Public Heroes, Private Felons: Athletes and Crimes Against Women" (Boston: North Eastern University Press, 1997).

297. M. A. Messner, and D. F. Sabo, *Sex, Violence & Power in Sports* (Freedom, CA: The Crossing Press, 1994): 33.

298. M. A. Messner, and D. F. Sabo, *Sex, Violence & Power in Sports* (Freedom, CA: The Crossing Press, 1994): 34.

299. D. Kamp, "Hey Kids, Suck on This!" *GQ* 70, n2 (February 1, 2000): 87-90.

Endnotes

Arbitrator

300. National Violence Study.Mediascope, Inc., February 1996: 88, 96.

301. National Violence Study.Mediascope, Inc., February 1996: 97.

302. M. Krcmar, and P. M. Valkenburg, "A Scale to Assess Children's Moral Interpretation of Justified and Unjustified Violence and its Relationship to Television Viewing," *Communication Research* 26, n5 (October 1999): 608-636.

303. J. P. Murray, "Children and Television Violence," *Journal of Law & Public Policy* 4, n3 (1995): 7-14.

304. C. J. Boyatzis, G. M. Matillo, and K. M. Nesbitt, "Effects of 'The Mighty Morphin Power Rangers' on Children's Aggression with Peers," *Child Study Journal* 25, n1 (January 1995): 45-54.

305. J. Tepperman, "Toxic Lessons: What Do Children Learn from Media Violence?" *Children's Advocate* (January/February 1997).

306. L. D. Eron, and L. R. Huesmann, "Television as a Source of Maltreatment of Children," *School Psychology Review* 16, n2 (1987): 195-202.

307. C. S. Clark, "One Viewer's Violence is Another Viewer's Action," *CQ Researcher* (March 26, 1993): 270.

308. The UCLA Television Violence Report, University of California Los Angeles, Center for Communication Policy, 1996.

309. J. Tepperman, "Toxic Lessons: What Do Children Learn from Media Violence?" *Children's Advocate* (January/February 1997).

310. W. Josephson, "Television Violence: A Review of the Effects on Children of Different Ages," Report prepared for the Department of Canadian Heritage, 1995.

311. B. J. Simmons, K. Stalsworth, and H. Wentzel, "Television Violence and Its Effects on Young Children," *Early Childhood Education Journal* 26, n3 (1999): 149-153.

312. O. Hatch, "Intoduction of S. 525, S. 526: The Child Health Insurance and Lower Deficit Act (CHILD)." Statement Before the U.S. Senate, April 8, 1997. www.senate.gov/~hatch/statement.state023.html.

313. R. D. Danielsen, "Adolescent Violence in America," *Clinician Reviews* 8, n5 (1998): 167-184.

314. V. C. Strasburger, *Adolescents and the Media: Medical and Psychological Impact* (Thousand Oaks, CA: Sage Publications, Inc. 1995).

315. V. C. Strasburger, *Adolescents and the Media: Medical and Psychological Impact* (Thousand Oaks, CA: Sage Publications, Inc. 1995).

316. D. Grossman, and G. DeGaetano, *Stop Teaching our Kids to Kill* (New York: Crown Publishers, 1999): 49.

317. D. Grossman, and G. DeGaetano, *Stop Teaching our Kids to Kill* (New York: Crown Publishers, 1999): 17.

318. L. D. Eron, and L. R. Huesmann. "Television as a Source of Maltreatment of Children," *School Psychology Review* 16, n2 (1987): 195-202.

319. L. D. Eron, and L. R. Huesmann. "Television as a Source of Maltreatment of Children," *School Psychology Review* 16, n2 (1987): 195-202.

320. D. Grossman, and G. DeGaetano, *Stop Teaching our Kids to Kill* (New York: Crown Publishers, 1999): 29-30.

321. "Children and Television Violence." Report by the American Psychological Association, 1997.

322. V. C. Strasburger, *Adolescents and the Media: Medical and Psychological Impact* (Thousand Oaks, CA: Sage Publications, Inc. 1995).

323. J. Tepperman, "Toxic Lessons: What Do Children Learn from Media Violence?" *Children's Advocate* (January/February 1997).

324. P. Meyer, "Believe It: TV Violence Stalks Streets of Littleton—And Your Town."

325. D. Grossman, and G. DeGaetano, *Stop Teaching our Kids to Kill* (New York: Crown Publishers, 1999): 31-32.

326. G. Gerbner, "Television Violence and the Art of Asking the Wrong Question," *The World & I: A Chronicle of Our Changing Era* (July 1994).

327. G. Gerbner, "Television Violence and the Art of Asking the Wrong Question," *The World & I: A Chronicle of Our Changing Era* (July 1994).

328. L. Ellerbee, moderator, *The American Family and Television: A National Town Hall Meeting,* Lucky Duck Productions, 1997.

329. K. Krumplitsch, and A. Brower, "Public Enemy No. 1? Most Adults are Offended by Television's Sex and Violence," *Mediaweek* 3, n44 (Nov. 1, 1993): 19-22.

330. G. Gerbner, "Television Violence and the Art of Asking the Wrong Question," *The World & I: A Chronicle of Our Changing Era* (July, 1994).

331. M. Medved, *Hollywood vs. America* (New York: HarperPerennial, 1993).

332. J. Tepperman, "Toxic Lessons: What Do Children Learn from Media Violence?" *Children's Advocate* (January-February 1997).

333. J. P. Murray, "Children and Television Violence," *Journal of Law & Public Policy* 4, n3 (1995): 7-14.

Friend

334. R. B. Adler, L. B. Rosenfeld, and N. Towne, *Interplay: The Process of Interpersonal Communication* (Fort Worth, TX: Harcourt Brace College Publishers, 1992): 273.

335. M. Mead, and K. Heymar, *Family* (New York: Macmillan Company, 1965): 167.

336. J. DeVito, *The Interpersonal Communication Book* (7th Edition) (New York: HarperCollins College Publisher, 1995): 422.

337. D. Helmering, as quoted in *Motivating Moments* (1998). www.motivations.com.teens4a.htm.

338. "Statistics in Brief: Child Care and Early Education Program Participation of Infants, Toddlers, and Preschoolers," National Center for Education Statistics, October 1996.

339. L. Mumford, *The City in History: Its Origins, Its Transformations, and Its Prospects* (New York: Harcourt Brace Jovanovich: 1961): 231.

340. F. DeCaro, "They Made It After All," *TV Guide* (February 5-11, 2000): 18(6).

341. G. F. Will, "Are Children Little Adults? And Why All Those Shows 'Seinfeld,' 'Ally McBeal,' 'Friends' About Childish Adults?" *Newsweek* (Dec. 6, 1999): 98.

342. M. McLuhan, *Understanding Media* (New York: New American Library, 1964): 277.

343. M. McLuhan, *Understanding Media* (New York: New American Library, 1964): 277.

344. J. Ellul, *Propaganda: The Formation of Men's Attitudes* (New York: Vintage Books, 1965): 175.

345. M. McLuhan, *Understanding Media* (New York: New American Library, 1964): 276.

346. G. J. Ellis, S. K. Streeter, and J. D. Engelbricht, "Television Characters as Significant Others and the Process of Vicarious Role Taking," *Journal of Family Issues* 2, n4 (June 1983): 370.

347. M. McLuhan, *Understanding Media* (New York: New American Library, 1964): 276.

348. V. C. Strasburger, *Adolescents and the Media: Medical and Psychological Impact* (Thousand Oaks, CA: Sage Publications, Inc. 1995).

349. J. O'Connor, and J. Seymour, *Introducing Neuro-Linguistic Programming: Psychological Skills for Understanding and Influencing People* (New York: Thorsons/HarperCollins, 1995).

350. L. D. Eron, and L. R. Huesmann, "The Role of Television in the Development of Prosocial and Antisocial Behavior," in Olweus, D., Block, J., and M. Radke-Yarrow (eds.), *The Development of Antisocial and Prosocial Behavior: Research, Theories, and Issues* (New York: Academic, 1986).

351. G. J. Ellis, S. K. Streeter, and J. D. Engelbricht, "Television Characters as Significant Others and the Process of Vicarious Role Taking," *Journal of Family Issues* 2, n4 (June 1983): 370.

352. M. Pipher, *Reviving Ophelia* (New York: Ballantine Books, 1994): 291.

353. T. Hine, "Buffy Saves the World, but She's Still a Teen," *The Denver Post*, November 16, 1997: 91-101.

354. T. Hine, "Buffy Saves the World, but She's Still a Teen," *The Denver Post*, November 16, 1997: 91-101.

355. T. Hine, "Buffy Saves the World, but She's Still a Teen," *The Denver Post,* November 16, 1997: 91-101.

356. M. Medved, *Hollywood vs. America* (New York: HarperPerennial, 1993): 222.

357. Because the idea of "abnormal" behavior is inherently subjective, and due to the relatively recent proliferation of talk shows, no reliable statistics are available regarding violence and unusual behaviors on these shows. Also, while these shows frequently discuss violent behaviors, only a few, like Jerry Springer, actually depict such behaviors first-hand.

358. "TV Viewing Top After-school Activity for Children," *Broadcasting* (January 11, 1988).

359. "TV Viewing Top After-school Activity for Children," *Broadcasting* (January 11, 1988).

360. "Where is Today's Child? Probably Watching TV," *New York Times*, Dec. 6, 1999: C18.

361. J. Ellul, *The Technological Society* (New York: Vintage Books, 1964): 379.

362. N. Postman, *The Disappearance of Childhood* (New York: Delacorte Press, 1982): 114.

363. R. W. Kubey, "Television and the Quality of Family Life," *Communication Quarterly* 38, n4 (Fall 1990): 312.

364. G. Brody, Z. Stoneman, and A. Sanders, "Effects of Television Viewing on Family Interactions: An Observational Study," *Family Relations* (April 1980): 216-220.

365. *Television and the Preparation of the Mind for Learning: Critical Questions on the Effects of TV on the Developing Brains of Young Children,* Conference sponsored by the Division of Children and Families of the U.S. Department of Health and Human Services (Washington, D.C., Oct. 2, 1996).

366. P. S, Jensen, D. Mrazek, P. K. Knapp, L. Steinberg, C. Pfeffer, J. Schowalter, and T. Shapiro, "Evolution and Revolution in Child Psychiatry: ADHD as a Disorder of Adaptation," *Journal of the American Academy of Child and Adolescent Psychiatry* 36, n1 (December, 1997): 1672-1679,

367. *Television and the Preparation of the Mind for Learning: Critical Questions on the Effects of TV on the Developing Brains of Young Children,* Conference sponsored by the Division of Children and Families of the U.S. Department of Health and Human Services (Washington, D.C., Oct. 2, 1996).

368. *Television and the Preparation of the Mind for Learning: Critical Questions on the Effects of TV on the Developing Brains of Young Children,* Conference sponsored by the Division of Children and Families of the U.S. Department of Health and Human Services (Washington, D.C., Oct. 2, 1996).

369. G. DeGaetano, "Visual Media and Young Children's Attention Spans," *Media Literacy Online Project*, College of Education, University of Oregon, 1998.

370. B. R. Fowles, "A Child and His Television Set: What is the Nature of the Relationship?" *Education and Urban Society* 10, n1 (1977): 89-102.

371. A. Poussaint, and S. Linn, "Say 'No' to Teletubbies," *Family Education Network*, 1999.

372. T. Robinson, "Reducing Children's Television Viewing to Prevent Obesity: A Randomized Controlled Trial," *The Journal of the American Medical Association* 282, n16 (1999): 1561-1567.

373. N. Hellmich, "Healthy Families Ease Heavy Burden," *USA Today*, August 31, 1999.

374. "Kid Couch Potatoes More Likely to be Obese," *Journal of the American Medical Association Science News Update,* (April 10, 1996).

375. M. Leslie, "For Kids, Reducing TV Viewing May Be A Key to Preventing Obesity," *Stanford Online Report*, (May 5, 1999).

376. R. McIlwraith, R. Jacobvitz, Smith, R. Kubey, and A. Alexander. "Television Addiction: Theories and Data Behind the Ubiquitous Metaphor," *American Behavioral Scientist* 35, n2 (November/December 1991): 104-121.

377. R. McIlwraith, R. Jacobvitz, Smith, R. Kubey, and A. Alexander, "Television Addiction: Theories and Data Behind the Ubiquitous Metaphor," *American Behavioral Scientist* 35, n2 (November/December 1991): 104-121.

Why Regulation Hasn't Worked

378. Three Telecommunications Laws: Their Impact and Significance, The Center for Educational Priorities, 1997.

379. Three Telecommunications Laws: Their Impact and Significance, The Center for Educational Priorities, 1997.

380. B. Watkins, "Improving Educational and Informational Television for Children: When the Marketplace Fails," *Yale Law and Policy Review* 5: 345-381.

381. "The Moral Significance of the V-Chip," The Center for Educational Priorities, 1997.

382. "The History of Education on the Airways," The Center for Educational Priorities, 1997.

383. Revision of Programming Policies for Television Broadcast Stations: Reply Comments of Center for Medical Education, American Association of School Administrators, Association for Library Service to Children/American Library Association, National Education Association, National PTA, et al. Federal Communications Commission, In the Matter of Policies and Rules Concerning Children's Television Programming, Docket No. 93-48, 1993.

384. Revision of Programming Policies for Television Broadcast Stations: Reply Comments of Center for Medical Education, American Association of School Administrators, Association for Library Service to Children/American Library Association, National Education Association, National PTA, et al. Federal Communications Commission, In the Matter of Policies and Rules Concerning Children's Television Programming, Docket No. 93-48, 1993.

385. D. A. Hayes, *The Children's Hour Revisited: The Children's Television Act of 1990,* Unpublished (The University of Indiana. 1993).

386. D. A. Hayes, *The Children's Hour Revisited: The Children's Television Act of 1990,* Unpublished (The University of Indiana. 1993).

387. Comments by the American Psychological Association, The Center for Educational Priorities, 1997.

388. "The Moral Significance of the V-Chip," The Center for Educational Priorities, 1997.

389. V-Chip Home Page. Federal Communications Commission, February 2000.

390. L. Ellerbee, moderator, *The American Family and Television: A National Town Hall Meeting,* Lucky Duck Productions, 1997.

391. *Kids, Television, and the Telcom Act of 1996,* The Center for Educational Priorities, 1997.

392. *President Clinton and National Broadcasters Sign Historic Commitment to Education,* The Center for Educational Priorities, 1997.

393. *Broadcasters Unveil New Rating System for TV,* The Center for Educational Priorities, 1997.

394. *The Telecom Act of 1996: First Annual Report on Five Key Issues,* The Center for Educational Priorities, 1997.

395. *President Clinton and National Broadcasters Sign Historic Commitment to Education,* The Center for Educational Priorities, 1997.

396. *President Clinton and National Broadcasters Sign Historic Commitment to Education,* The Center for Educational Priorities, 1997.

397. Kaiser Family Foundation, *New National Surveys of Parents and Children on TV Rating System,* Press Release (May 27, 1998).

398. Gallup/CNN/USA Today poll (September 10-14, 1999).

399. S. Riley, "V-chip to Regulate Canadian Television Viewing," *Southam Newspapers*, March 15, 1996.

400. *Kids, Television, and the Telcom Act of 1996,* The Center for Educational Priorities, 1997.

401. *The Paradox of Censorship,* The Center for Educational Priorities, 1997.

402. K. Zinmeister, "TV-Free: Real Families Describe Life Without the Tube," *The American Enterprise* 8, n5 (September-October 1997): 63(9).

403. *The Moral Significance of the V-Chip,* The Center for Educational Priorities, 1997.

404. J. Brinkley, "PC Industry Calls for a Truce in TV Wars," *New York Times,* July 7, 1997: D-2.

405. R. D. Hof, and G. McWilliams, "Digital TV: What Will it Be?" *Business Week* (April 21, 1997): 34-36.

406. E. Lesly, and R. D. Hof, "Is Digital Convergence for Real?" *Business Week* (June 23, 1997): 42-43.

407. E. Lesly, and R. D. Hof, "Is Digital Convergence for Real?" *Business Week* (June 23, 1997): 42-43.

408. H. Rheingold, *The Virtual Community: Homesteading on the Electronic Frontier* (Reading, MA:Addison-Wesley, 1993).

409. Reno v. ACLU. Supreme Court of the United States, No. 96-511, 1997.

410. Reno v. ACLU. Supreme Court of the United States, No. 96-511, 1997.

411. Reno v. ACLU. Supreme Court of the United States, No. 96-511, 1997.

Take Back Control

412. L. Ellerbee, moderator. *The American Family and Television: A National Town Hall Meeting,* Lucky Duck Productions, 1997.

413. Pew Research Center for the People & the Press, Princeton Survey Research Associates, May 12-16, 1999.

414. The Harris Poll, June 10-15, 1999.

415. M. Winn, *The Plug-in Drug: Children and the Family* (New York: Viking Press, 1977): 271.

416. G. Comstock, *Television in America* (Beverly Hills: Sage Publications, 1980).

417. M. Mohler, "Unplugged!" *Ladies Home Journal* (March 1994): 94-104.

418. M. Mohler, "Unplugged!" *Ladies Home Journal* (March 1994): 94-104.

419. M. Mohler, "Unplugged!" *Ladies Home Journal* (March 1994): 94-104.

420. M. Mohler, "Unplugged!" *Ladies Home Journal* (March 1994): 94-104.

421. M. Mohler, "Unplugged!" *Ladies Home Journal* (March 1994): 94-104.

422. M. Mohler, "Unplugged!" *Ladies Home Journal* (March 1994): 94-104.

423. M. Mohler, "Unplugged!" *Ladies Home Journal* (March 1994): 94-104.

424. M. Mohler, "Unplugged!" *Ladies Home Journal* (March 1994): 94-104.

425. N. N. Minnow, and C. L. Lamay, *Abandoned in the Wasteland* (New York: Hill & Wang: 1995): 118.

426. V. Fahey, "TV by the Numbers," *Health* (December/January 1992): 35.

427. V. Fahey, "TV by the Numbers," *Health* (December/January 1992): 35.

428. William J. Doherty, *The Intentional Family, How to Build Family Ties in Our Modern World* (Reading, MA: Addison Wesley Publishing Company, 1997).

429. "Improving Your Child's TV Habits," *KidsHealth* (American Medical Association, 1999).

430. S. Sherman, "A Set of One's Own: TV Sets in Children's Bedrooms," *Journal of Advertising Research* 36, n6 (November/December 1996).

431. Kaiser Family Foundation, *New National Surveys of Parents and Children on TV Rating System,* Press Release (May 27, 1998).

432. Kaiser Family Foundation, *New National Surveys of Parents and Children on TV Rating System,* Press Release (May 27, 1998).

433. S. Mann, "What the Survey of American College Freshmen Tells Us About Their Interest in Politics and Political Science," *The American Political Science Association News* (June 1999).

434. *Associated Press*, January 27, 1997.

435. J. Bryant, *Television and the American Family* (Hillsdale, NJ: Lawrence Erlbaum Associates, 1999): 349.

436. M. Medved, *Hollywood vs. America* (New York: HarperPerennial, 1993): 22.

437. N. Postman, *The Disappearance of Childhood* (New York: Delacorte Press, 1982).

438. M. Medved, *Hollywood vs. America* (New York: HarperPerennial, 1993): 328.

439. S. Allen, "A Parents' Appeal to TV Sponsors," *Boulder Daily Camera*, June 24, 1999: 9C.

440. K. Kranhold, "Big Advertisers to Commission TV Scripts for Families," *The Wall Street Journal*, August 11, 1999: B1.

441. K. Kranhold, "Big Advertisers to Commission TV Scripts for Families," *The Wall Street Journal*, August 11, 1999: B1.

442. V. C. Strasburger, *Adolescents and the Media: Medical and Psychological Impact* (Thousand Oaks, CA: Sage Publications, Inc. 1995): 63.

Bibliography

A.C. Nielsen Company. *Nielsen Report on Television*. Northbrook, Ill.: A.C. Nielsen Company, 1982.

Adler, R.B.;L.B. Rosenfield; and N. Towne. *Interplay: The Process of Interpersonal Communication*. Fort Worth, TX: Harcourt Brace College Publishers, 1992.

Albinlak, P. "Beat it Kid, I'm Watching TV." *Broadcasting & Cable* 128, n30 (July 20, 1998).

Allen, S. "A Parents' Appeal to TV Sponsors." *Boulder Daily Camera*, June 24, 1999: 9C.

"America's Smallest School: The Family." *Educational Testing Service*, (1992).

Anderson, R. E., and I. E. Carter. *Human Behavior in the Social Environment*. Chicago: Aedine, 1974.

"Are We Failing Our Children?" *Rocky Mountain News* (September 3, 1989).

Ariés, P. Centuries of Childhood: *A Social History of Family Life*. New York: Vintage Books, 1962.

Armstrong, G.B., and B.S. Greenberg. "Background Television as an Inhibitor of Cognitive Processing." *Human Communication Research* 16, n3 (Spring 1990).

Armstrong, S. "Media: Hollywood Examined on Minority Roles." *The Christian Science Monitor* 85, n146 (June 24, 1993).

Associated Press, January 27, 1997.

Bandura, A. *Social Learning Theory*. Englewood Cliffs, N. J.: Prentice-Hall, 1977.

Bandura, A.; D. Ross; and S. A. Ross. "Imitation of Film—Mediated Aggressive Models." *Journal of Abnormal and Social Psychology* 66 (1963).

Barcus, E. *Images of Life on Children's Television: Sex Roles, Minorities, and Families*. New York: Praeger Publishers, 1983.

Benedict, J. *Public Heroes, Private Felons: Athletes and Crimes Against Women.* Boston: North Eastern University Press, 1997.

Benedict, J., and D. Yaeger. *Pros and Cons.* New York: Warner Books, 1998.

Berry, B.T., and C.L. Manning-Miller (eds.). *Mediated Messages and African-American Culture.* Thousand Oaks, Calif.: Sage Publications, 1996.

Berry, G. L., and J. K. Asamen. *Children and Television: Images in a Changing Sociocultural World.* Newbury Park, Calif.: Sage Publications, 1993.

"Bill Cosby Blasts Hollywood's Portrayal of Blacks on Television." *Jet* 95, n19 (April 12, 1999).

Bogart, L. *The Age of Television.* 3d ed. New York: Frederick Ungar, 1972.

Bond, L., and B. Wagner. *Families in Transition.* Beverly Hills: Sage Publications, 1988.

Boszormenyi, N. I., and G. M. Spark. *Invisible Loyalties.* New York: Brunner/Mazel, 1984.

Bowen, M. *Family Theory in Clinical Practice.* New York: Jason Aronson, 1985.

Bower, R. T. *Television and the Public.* New York: Holt, Rinehart & Winston, 1973.

Boyatzis, C.J.; G.M. Matillo; and K.M. Nesbitt. "Effects of 'The Mighty Morphin Power Rangers' on Children's Aggression with Peers." *Child Study Journal* 25. n1 (January 1995).

"Boys to Men: Messages About Masculinity. A National Poll of Children, Focus Groups and Content Analysis of Sports Programs and Commercials." *Children Now* (September 1999).

Brinkley, J. "PC Industry Calls for a Truce in TV Wars." *New York Times*, July 7, 1997: D-2.

Brinson, S.L. "The Use and Opposition of Rape Myths in Prime-time Television Dramas." *Sex Roles* 27, n7/8 (1992).

Broadcasters Unveil New Rating System for TV. The Center for Educational Priorities. 1997.

Brody, G. H., and Z. Stoneman. "The Influence of Television Viewing in Family Interactions and a Contextualist Framework." *Journal of Family Issues* 4, n2 (June 1983): 329-348.

Brody, G.; Z. Stoneman; and A. Sanders. "Effects of Television Viewing on Family Interactions: An Observational Study." *Family Relations* (April 1980): 216-220.

Bronfenbrenner, U. *The Ecology of Human Development: Experiments of Nature and Design.* Cambridge, MA: Harvard University Press, 1979.

Bronfenbrenner, U., and M. Mahoney (eds.). *The Origins of Alienation: Influences on Human Development.* Hindsdale, IL: Dryden, 1975.

Brooks, T., and E. Marsh. *The Complete Directory to Prime Time Network TV Shows 1946-Present.* New York: Ballantine Books, 1995.

Bibliography

Brown, B. "Gender Stereotypes in Advertising on Children's Television in the 1990s: A Cross-national Analysis." *Journal of Advertising*, vol. 27, no. 1 (Spring 1998).

Brown, J.; K. Childers; K. Bauman; and G. Koch. "The Influence of New Media and Family Structure on Young Adolescents' Television and Radio Use." *Communication Research* 17, n1 (Feb. 1990): 65-82.

Browne, B. "Gender Stereotypes in Advertising on Children's Television in the 1990s: A Cross-national Analysis." *Journal of Advertising* 27, n1 (Spring 1998): 83-96.

Bryant, J. and D. Zillmann (eds.). *Perspective on Media Effects.* Hillsdale, N.J.: Lawrence Erlbaum Associates, 1986.

Bryant, J. *Television and the American Family.* Hillsdale, N.J.: Lawrence Erlbaum Associates, 1990.

Bryce, J. W., and H. J. Leichter. "The Family and Television—Forms of Mediation." *Journal of Family Issues* 4, n2 (1983).

Cantor, J., S. Stutman, and V. Duran. *What Parents Want in a Television Rating System: Results of a National Survey.* Washington D.C.: Children First, National PTA, 1997.

Cantwell, R. "TCI, Microsoft Join Forces." *Rocky Mountain News* January 11, 1998: 3A, 52A.

Cash, T.F., and T.A. Brown. "Gender and Body Images: Stereotypes and Realities." *Sex Roles: A Journal of Research* 21, n5/6 (1989).

"Children and Television Violence." American Psychological Association Statement (1997).

Children First. *Agreement on Modifications to the TV Parental Guidelines.* Washington D.C.: National PTA, July 10, 1997.

Clark, C. "TV Violence." *CQ Researcher* 3, n12 (March 26, 1993).

Clark, C.S. "One Viewer's Violence is Another Viewer's Action." *CQ Researcher* (March 26, 1993).

Clark, P. "Some Proposals for Continuing Research on Youth and the Mass Media." in *Mass Communications and Youth: Some Current Perspectives.* Vol. 4. Edited by F. G. Kline and P. Clark (1984): 11-20.

Coffin, T. E. "Television's Impact on Society." *American Psychologists* 10, n10 (1955): 630-641.

Collins, G., moderator. "A Couple of Kingmakers Talk Shop." (Q & A session) *The New York Times Magazine* (January 11, 1998): 24-27.

Comments by the American Psychological Association. The Center for Educational Priorities. 1997.

Comstock, G. *Television in America.* Beverly Hills: Sage Publications, 1980.

Comstock, G., and G. Lindsey. *Television and Human Behavior: The Research Horizon, Future and Present.* Santa Monica, Calif.: Rand Corp., 1975.

Comstock, G., and M. Fisher. *Television and Human Behavior: A Guide to the Pertinent Scientific Literature*. Santa Monica, Calif.: Rand Corp., 1975.

Comstock, G.; S. H. Chafee; N. Katzman; M. McCombs; and D. Roberts. *Television and Human Behavior*. New York: Columbia University Press, 1978.

Comstock J. and K. Strzyewski. "Interpersonal Interactions on Television: Family Conflict an djealousy on Primetime." *Journal of Broadcasting & Electronic Media* 34, n3 (Summer 1990): 263–82.

Cooke, P. "TV or Not TV." *Health* (December/January, 1992): 33-43.

Cordellan, W. "Television and Children: Towards the Millennium." *Communication Research Trends* 10, n3 (1990).

Corpus, L. "Violence: The Mainstreaming of Mayhem." *Unholy Hollywood*, 1991.

Craig, S. (ed.). *Men, Masculinity, and the Media*. Newbury Park, Calif.: Sage Publications, 1992.

Crime Magazine, International Fans, 1999.

Crissey, M. "Cronkite, Moyers Speak at Newspaper's Centennial." *Associated Press*, Oct. 1, 1999.

Curtis, G. "Leave Ozzie and Harriet Alone." *The New York Times Magazine* (January 19, 1997): 40-41.

Cutler, B. "Where Does the Free Time Go?" *American Demographics* (November 1990): 36-39.

Danielsen, R.D. "Adolescent Violence in America." *Clinician Reviews* 8, n5 (1998): 167-184.

Davis, D. K., and R. Abelman. "Families and Television: An Application of Name Analysis Theory." *Journal of Family Issues* 4, n2 (June 1983): 385-404.

Davis, D.M. "Portrayals of Women in Prime-Time Network television: Some Demographic Characteristics." *Sex Roles: A Journal of Research* 23, n5/6 (1990).

DeCaro, F. "They Made it After All." *TV Guide* 6, n18 (February 5-11, 2000).

DeGaetano, G. "Visual Media and Young Children's Attention Spans." *Media Literacy Online Project*, College of Education, University of Oregon, 1998.

DeGraaf, J., and V. Boe. *Affluenza*. Seattle: KCTS-TV and Oregon Public Broadcasting, 1997.

DeVito, J. *The Interpersonal Communication Book* (7th Edition). New York: HarperCollins College Publisher, 1995.

DeWolf, R. "Group: Women and Work/Family Issues Shorted on TV." *The Denver Post*, June 28, 1998: 8J.

Dickinson, A. "Must-See TV? Too Much Media—Television Especially—Can be an Isolating Experience. Get It Under Control." *Time* 154, i22 (Nov. 29, 1999): 114.

Dines, G., and J. M. Humez. *Gender, Race and Class in Media*. Thousands Oaks, Calif.: Sage Publications, 1995.

Bibliography

Douglas, S. *Where the Girls Are*. New York: Times Books, 1994.

Douglas, W. "The Fall from Grace? The Modern Family on Television." *Communication Research* 23, n6 (December 1996): 675-702.

Douglas, W., and B. Olson. "Subversion of the American Family? An Examination of Children and Parents in Television Families." *Communication Research* 23, n1 (February 1996): 73-99.

Doherty, William J. *The Intentional Family, How to Build Family Ties in Our Modern World*. Reading, MA: Addison Wesley Publishing Company, 1997.

Dow, B.J. "Hegemony, Feminist Criticism and The Mary Tyler Moor Show." *Critical Studies in Mass Communication* 7 (1990).

Drew, E. *Portrait of an Election: The 1980 Presidential Campaign*. New York: Simon and Schuster, 1981.

Dunn, G. *The Box in the Corner*. New York: Macmillan, 1977.

Dunn, T.; Josepsson; and J.G. Wells. "Television and the Adjustment of Icelandic Children to Family and Peers." *Journal of Comparative Family Studies* 7, n1 (1976): 87-95.

Dutta, M.B. "Taming the Victim: Rape in Soap Opera." *Journal of Popular Film and Television* 27 (Spring 1999): 34(6).

Duvall, E. M. *Marriage and Family Development*. Philadelphia: J. B. Lippincott, 1977.

Eicher, D. "Evolution of the Television Mom: Attitudes Change, Realistic Families of '90s Disappear." *The Denver Post*, May 9, 1999: G1(2).

Eisenstein, E. L. *The Printing Press as an Agent of Change*. New York: Cambridge University Press, 1979.

Elasmar, M.; H. Kazumi; and M. Brain. "The Portrayal of Women in U.S. Prime Time Television." *Journal of Broadcasting & Electronic Media* 44, n1 (Winter 1999): 20-34.

Elias, M. "Fathers Focus Increased Care on Boys." *USA Today*, June 14, 1999: 6D.

Ellerbee, L., moderator. "The American Family and Television: A National Town Hall Meeting." Lucky Duck Productions, 1997.

Ellis, G. J. "Television and the Family." *Journal of Family Issues* 4, n2 (June 1983).

Ellis, G. J.; S. K. Streeter; and J. D. Engelbricht. "Television Characters as Significant Others and the Process of Vicarious Role Taking." *Journal of Family Issues* 2, n4 (June 1983): 370.

Ellul, J. *Propaganda: The Formation of Men's Attitudes*. New York: Vintage Books, 1965: 175.

Ellul, J. *The Technological Society*. New York: Vintage Books, 1964.

Eron, L.D., and L. R. Huesmann. "Television as a Source of Maltreatment of Children." *School Psychology Review* 16, n2 (1987): 195-202.

Eron, L.D., and L.R. Huesmann. "The Role of Television in the Development of Prosocial and Antisocial Behavior." In *The Development of Antisocial and Prosocial Behavior: Research, Theories, and Issues.* Olweus, D.; J. Block; and M. Radke-Yarrow (eds.). New York: Academic, 1986.

Evertt, R., and F. Balle (eds.). *The Media Revolution in America and Western Europe.* Norwood, N.J.: Ablex Publishing Co., 1985.

Fahey, V. "TV by the Numbers."*Health* (December/January 1992): 35.

Fallis, S. F.; M. A. Fitzpatrick; and S. Friestad. "Spouses' Discussion of Television Portrayals of Close Relationships." *Communication Research* 12, n1 (January 1985): 59-81.

"Family Hour: Worse than Ever and Headed for New Lows." Parents Television Council Special Report, August 31, 1999.

Farrell, W. *Why Men Are the Way They Are.* New York: Berkley Publishing Group, 1990.

Fejes, F.J. "Masculinity as Fact." *Past Study on Men and the Media*, Part I.

Ferguson, M. "Images of Power and the Feminist Fallacy." *Critical Studies in Mass Communication* 7 (1990).

Fields, S. "Harriet's Back in Feminist Form." *Insight on the News* 14, n17 (May 11, 1998): 48(1).

Fiske, J. *Television Culture.* New York: Routledge, 1987.

Flint, J. "Fade to White." *Entertainment Weekly* (April 23, 1999): 8-9.

Forsay, S. D. "The Influences of Family Structures Upon the Patterns and Effects of Family Viewing." In *Television and Human Behavior: Tomorrow's Research in Mass Communication*, eds. L. Arons and A. May, New York: Appleton-Century Crafts, 1963, 64-80.

Fowles, B.R. "A Child and His Television Set: What is the Nature of the Relationship?" *Education and Urban Society* 10, n1 (1977): 89-102.

Frazer, C. F. "The Social Character of Children's Television Viewing." *Communication Research* 8, n3 (1981): 307-322.

Gallup/CNN/*USA Today* poll. September 10-14, 1999.

Gardner, M. "Children Say Television Distorts its Portrayals of Minorities." *The Christian Science Monitor* (May 14, 1998): 13.

Garner, D.M.; P.E. Garfinkel; D. Schwartz; and M. Thompson. "Cultural Expectations of Thinness in Women." *Psychological Report* 47 (1980): 483-491.

Gerbner, G. "A Look at the Characters on Prime time and Daytime Television from 1994–1997." *The 1998 Screen Actors Guild Report: Casting the American Scene Fairness and Diversity in Television: Update and Trends since the 1993 Screen Actors Guild Report Women and Minorities on Television*, 1998.

Gerbner, G. "Study Guide: Crisis of the Cultural Environment." Media Education Foundation, 1998.

Bibliography

Gerbner, G. "Television Violence and the Art of Asking the Wrong Question." *The World & I: A Chronicle of Our Changing Era* (July 1994).

"Getting the Skinny on TV." *Discover* 20, n12 (December 1999).

Gilbert, S. "Study Stresses Family Role: Home May Be as Vital as Peers to Teenagers." *Denver Post*, September 19, 1997: 15A.

Gilder, G. *Life After Television: The Coming Transformation of Media and American Life*. New York: W. W. Norton & Co., 1992.

Globus, S. "Athletes as Role Models." *Current Health* 24, n6 (February 1998): 25(3).

Goffman, E. *Gender Advertisements*. Cambridge, MA: Howard University Press, 1979.

Goode, E. "TV Cuts Weight in Fiji." *The Denver Post*, May 20, 1999.

Goodman, I. F. "Television's Role in Family Interaction: A Family Systems Perspective." *Journal of Family Issues* 4, i2 (June 1983): 416.

Goodstein, L. "Has Television Found Religion? Not Exactly." *The New York Times*, November 30, 1997: 37, 43.

"Greatest Gifts We Can Give Our Children: A Report from the Ad Council." *Reader's Digest* (June 1998).

Greenberg, B.S.; P.M. Ericson; and M. Vlahos. "Children's Television Behavior as Perceived by Mother and Child." In *Television and Social Behavior*, Vol. 4: "Television Day-To-Day Life: Patterns of Use," eds. E. A. Rubinstein; G. A. Comstock; and J. P. Murray. Washington D.C.: U.S. Government Printing Office, 1972.

Greenberg, B.S., and L. Collette. "The Changing Face on TV: A Demographic Analysis of Network Television's New Seasons, 1966–1992." *Journal of Broadcasting & Electronic Media* 41 (Winter 1997): 1-13.

Greenberg, B.S., and R.W. Busselle. "Soap Operas and Sexual Activities: A Decade Later." *Journal of Communication* 46, n4 (1996).

Grossman, D. and G. DeGaetano. *Stop Teaching our Kids to Kill*. New York: Crown Publishers, 1999.

Grube, J.W., and L. Wallack. "Television Beer Advertising and Drinking Knowledge, Beliefs, and Intentions Among School Children." *American Journal of Public Health* 84 (1994): 254-259.

Gumpert, G., and R. Cathcart. *Inter/Media—Interpersonal Communication in a Media World*. New York: Oxford University Press, 1982.

Gurman, E.; S. Ala; and D. P. Kniskern. *Handbook of Family Therapy*. New York: Brunner/Mazel, 1981.

Haaf, L. "Role-Sharing Couples." In *Marriage and Family in a Changing Society*. J.M. Henslin (ed.). New York: MacMillian.

Hales, D. "What Friends Are For." *Woman's Day* (March 31, 1987).

Hamilton, R., and R. Lawless. "Television Within the Social Matrix." *Public Opinion Quarterly* 20 (1956): 393-403.

Harris, L. *Inside America*. New York: Vintage, 1987.

Harris Poll. June 10-15, 1999.

Hatch, O. "Introduction of S. 525, S. 526: The Child Health Insurance and Lower Deficit Act (CHILD)." Statement Before the U.S. Senate, April 8, 1997.

Hawkins, R. "The Dimension Structure of Children's Perceptions of Television Reality." *Communication Research* 3 (1977): 299-320.

Hayes, D.A. *The Children's Hour Revisited: The Children's Television Act of 1990*. Unpublished. The University of Indiana. 1993.

Hazan, A.R., Lipton, H.L., and S.A. Glanz. "Popular Films do not Reflect Current Tobacco Use." *American Journal of Public Health* 84: 998-1000.

Heintz-Knowles, K. "Balancing Acts: Work/Family Issues on Prime-Time TV." National Partnership for Women & Families, 1998.

Hellmich, N. "Healthy Families Ease Heavy Burden." *USA Today*, August 31, 1999.

Helmering, D. Quotation in *Motivating Moments*. 1998.

Henry J. Kaiser Family Foundation, 1996.

Hill, G., L. Raglin and C.F. Johnson. *Black Women in Television: An Illustrated Bibliography*. New York: Garland Publishing. 1990.

Hill, J.R., and D. Zillmann. "The Oprahization of America: Sympathetic Crime Talk and Leniency." *Journal of Broadcasting & Electronic Media* 43, n1 (Winter, 1999).

Himmelstein, H. *Television: Myth and the American Mind*. New York: Praeger, 1984.

Himmelweit, H. T.; A. N. Oppenheim; and P. Vince. *Television and the Child*. London: Oxford University Press, 1958.

History of Education on the Airway, The. The Center for Educational Priorities. 1997.

Hine, T. "Buffy Saves the World, but She's Still a Teen." *The Denver Post*, Nov. 16, 1997: 91-101.

"HIV/AIDS among Adolescents & Teens." *Why We Should Care: The 1997 World AIDS Day Resource Booklet*, 1997.

Hochschild, A. "The Second Shift: Employed Women are Putting In Another Day of Work." *UTNE Reader* 190 (March/April 1999): 66-73.

Hof, R.D., and G. McWilliams. "Digital TV: What Will it Be?" *Business Week*, April 21, 1997: 34-36.

Huston, A.C.; C. Wright; J. Marquis; and S.B. Green. "How Young Children Spend their Time: Television and Other Activities." *Developmental Psychology* v35, n4 (July 1999): 912(1).

Ianni, F. A. J. "Home, School and Community in Adolescent Education." *Clearinghouses on Urban Education* (1983): 84.

Bibliography

Iijima Hall, C.C., and M.J. Crum. "Women and 'Body-isms' in Television Beer Commercials." *Sex Roles* 31, n5/6 (1994): 329-337.

Illinois Department of Public Health, 1998.

"Improving Your Child's TV Habits." *KidsHealth.* American Medical Association, 1999.

Jackson, D. D. "The Study of the Family." *Family Process* 4 (1965): 1-20.

Jacoby, J. "TV has Destroyed Presidential Dignity." *Rocky Mountain News,* January 17, 1998: 55A.

Jacoby, J. "You Never Saw Harry Truman in Jogging Shorts." *The Boston Globe,* January 13, 1998.

Jacoby, S. "Great Sex: What's Age Got to do With It?" *Modern Maturity* (September/October 1999).

Jensen, P.S.; D. Mrazek; P.K. Knapp; L. Steinberg; C. Pfeffer; J. Schowalter; and T. Shapiro. "Evolution and Revolution in Child Psychiatry: ADHD as a Disorder of Adaptation." *Journal of the American Academy of Child and Adolescent Psychiatry* 36, n12 (December, 1997): 1672-1679.

Johnson, D. "Europe Still Hot for U.S. Shows: Although Prime Time Slots are Scarce, Hit Still Find a Home." *Broadcasting & Cable* 127, n2 (Jan. 13, 1997): 92(2).

Josephson, W. "Television Violence: A Review of the Effects on Children of Different Ages." Report prepared for the Department of Canadian Heritage, 1995.

Kaiser Family Foundation. *New National Surveys of Parents and Children on TV Rating System.* Press Release: May 27, 1998.

Kaiser Family Foundation. *Sex on TV: Content and Context: A Biennial Report to the Kaiser Family Foundation.* 1999.

Kaiser Family Foundation. "So-called 'Family TV Hour' Pretty Racy." *Media Report to Women* (Winter, 1997).

Kamp, D. "Hey Kids, Suck on This!" *GQ* 70, n2 (February 1, 2000): 87-90.

Kanner, B. "Dynasty Dollars." *New York.* Aug. 6, 1984.

Kantrowitz, B. "High School Homeroom." *Newsweek* (June 1990): 50-54.

Katz, E. and D. Faulkes. "On the Use of Mass Media as 'Escape.'" *Public Opinion Quarterly* 4 (1962): 377-388.

Kaufman, L. "Prime Time Nutrition." *Journal of Communications* 30, n3 (1980): 37-46.

Kenrick, D.T., and S.E. Gutierres. "Contrast Effects and Judgments of Physical Attractiveness: When Beauty Becomes a Social Problem." *Journal of Personality and Social Psychology* 38, n131 (1980).

"Kid Couch Potatoes More Likely to be Obese." *Journal of the American Medical Association Science News Update* (April 10, 1996).

Kids, Television, and the Telcom Act of 1996. The Center for Educational Priorities. 1997.

Knapp, M. L. *Social Intercourse: From Greeting to Goodbye*. Boston: Allyn & Bacon, 1978.

Koolstra, C.M., and T.H. Van Der Voort. "Longitudinal Effects of Television on Children's Leisure-time Reading: A Test of Three Explanatory Models." *Human Communication Research* 23, n1 (Sept. 1996): 4(32).

Kotulak, R. "Youngsters Lose Way in Maze of Family Instability." *Chicago Tribune*, Dec. 14, 1986: 6-1(3).

Kranhold, K. "Big Advertisers to Commission TV Scripts for Families." *The Wall Street Journal*, August 11, 1999: B1.

Krcmar, M., and P.M. Valkenburg. "A Scale to Assess Children's Moral Interpretation of Justified and unjustified Violence and its Relationship to Television Viewing." *Communication Research* 26, n5 (October 1999): 608-636.

Krumplitsch, K. and A. Brower. "Public Enemy No. 1? Most Adults are Offended by Television's Sex and Violence." *Mediaweek* 3, n44 (Nov. 1, 1993): 19-22.

Kubey, R., and M. Csikszentmihalyi. *Television and the Quality of Life: How Viewing Shapes Everyday Experience*. Hillsdale, N.J.: Lawrence Erlbaum Associates, 1990.

Kubey, R.W. "Television and the Quality of Family Life." *Communication Quarterly* 38, n4 (Fall 1990): 312-324.

Kubey, R.W. "Television Use in Everyday Life: Coping with Unstructured Time." *Journal of Communication* (Summer 1986): 109-123.

Kunkel, D.; K.M. Cope; and E. Biely. "Sexual Message of Television: Comparing Findings from Three Studies." *The Journal of Sex Research* 36, n3 (August 1999): 230-236.

Lamb, S. *Denver Post*. Aug. 26, 1995: 7E.

Langrehr, D. "A Critical Reading of Television Commercials." Unpublished manuscript. Florida State University, Department of Education Theory and Practice, 1999.

Larson, M. "Sex Roles and Soap Operas: What Adolescents Learn About Single Motherhood." *Sex Roles: A Journal of Research* 35, n1-2 (July 1996).

"Latest Trend: The New Traditionalism." *Rocky Mountain News,* March 19, 1988.

"Latinos Talk Back to TV Through a National Survey." *La Prensa* San Diego 22, n39 (October 2, 1998).

Lauzen, M.M., and D.M. Dozier. "Making a Difference in Prime Time: Women On Screen and Behind the Scenes in the 1995–1996 Television Season." *Journal of Broadcasting & Electronic Media* 43, n1 (Winter 1999): 1–19.

Lawrence, F.C.; G.E. Tasker; C.T. Daly; A.L. Orhiel; and P.H. Wozniak. "Adolescents' Time Spent Viewing Television." *Adolescence* 21, n82 (Summer, 1986).

Leo, J. "It's all Relative." In "That's Outrageous," *The Readers Digest* (February 1998): 75.

Leslie, M. "For Kids, Reducing TV Viewing May Be A Key to Preventing Obesity." Stanford Online Report: May 5, 1999.

Bibliography

Lesly, E., and R.D. Hof. "Is Digital Convergence for Real?" *Business Week* (June 23, 1997): 42-43.

Lewis, A. "Helping Young Urban Parents Educate Themselves and Their Children." *ERIC/CUE Digest*, n85 (Dec. 1992).

Lichter, S.R.; L.S. Lichter; and D. Amundson. "Merchandising Mayhem: Violence in Popular Culture." Washington: Center for Media and Public Affairs, September 1999.

Lichter, S. R.; L. S. Lichter; and S. Rothman. *Prime Time*. Washington: Regnery Publishing, Inc., 1994.

Lichter, S.R. and D. R. Amundson. "Don't Blink: Hispanics in Television Entertainment." For the National Council of La Raza, April 1996.

Liebelt, J. "You've Come a Long Way Baby: Or Have You? An Examination of Hegemony for Women Nonverbal Communication on Television." Unpublished Thesis, University of Northern Colorado, 1999.

Lofland, J. F., and L. Lofland. *Analyzing Social Settings*. Belmont, CA: Wadsworth Publishing Co., 1984.

LoSciuto, L. "A National Inventory of Television Viewing Behavior." In *Television and Social Behavior,* v4. eds. E. Rubenstein; G. Comstock; and J. Murray. Washington, D.C.: U.S. Government Printing Office.

Lull, J. "The Social Uses of Television." In *Inter/Media—Interpersonal Communication in a Media World*. eds. G. Gumpert, and R. Cathcart. New York: Oxford University Press, 1982, 566-579.

Lyle, L. and H. Hoffman. "Children's Use of Television and Other Media." In *Television and Social Behavior,* v4. eds. E. Rubenstein; G. Comstock; and J. Murray. Washington, D.C.: U.S. Government Printing Office, 1972, 129-256.

Maccoby, E. "Television: Its Impact on School Children," *Public Opinion Quarterly* 15 (Fall 1951): 421-444.

Mander, J. *Four Arguments for the Elimination of Television*. New York: Morrow Quill, 1978.

Mann, S. "What the Survey of American College Freshmen Tells Us about Their Interest in Politics and Political Science." *The American Political Science Association News* (June 1999).

"Married People Claim They're Faithful." *San Francisco Chronicle*, June 29, 1991: A7.

Mauro, T. "National Trending Toward Do-It-Yourself Censorship." The Freedom Forum First Amendment Center, 1997.

Mayes, S.L., and K.B. Valentine. "Sex Roles Stereotyping in Saturday Morning Cartoon Shows." *Journal of Broadcasting* 23, n1 (1979): 41-50.

McBride, B.A., and G. Mills. "A Comparison of Mother and Father Involvement with their Preschool-age Children." *Early Childhood Research Quarterly* 8 (1993): 457-477.

McFarling, U.L. "Muscle-minded Boys Look Up to GI-ant Joes." *The Denver Post*, May 19, 1999: 2A, 8A.

McIlwraith, R.; R. Jacobvitz; Smith; R. Kubey; and A. Alexander. "Television Addiction: Theories and Data Behind the Ubiquitous Metaphor." *American Behavioral Scientist* 35, n2 (November/December 1991): 104-121.

McLeod, J.; C. K. Atkin; and S. H. Chaffee. "Guiding Perspective of a Loose Collaboration." Paper presented to the Theory and Methodology Division of the Association for Education in Journalism Connection, Houston, 1979.

McLuhan, M. *Understanding Media*. New York: New American Library, 1964.

Mead, G. H. *Mind, Self and Society*. Chicago: University of Chicago Press, 1934.

Mead, M. *Culture and Commitment: A Study of the Generation Gap*. Garden City, N.Y.: Doubleday & Co., 1970.

Mead, M., and K. Heyman. *Family*. New York: MacMillan Co., 1965.

Medrick, E. "Constant Television: A Background to Family Life." *Journal of Communication* 29, n2 (1979): 171-176.

Medrick, E., and N. Waxler. *Interaction in Families*. New York: John Wiley, 1968.

Medved, M. *Hollywood vs. America*. New York: HarperPerennial, 1993.

Mendelsohn, H. "Sociological Perspectives on the Study of Mass Communications." In *People, Society and Mass Communications*. eds. L. A. Dexter and D. M. White. New York: Free Press, 1964.

"Messages Reinforce Sexual Stereotypes." *USA Today* 126, n2631, December 1997.

Messaris, P. "Family Conversations About Television." *Journal of Family Issues* 4, n2 (June 1983): 293-308.

Messner, M.A., and D.F. Sabo. *Sex, Violence & Power in Sports*. Freedom, CA: The Crossing Press, 1994.

Meyer, P. "Believe It: TV Violence Stalks Streets of Littleton—And Your Town."

Meyers, P., and F.A. Biocca. "The Elastic Body Image: The Effect of Television Advertising and Programming on Body Image Distortions in Young Women.." *Journal of Communication* 42, n3 (Summer, 1992).

Meyrowitz, J. *No Sense of Place*. New York: Oxford University Press, 1985.

Miller, G. R. "A Neglected Connection: Mass Media Exposure and Interpersonal Communicative Competency." In *Inter/Media —Interpersonal Communication in a Media World*. eds. A.G. Gumpert, and R. Cathcart. New York: Oxford University Press, 1982, 49-56.

Minnow, N.N., and C.L. Lamay. *Abandoned in the Wasteland*. New York: Hill & Wang, 1995.

Mohler, M. "Unplugged!" *Ladies Home Journal* (March 1994): 94-104.

Mohr, P. J. "Parental Guidance of Children's Viewing of Evening Television Programs." *Journal of Broadcasting* 23, n2 (1972): 213-218.

Bibliography

Moody, K. *Growing Up on Television: The TV Effect*. New York: Times Books, 1980.

Moos, R. and B. Moss. "Typology of Family Social Environment." *Family Process* 15 (1976): 357-361.

Moral Significance of the V-Chip, The. The Center for Educational Priorities. 1997.

Morgan, M.; S. Leggett; and J. Shanahan. "Television and Family Values: Was Dan Quayle Right?" *Mass Communication & Society* 2 (Winter/Spring 1999): 47-63.

Morris, N. S. *Television's Child*. Boston: Little, Brown & Company, 1971.

Mumford, L., and J. N. Morgan. "Some Pilot Studies of Communication and Consensus in the Family." *Public Opinion* 8, n32 (1968): 113-121.

Mumford, L. *The City in History*. New York: H. B. J. Bond, 1961.

Mumford, L. *The City in History: Its Origins, Its Transformations, and Its Prospects*. New York: Harcourt Brace Jovanovich: 1961.

Murray, J.P. "Children and Television Violence." *Journal of Law & Public Policy* 4, n3 (1995): 7-14.

Myers, P.N., and F.A. Biocca. "The Elastic Body Image: The Effect of Television Advertising and Programming on Body Image Distortions in Young Women." *Journal of Communication* 42, n3 (Summer 1992): 108-133.

Napier, G., and C. Whitaker. *The Family Crucible*. New York: Harper and Row, 1978.

National Commission on Working Women. *Women, Work and Family: Working Mothers Overview*. Washington, D.C.: Fall/Winter, 1992.

National Institute of Mental Health. *Television and Behavior: Ten Years of Scientific Progress and Implications for the Eighties*. DHHS Publication No. ADM 82-1195. Washington, D.C.: U.S. Government Printing Office, 1982.

National PTA, National Cable Television Association, and Cable in the Classroom. *Taking Charge of Your TV*. Family and Community Critical Viewing Project, HBO, 1997.

National Science Foundation. *Research on the Effects of Television Advertising on Children*. Washington, D.C.: U.S. Government Printing Office, 1973.

National Violence Study. Mediascope, Inc., February 1996.

Newcomb, H., ed. *Television: The Critical View*. New York: Oxford University Press, 1979.

"New Season: UPN Wednesdays." www.upn.com, 1999.

Nobel, G. *Children in Front of the Small Screen*. Beverly Hills: Sage Publications, 1975.

Nystrom, C. Class Lecture, New York University, 1999.

Nystrom, C. *Media and Children*. Conference conducted at Tel Aviv University, Israel, 1987.

O'Connor, J., and J. Seymour. *Introducing Neuro-Linguistic Programming:*

Psychological Skills for Understanding and Influencing People. New York: Thorsons/HarperCollins, 1995.

Ong, W. J. "Interfaces of the World: Television as an Open System." In *Inter/Media — Interpersonal Communication in a Media World.* eds. A.G. Gumpert and R. Cathcart. New York: Oxford University Press, 1982, 93-109.

Orrick, A. "Success & Failures of Working Women on Television." *Working Women* 5 (Nov., 1980).

Ostrow, J. "'Action' Risqué but Realistic." *The Denver Post Online*, August 24, 1999.

Ostrow, J. "It's 'Teletubbies' Time." *The Denver Post*, January 18, 1998: 1H, 12H.

Palmer, E. L.; A. B. Hockett; and W. W. Dean. "The Television Family and Children's Fright Reactions." *Journal of Family Issues* 4, v2 (June 1983): 279-292.

Palmer, E.; T. Smith; and K. Strawser. "Rubik's Tube—Developing a Child's Television Worldview." In *Children and TV.* eds. Gordon Berry and Joy Keiko Asamen. Newbury Park, Calif.: Sage Publications, 1993.

Paradox of Censorshi, The. The Center for Educational Priorities. 1997.

Pearce, W. B. "The Coordinated Management of Meaning: A Rules Based Theory of Interpersonal Communication." *Explorations in Interpersonal Communication*, v17. *Sage Annual Review of Communication Research* 5 (1976).

Pearl, D.; L. Bouthilet; and J. Lazar. *Television and Behavior—Ten Years of Scientific Progress and Implications for the Eighties*, 1982a: 1. (DHHS Publication 82-1195) Rockville, Md.: U.S. Department of Health and Human Services. 1982b: 2. (DHHS Publication 82-1196.) Rockville, Md.: U.S. Department of Health and Human Services, 1982.

Peterson, J.L.; K.A. Moore; and F.F. Furstenberg, Jr.. "Television Viewing and Early Initiation of Sexual Intercourse: Is there a Link?" *Journal of Homosexuality* 21 (1991): 93-188.

Pew Research Center for the People & the Press, Princeton Survey Research Associates, May 12-16, 1999.

Pipher, M. *Reviving Ophelia.* New York: Ballantine Books, 1994.

Pogrebin, L. C. *Family Politics.* New York: McGraw Hill, 1983.

Pollack, W. *Real Boys.* New York: Henry Holt and Company, 1998.

Popenoe, D. *Life Without Father.* New York: The Free Press, 1996.

Postman, N. *Amusing Ourselves to Death: Public Discourse in the Age of Show Business.* New York: Viking Penguin, 1985.

Postman, N. Class Lecture. New York University, 1994.

Postman, N. *Conscientious Objections: Stirring Up Trouble About Language, Technology, and Education.* New York: Alfred A. Knopf, 1988.

Postman, N. *Teaching as a Conserving Activity.* New York: Dell Publishing, 1979.

Postman, N. *The Disappearance of Childhood.* New York: Delacorte Press, 1982.

Bibliography

Postman, N.; C. Nystrom; L. Strate; and C. Weingartner. *Myths, Men & Beer: An Analysis of Beer Commercials on Broadcast Television*. Washington, D.C.: AAA Foundation for Traffic Safety, 1987.

Postman, Neil. *Technopoly: The Surrender of Culture to Technology*, New York: Vintage Books, 1992.

Poussaint, A., and S. Linn. "Say 'No' to Teletubbies." Family Education Network. 1999.

President Clinton and National Broadcasters Sign Historic Commitment to Education. The Center for Educational Priorities. 1997.

"Problem with Kids' TV." Center for Educational Priorities, 1997.

Quayle, D. Speech to the Commonwealth Club of San Francisco, May 19, 1992.

Reno v. ACLU. Supreme Court of the United States, No. 96-511, 1997.

Revision of Programming Policies for Television Broadcast Stations: Reply Comments of Center for Medical Education, American Association of School Administrators, Association for Library Service to Children/American Library Association, National Education Association, National PTA, et al. Federal Communications Commission, In the Matter of Policies and Rules Concerning Children's Television Programming, Docket No. 93-48, 1993.

Rheingold, H. *The Virtual Community: Homesteading on the Electronic Frontier*. Reading, MA: Addison-Wesley, 1993.

Riley, J.; F. Cantewell; and K. Ruttiger. "Some Observations on the Social Effects of Television." *Public Opinion Quarterly,* n13 (1949): 223-234.

Riley, S. "V-chip to Regulate Canadian Television Viewing." *Southam Newspapers*, March 15, 1996.

Robinson, J. P. "Television and Leisure Time: Yesterday, Today and (Maybe) Tomorrow." *Public Opinion Quarterly,* n33 (1969): 210-223.

Robinson, J.P. "I Love My TV." *American Demographics* (Sept. 1990).

Robinson, T. "Reducing Children's Television Viewing to Prevent Obesity: A Randomized Controlled Trial." *The Journal of the American Medical Association* 282, n16 (1999): 1561-1567.

Rojano, R. *Denver Post*. Aug. 26, 1995: 7E.

Romeo, F. "Adolescent Boys and Anorexia Nervosa." *Adolescence* v29, n115 (Fall 1994).

Rosenblatt, P. C., and M. R. Cunningham. "Television Watching and Family Tensions." *Journal of Marriage and Family* 2, n38 (1976): 105-111.

Rubin, R. "Pregnancy No Longer Pushes Women to Wed." *USA Today*, Nov. 9, 1999: D1.

Rubinstein, E. "Television and the Young Viewer." *Charlotte Observer*, April 1986.

St. Peters, M.; M. Fitch; A. Huston; J.C. Wright; and D. Eskins. "Television and Families: What Do Young Children Watch with Their Parents?" *Child Development* 62, n6 (Dec. 1, 1999): 1409-1423.

Sapolsky, B.S., and J.O. Tabarlet. "Sex in Prime-time Television: 1979 Versus 1989." *Journal of Broadcasting & Electronic Media* 35, n4 (Fall 1991): 505-516.

Saunders, D. "Fox Comedy Pushes the Raunch Envelope." *Rocky Mountain News,* July 26, 1999: 2D.

Saunders, D. "Fox Execs Know how to Exploit X-philes: Wish Comes True." *Rocky Mountain News,* January 13, 1998: 2D.

"School Changes Name from 'South Park' After Movie Release." *Associated Press*, August 30, 1999.

Schramm, W. J. Lyle, and E. B. Parker. *Television in the Lives of Our Children.* Stanford, Calif.: Stanford University Press, 1961.

Schudson, M. "The Idea of Conversation in the Study of Mass Media." In *Inter/Media— Interpersonal Communication in a Media World.* eds. A.G. Gumpert and R. Cathcart. New York: Oxford University Press, 1982.

Scwartz, P. "Behind the Curtain and Into the Brutal Land of Oz." *New York Times*, July 12, 1998.

Semenauer, J., and Carroll, D. *Singles: The New Americans.* New York: Simon and Schuster, 1982.

"Sexuality, Contraception, and the Media" (RE9505). *Pediatrics* v95, n2 (February 1995): 298-300.

Sherman, S. "A Set of One's Own: TV Sets in Children's Bedrooms." *Journal of Advertising Research* 36, n6 (November/December 1996).

Shorter, E. *The Making of the Modern Family.* New York: Basic Books, 1977.

Signorielli, N. (ed.). *Role Portrayal and Stereotyping on Television.* Westport, Conn.: Greenwood Press, 1985.

Signorielli, N. "Reflections of Girls in the Media: A Content Analysis Across Six Media and a National Survey of Children." Kaiser Family Foundation, Children NOW, (#1260), April 1997.

Signorielli, N. "Television's Contribution to Sex-Role Socialization." Paper presented to the Seventh Auunal Telecommunications Policy Research Conference: Skytop, PA, April 1979.

Signorielli, N., and M. Lears. "Children, Television, and Conceptions about Chores: Attitudes and Behaviors." *Sex Roles* 27, n3/4 (1992): 157-170.

Simmons, B.J.; K. Stalsworth; and H. Wentzel. "Television Violence and Its Effects on Young Children." *Early Childhood Education Journal* 26, n3 (1999): 149-153.

Simons, S. "Affluenza." PBS, September 15, 1997.

Skill, T., and J.D. Robinson, "Four Decades of Families on Television: A Demographic Profile, 1950–1989." *Journal of Broadcasting and Electronic Media* (Fall 1994): 449-464.

"A Spoonful of Sugar—Television Food Advertising Aimed at Children: An International Comparative Survey." *Consumer International*, (1996).

Bibliography

"Sports Fans Get Testosterone Rush." *Kaleidoscope Interactive News & Features* (May 19, 1998).

"Statistics in Brief: Child Care and Early Education Program Participation of Infants, Toddlers, and Preschoolers." National Center for Education Statistics, October 1996.

Steenland, S. *What's Wrong With This Picture: The Status of Women on Screen and Behind the Camera in Entertainment TV.* Washington, D.C.: National Commission on Working Women on Wider Opportunities for Women, 1990.

Stone, L. A. *Comments Regarding Standards Set Forth in Section 551(e) of the Telecommunications Act of 1996.* American Academy of Child & Adolescent Psychiatry, April 8, 1997.

Stossel, J., P. Fleming and R. Schlenker. "TV Sports Junkies." *20/20.* New York: ABC News, Nov. 8, 1996.

Strasburger, V. C. *Adolescence and the Media: Medical and Psychological Impact.* Thousand Oaks, Calif.: Sage Publications, 1995.

Strasburger, V.C. "Adolescent Sexuality and the Media." *Pediatric Clinics of North America* 36, n3 (June 1989): 747-773.

Strasburger, V.C. "Tuning in to Teenagers." *Newsweek* (May 19, 1997).

"Study of Worldwide Rates of Religiosity, Church Attendance." University of Michigan News and Information Service, 17, December 10, 1997.

Stuller, J. "Uniquely American." *The American Legion Magazine* (September, 1998).

Taylor, E. "From the Nelsons to the Huxtables: Genre and Family Imagery in American Network Television." *Qualitative Sociology* 12, n1 (Spring 1989): 13-27.

Taylor, E. *Prime Time Families.* Berkeley, Calif.: University of California Press, 1989.

Taylor, F. G. "Sexual Message to Kids Studied by Experts." *The Denver Post,* August 26, 1995: 7E.

Tedesco, N. "Patterns in Prime Time." *Journal of Communication* (Spring 1974).

Telecom Act of 1996: First Annual Report on Five Key Issues, The. The Center for Educational Priorities. 1997.

Television and the Preparation of the Mind for Learning: Critical Questions on the Effects of TV on the Developing Brains of Young Children. Conference sponsored by the Division of Children and Families of the U.S. Department of Health and Human Services, Washington, D.C., Oct. 2, 1996.

"Television Statistics and Sources," TV-Free America. 1999.

Tepperman, J. "Toxic Lessons: What Do Children Learn from Media Violence?" *Children's Advocate* (January/February 1997).

Three Telecommunications Laws: Their Impact and Significance. The Center for Educational Priorities. 1997.

Tims, A. R., and J. L. Masland. "Measurement of Family Communication Patterns." *Communication Research* 12, n1 (January 1985): 35-57.

Traudt, P. *Families and Television: Guidelines for an Ethnographic Procedure*. Paper presented at the annual meeting of the Association for Education in Journalism, Houston, August 1979.

"TV Viewing and Parental Guidance." *Office of Research Education Consumer Guide*, n10. U.S. Department of Education, October 1994.

"TV Viewing Top After-school Activity for Children." *Broadcasting* (January 11, 1988).

UCLA Television Violence Report, The. University of California Los Angeles, Center for Educational Priorities. 1997.

U.S. Senate. *TV Ratings*. Washington, D.C.: Testimony before the Senate Commerce Committee, February 27, 1997.

Uniform Crime Reports. Federal Bureau of Investigation, 1991.

Vann, A.S. "Kids, Media, and Family Values." *The Education Digest* (March 1996): 23-25.

V-Chip Home Page. Federal Communications Commission, February 2000.

Veith, G.E. "Not Suitable for TV." *World* 27, n8 (Feb. 27, 1999).

Velknap, P., and W.M. Leonard II. "A Conceptual Replication and Extension of Erving Goffman's Study of Gender Advertisements." *Sex Roles* 25, n3/4 (1991): 103-188.

Vogel, E., and N. Bell. *The Emotionally Disturbed Child as Family Scapegoat: A Modern Introduction to the Family*. New York: Macmillan, 1968.

Von Bertalanffy, L. *Modern Theories of Development—An Introduction to Theoretical Biology*. London: Oxford University Press, 1934.

Vorman, J. "Media Can't Seem to Get Enough, Critics Say." *The Rocky Mountain News*, January 28, 1998: 3A, 49A.

Walsh, F., ed. *Normal Family Processes*. New York: Guilford Press, 1982.

Walters, J., and V. Stone. "Television and Family Communication," *Journal of Broadcasting* 15, n4 (Fall 1971): 409-414.

Ward, M., and R. Rivadeneyra. "Contributions of Entertainment Television to Adolescents' Sexual Attitudes and Expectations: The Role of Viewing Amount Versus Viewer Involvement." *The Journal of Sex Research* 36, n3 (August 1999): 237-249.

Watkins, B. "Improving Educational and Informational Television for Children: When the Marketplace Fails." *Yale Law and Policy Review* 5 (345-381).

Watzlawick, P.; J. H. Beavin; and D. D. Jackson. *Pragmatics of Human Communication*. New York: W. W. Norton & Co., 1967.

"Where is Today's Child? Probably Watching TV." *New York Times*. Dec. 6, 1999: C18

Whitehead, B. "Dan Quayle was Right." *The Atlantic Monthly* (1993): 47(19).

Whitmire, T. "Sexy Soaps Set Bad Example, Study Finds." *The Denver Post,*. September 8, 1996.

Will, G.F. "Are Children Little Adults? And Why All Those Shows 'Seinfeld,' 'Ally McBeal,' 'Friends' About Childish Adults?" *Newsweek* (Dec. 6, 1999): 98.

Bibliography

Wilson, P., and E.S. Christopher. "The Home-Television Environment: Implications for Families." *Journal of Home Economics* (Winter, 1992).

Winn, M. *The Plug-in Drug, Children and the Family*. New York: Viking Press, 1977.

Witt, S. "Parental Influences on Children's Socialization to Gender Roles." *Adolescence* 32, n126 (Summer 1997).

Wolf, N. *The Beauty Myth*. New York: William Morrow, 1991.

Wollenberg, S. "Holiday Inn Ad Died Quickly." *Rocky Mountain News,* January 20, 1998: 6B.

Wood, J. "Gendered Patterns of Family Roles." *Gendered Patterns in Family Communication*: 64-72.

Wright, L. "Television and American Parents." *The World & I* (May 1990): 573.

Writers Guild of America, West, Inc., v. Federal Communications Commission, et al. U.S. District Court for the Central District of California, Nov. 4, 1976.

Zillmann, D., J. Bryant, and A. C. Huston (eds.). *Media, Children and the Family*. Hillsdale, N.J.: Lawrence Erlbaum Associates, 1994.

Zinmeister, K. "TV-Free: Real Families Describe Life Without the Tube."*The American Enterprise* 8, n5 (September-October 1997): 63(9).

Zwingle, E. "Women and Population." *National Geographic* (October 1998): 50.

Index

Index

Index

Index

impact of electronic media on, 18–19; impact of stereotyping on, 82–83, 90–91; impact of television on views of sex, 123; impact of television viewing on, 51–52, 117; impact of television violence on, 146–149; lessons taught to minority, 83; living apart from fathers, 109; on soap operas, 121; power of sexual messages for, 117–19; removing television from bedrooms of, 198; target of advertising, 66, 67, 95, 164; television as afterschool activity for, 167–68; time spent viewing television, 50–53, 167, 200; use of television as reward or punishment for, 63, 197; value of friendship for, 154–55; viewing of adult programming, 56; viewing of cartoons, 170. *See also* adolescents

Children Now, 82–83, 210

children's programs: demanding higher quality of, 205; offensiveness of, 176–77; sexual behavior in, 112; Telecommunications Act, 179; violence in, 146–149. *See also* cartoons; educational programs

Children's Television Act (1990), 176–77

Children's Television Workshop, 50–51

Christian Action Network, 210

Christian Coalition, 210

Christian Voice, 210

Citizens for Media Literacy, 210

Clinician Reviews, 171

Clueless, 164

cohabitation, 42–43

Collins, Joan, 100

Collins, Stephen, 39–40

Colombia Journalism Review, 210

Combat, 92, 157

comedies: adult-oriented, 38; career depiction on, 105; gender on, 92, 95, 96–97; reality-based, 37–39, 45; slapstick, 26.

See also situation comedies

comic book characters, 131

Commish, The, 69

communication, technology of, 9–12

Communication Act (1934), 175–76

Communication Research, 145

Communications Consortium, 210

Communications Decency Act (1996), 184

Communications Research, 44

computers, 19–20, 184

confidants, role of, 165–67

conflicts: conversations in resolving, 207; depiction of, 58–63, 143–44, 159; in families, 143; in situation comedies, 42; in talk shows, 34; television as basis of, 58–63, 70

Consumer International, 66

consumerism: children as target, 64–65; depiction of, 37; in redefining family values, 68–70; television's export of, 75–77. *See also* advertising

conversations: depiction of, 158; discussing conflicts in, 207; effect of television viewing on, 168–69, 189; exchange of ideas in, 169–70; television programs in, 55, 57–58, 192–94

coping mechanism, television as, 59, 172

COPS, 80

Cosby, Bill, 36, 78

Cosby Show, The, 36, 44, 45, 79

counterculture, heroes in, 129

Courtship of Eddie's Father, 29, 31, 81

Cox Arquette, Courtney, 101

Creating Critical Viewers, 210–11

creativity, impact of television on, 51

criminal jury candidates, 135

critical thinking, 170

Cronkite, Walter, 30, 138

Index

Index

Index

Index

Index

Index

printing press, 5, 10, 11–12, 14–16, 71

print media, 18–19

problem solving, 144

Procter & Gamble, 204, 205

profanity: in advertising, 74; in movies and television, 73; in prime-time programs, 73. *See also* language

professional dramas, women in, 101

promiscuity, 125–127

Promised Land, 39–40, 84, 85, 202

prosperity, 69–70

Protestant Reformation, 15–16

Providence, 101

Prozac television, 130, 172

Public Broadcasting System, 170

public officials, depiction of, 134–35

public service spots, 205–206

punishment, use of television as, 63, 197

Q

Quayle, Dan, 33

Queen for a Day, 98

Quirk, Kevin, 61

R

radio, 17; transition of soap operas from, 24; Radio-Television News Directors Association, 213; *War of the Worlds,* 17

rape: in prime-time programs, 120, in soap operas, 120, television violence as cause of, 94–95

Raphael, Sally Jessy, 34, 166

Rashad, Phylicia, 36

ratings. *See* television ratings

reading habits, 51

Reagan, Ronald, 136

reality programming, 33–34; in comedies, 37–39, 45; in family programs, 27, 45; friendships on, 161; Hispanics on, 80; as theme, 34–39; violence on, 145

Real McCoys, The, 30, 80

Real World, The, 161

Recasner, Eldridge, 140

recurrent themes on television, 43–45

Red Skeleton Show, The, 25

regional diversity, 72–73

regulations: attempt to institute family viewing hour restrictions, 35–36; reasons for failure of, 175–85; survey on desire for more, 149; V-chips in, 179–80, 199. *See also* television ratings

Reiser, Paul, 82

religion, 201

religious programs: messages on, 83–85; redefining of family values and, 68–70; television ratings for, 84–85

remote control, 195

Reuben, Gloria, 101

reverse anorexia, 107

reward, use of television as, 63, 197

Ribeiro, Alfonso, 79–80

Richards, Michael, 158

Rison, Andre, 140

Roberts, Tanya, 99

Robinson, James D., 31

Robinson, Thomas, 171–72

Roe v. *Wade,* 104

Rogers, Roy, 131

Rojano, Ramon, 122

Roseanne, 38, 44, 45, 90, 114

Rosenblatt, P. C., 59

Rosenfield, Lawrence B., 153

Index

Rothman, Stanley, 112, 113, 116, 134–35, 136, 150, 164

Rowan, Dan, 98

Rowan and Martin's Laugh-In, 98

Roy Rogers Show, The, 131

Rubble, Barney, 28

Rubble, Betty, 28

Ruth, Babe, 139

S

Sagal, Katey, 38

Saint James, Susan, 159

Sanford, Isabel, 34

SanGiacomo, Laura, 105

Santiago, Saundra, 81

Sapo, Donald F., 140

Sargent, Dick, 29

Savage, Fred, 36

schedule: creating, for television viewing, 196–97; as framework for family, 54

Schlitz Playhouse of Stars, 130

Schultz, Dwight, 93

Schwarzenegger, Arnold, 132

Segalowitz, Sidney, 53

Seinfeld, 40, 82, 101, 115–16, 158–60

Seinfeld, Jerry, 82, 116, 158

self-control, 118

self-monitoring, 53

Sellers, Larry, 82

sensationalism, on television news, 138

Sesame Street, 53, 64, 170, 176, 177, 180, 205

77 Sunside Strip, 97

7 Days, 128

7th Heaven, 39–40, 68–69, 202

Sex Roles, 120

sex/sexuality: in children's programs, 112; defining satisfying, 112–13; in family programs, 112–13; in gender stereotyping, 94; heavy television viewing and, 111–12; influence of television on children's views of, 123; institution of family viewing hour and, 35–36; irresponsibility of, on television, 118–21; mixing with alcohol consumption, 96; in music videos, 94; portrayal of, 113; power of, as message for children, 117–18; in prime-time programs, 111, 112, 118; promiscuity in, 42–43; role of television as advisor in, 111–26; role of television in planting seeds of discontent in, 125–26; separating, from emotion, 113–14; in soap operas, 111, 115, 119, 120; stimulation of curiosity on, 58

Seymour, Jane, 101

Shasta McNasty, 123

Shatner, William, 93

shock value, 166–67

Shorter, Edward, 21–22

siblings, friendships with, 153

Signorielli, Nancy, 103, 108

Simenauer, Jacqueline, 116

Simpson, Bart, 144

Simpson, Marge, 107

Simpson, O. J., 139–140

Simpsons, The, 38, 45, 75, 95, 107, 158

singlehood, 115–16

single parents, 30–33, 121

situation comedies: African-Americans on, 79–80; conflicts in, 42; employment on, 69; families in, 24–25, 114; financial theme in, 37; friendships on, 152–53, 157, 159; reality base of, 37–39; surrogate families in, 40

Index

Index

About the Author

Cheryl Pawlowski received a Ph.D. in media ecology from New York University in 1990. As a media ecologist, she studies how media of communication affect human perception, feelings, understanding, and values, and how transactions with media facilitate or impede chances of survival. She has participated in various programs focusing on family communication theories and holds undergraduate and graduate degrees in media theory, corporate and political communication, anthropology, and communication. Currently, she is an assistant professor of speech communication at the University of Northern Colorado in Greeley, Colorado.